D1569508

They'll Have to
Catch Me First

They'll Have to *Catch* Me First

*An Artist's Coming of Age
in the Third Reich*

They'll Have to *Catch* Me First

*An Artist's Coming of Age
in the Third Reich*

Irene Awret

Foreword by Walter Laqueur

THE UNIVERSITY OF WISCONSIN PRESS / DRYAD PRESS

The University of Wisconsin Press
1930 Monroe Street, 3rd Floor
Madison, Wisconsin 53711-2059
www.wisc.edu/wisconsinpress/

Dryad Press
Post Office Box 11233
Takoma Park, Maryland 20913
dryadpress@yahoo.com

3 Henrietta Street
London WC2E 8LU, England

Printed in the United States of America

Cover painting, "Redhaired Girl in a Green Coat," and half-title page drawing, "From the Window of the Painters' Workshop," by Irene Awret
Book and cover design by Sandy Rodgers

Text is typeset in Bembo 12 points on 15.

Please see page 323 for credits and permissions.

The paper used in this publication meets the minimum requirements of American National Standard for Information Sciences — Permanence of paper for Printed Library Materials, ANSI Z39.48

Library of Congress Cataloging-in-Publication Data
Awret, Irene, 1920–
    They'll have to catch me first : an artist's coming of age in the Third Reich
    / Irene Awret ; forward by Walter Laqueur.
        p. cm.
    ISBN 0-299-18830-2 (alk. paper)
        1. Awret, Irene, 1920—Childhood and youth. 2. Jewish artists—United
    States—Biography. I. Title.
    N6537.A95A97   2003
    943.086'092—dc21   2003045832
    [B]

Acknowledgments

My heartfelt thanks to my lifelong partner Azriel Awret and my old friend Eve Fastag-Dobruszkes who tirelessly helped me to collect the notes needed to write the latter part of this memoir. Traveling together, our search for survivors of the Mechelen Gestapo camp willing to share their memories led us to Brussels and Antwerp, to elegant flats and to subsidized retirement homes.

I also give a hug to the three guardian angels who looked over my shoulder onto every page of my translation from the original German manuscript into English, my good friends Gruine Robinson, Florence Nelson and Michlean Amir. In addition I want to thank Dr. Guenter Lewy for his invaluable help. When all was said but not done, I found Merrill Leffler or he found me. He became my publisher and friend; with uncanny insight and indefatigable perseverance, he pulled everything together and brought it to fruition.

Contents

Foreword

As the chronicler of the generation which Irene Awret belongs to, I think I have read more stories of survivors, published and unpublished, than most. I still find every one of absorbing interest because no two stories are alike. The first part of Irene Awret's account of her youth is only too familiar to me personally — the German Jewish background, middle class life in Berlin, family, school, youth movement. I was born the same year as she, I belonged to the same youth group, the Werkleute, and I write these lines at the Institute of Advanced Studies in Berlin Grunewald, some five minutes from Uncle Tom's Cabin where Mrs. Awret grew up. The songs and poems she mentions are familiar to me as well, as is the whole atmosphere in which we then lived, witnessing the transition from Weimar to the Third Reich.

The lakes and the trees in Berlin have changed little nor the main roads and the Grunewald railway station from which the deportations of the Berlin Jews took place is still there with a drug store and a news-paper kiosk in front. From time to time classes of school children turn up to see this place as part of their curriculum in the field of civics. There is nothing very exciting to be seen in Uncle Tom's Cabin except the temporary buildings of the post-war U.S. occupation administration, now largely empty.

It must be very difficult for these school children born ten or fifteen years ago even to begin to understand what happened there once upon a time and Mrs. Awret's recollections could add to their understanding.

She and her family waited too long with their emigration — not without reason, for there was nowhere to go. After *Kristallnacht* in November 1938, they were taken by smugglers over the so-called "green border" and ended up in Brussels. But like thousands of other German Jews they had not escaped far enough because in late spring of 1940, the Nazi armies invaded Holland and Belgium. For the next three years Irene Awret survived in the Belgium capital much of the time with false identity papers, in dire poverty but still persisting in pursuing her drawing and painting classes at least part of the time.

Unlike the great majority of Dutch Jews, who were rounded up, deported and perished, a considerably higher proportion of Belgian Jews survived. One does not have to look very far for an explanation — some 90 percent or more were recent arrivals, mainly from Poland, whereas most Dutch Jews were quite assimilated, their families having settled in the country generations earlier. This meant that Dutch Jews behaved like good citizens obeying without questioning the order of the authorities, whereas the East European Jews in Belgium had the traditional (and quite justified) distrust of authority which they had brought from their countries of origin.

It is also true that Belgium (in contrast to Holland) had a German military administration to carry out the Nazi instructions for eliminating the Jews; but the local army officers had other priorities and did not overexert themselves in this respect. In both countries help was extended to the Jews and thousands of children were hidden, though there was also a good deal of collaboration, spying and informing, with the occupying forces and there were sizeable Nazi movements in both countries.

Those who survived owe their life largely to accident and luck. Mrs. Awret's arrest by the Gestapo came in 1943 after the mass deportations in the summer of 1942 had already taken place.

The newly arrested were taken to concentration camps that served as transit stations for deportation to the gas chambers in Poland. A great deal has been written about Westerbork, the Dutch camp, but little if anything about Mechelen (Malines in French), the Belgian transit camp, formerly a military installation. Irene Awret's account with her drawings and oil paintings are a unique contribution to one of the chapters in the story of these dark years.

Mechelen is located not far from Brussels — it is known today mainly for its soccer club, its medieval buildings its cathedral (it is the seat of the primate of the Catholic church in Belgium) and the site of various festivals. But there is also a museum in remembrance of deportations and resistance.

In this camp in which Irene Spicker met her future husband Azriel Awret, also an artist, she survived for more than a year painting numbers for the authorities. Many of the inmates were gradually sent on to the East and to certain death. It is doubtful whether any of the inmates would have survived, if the war had lasted much longer but in the summer of 1944 Brussels and most of Belgium were liberated and the Jews in the Mechelen camp were again free.

After the liberation the young couple had to register with the Belgian authorities who in their wisdom decided that since (technically) the Mechelen camp though located inside Belgium had been under German jurisdiction during the occupation, the Awrets were still foreigners with no right of legal residence in Belgium, whereupon they emigrated. Thus ends this moving and fascinating personal account.

What irony of history — nearly sixty years after the events described in this memoir Belgian society is confronted with hundreds of thousands of foreign residents who, in contrast to the refugees of the 1930s, have no wish to be assimilated into its culture, language, customs and way of life and who in the inner part of some of the large cities will soon constitute the majority.

But this is another story. Mrs. Awret's memoir does not deal with high politics, but is the unvarnished account of the fate of a single human being who had the good luck to survive at a time when so many of her contemporaries perished.

Walter Laqueur
Washington D.C. / Berlin

Introduction

Some years ago, our good friend Gruine Robinson, a retired newspaper reporter, invited my husband and me to accompany her to a lecture at the Belgian embassy in Washington, D.C. where she had been invited together with a large group of her colleagues. As former inhabitants of Brussels, we accepted gladly. We had often driven by the handsome embassy building and wondered about the interior.

A young lady with a charming French accent — she may have been the cultural attaché — gave a talk about education in Belgium. The audience clapped politely and champagne was served. Glass in hand, I attempted to show off my French and went over to her corner, inquiring where in Belgium she came from.

"From Malines," she answered. It was a name that made me gasp. "Do you know it? A lovely town. I grew up there . . . beautiful cathedral."

"Do I know it?" I drew out the words. "Yes and no, not the cathedral though I know Malines only from the inside." From the way she frowned, I must have sounded strange.

"You know it only from the inside?" she asked. "What do you mean?"

"From inside the old barracks of the Casern Dossin. I was imprisoned there for a year and a half," I said. "You know, the Gestapo camp the Germans called Mecheln." [In English, Mechelen.] The young lady's face was blank.

"In Malines? Are you sure?" she said. "I have never heard of such a place."

Her lack of awareness left me speechless. Were Jewish lives still expendable, did all those shadowy figures of the past shoved into cattle cars count for nothing? There was one big difference between then and now. Now I was free to open my mouth. I carried my champagne over to the ambassador who was talking to some guests, my Gallic veneer of politeness having suddenly evaporated, and interrupted him rudely.

"How is this possible," I asked, "that an educated person like your lecturer, born and raised in Malines, never heard of the infamous Casern Dossin, the Gestapo camp? More than twenty-five thousand men, women and children living in Belgium were shipped from there to Auschwitz, and no teacher of that town ever mentioned that fact to the young lady? True, they were only Jews and Gypsies," I added with a sneer. "It is not her fault that she was not told, but what do all those institutes of education she mentioned teach?"

I had to catch my breath, people were staring. The ambassador was searching for words. Poor man, it was not his fault either. An old career diplomat, all he could come up with was the classic apology, "Some of my best friends are Jews!"

It was then I promised myself that I would write my memories of the camp. It took me several years until I finally sat down to do it, beginning with my arrest in Brussels in 1943. That turned out to be a false start. I had to explain what had led up to my incarceration. Then I had to add why I had fled to Belgium in the first place. In the end, I had to start at the beginning, my birth.

I am happy to say that much has changed since that evening at the embassy. Not too long ago, the little Kingdom of Belgium, its Jewish community and the town of Malines pooled their resources to commemorate the dead in one corner of the old Casern Dossin barracks that were left standing, the Musée de la Déportation et la Résistance. Small but well conceived, it attracts Jews and non-Jews alike. School teachers from all over the country bring their students.

Scant material remains and ever decreasing numbers of survivors are left to bear witness to the events of those days in Belgium. This was especially true of Mechelen. I wanted to fill in some of the gaps and to keep alive the memory of those who perished. Towards this end I have tried to give a picture of childhood recollections and the experience of twelve years under the Nazi boot.

While I knew Malines from my own experience, I later used my visits with family and friends in Belgium to interview other inmates and to tape our conversations. On some of these occasions our friend Evi Dobruszkes-Fastag came from France to help us in our search and often the direct quotes in the book draw upon these interviews. I also consulted the works *La Traque des Juifs* and *Les Cent Jours de la Déportation* by the eminent Belgian historian Maxime Steinberg.

Finally I want to say a word about the art in this book. Unlike the majority of prisoners in Mechelen/Malines who were sent on transports to Auschwitz, we were not only fortunate to survive, we were fortunate to be able to make drawings and to paint. It may seem strange under the conditions we lived in, but many of the inmates were pleased to sit for their portraits. The day after the Allied liberation of Mechelen I was able to retrieve my few personal effects and the artwork that remained in the Malerstube, the painter's studio, my own as well as pieces by my husband Azriel, Lon Landau and Jacques Ochs. These works are but a small record of a few artists. May they testify to the indomitable spirit of the many nameless artists who perished under Nazi brutality.

Irene Awret
Fairfax, Virginia and Safad, Israel

Drawings and Paintings

PART ONE

Berlin

Overleaf. A view of Onkel Tom's Hütte (Uncle Tom's Cabin), the large suburban housing development designed in the Bauhaus style for working class families. We moved there in 1927, before construction was completed. (Stiftung Archiv der Akademie der Künste, Germany)

One

———

IN THE BEGINNING my story is quite ordinary. A normal birth, normal weight, and my mother who tied the dark fuzz on my head in a little pink bow. After the childless rift of World War I, which my father had spent in the trenches of France, I was welcomed warmly as a bonus of the great inflation.

My entire family, down to the last great-cousin, a bachelor who kept guinea pigs in his bathtub, lived in Berlin, all staunch German citizens of the Mosaic faith, as we were called by the authorities. With Jewish temperament and Prussian discipline rubbing like tectonic plates against each other, slight neuroses were inevitable. On the whole the prognosis for my future looked normal: an existence in the lap of the family, winding through holidays, weddings, funerals and bar mitzvahs along the Spree River. Maybe with time I could have made a modest name for myself as an artist, a painter of the Spree perhaps, for already as a small child I was fascinated by the glittering lights that trembled on her murky waters.

Things were to turn out differently. Born on a Sunday I was told I would have luck in life, a prediction which in some ways was to prove correct, for otherwise my biography would have ended fifty years ago. My birthday fell on Sunday, the thirtieth of January, 1921, twelve years to the day before Hitler came to power. Part of my family would perish in death camps, the rest would be dispersed over four continents by the brutal fist of Nazism — my only relative left in Berlin is a half-Jewish niece. But who at that time was paying attention to the hysterical drivel of an anti-Semitic corporal from Austria? One had other things to worry about.

"Careful with the butter, Grandma," my father shouted at dinner into my great-grandmother's ear. "This morning we paid thirteen million marks for half-a-pound. By now the cost may be up to a billion."

"Is that so? Well, then the Almighty will forgive us if we eat lard," the old woman was said to have answered.

Germany had been brought to its knees, vanquished, impoverished. The newborn Weimar Republic lay as helplessly kicking on its back as I did in my baby carriage. While the bellies of his former subjects rumbled and the German currency was so worthless that banknotes were used to paper walls, the Kaiser was away in Holland chopping wood. Whoever had not yet had enough of war, mostly extremists of the left or right, continued their battles in the streets of Berlin.

One morning on her way to a walk in the Tiergarten, a large park in the center of Berlin, my mother had been caught up in such a battle. Holding my sister and brother each by a hand, and pregnant with me, she was hurrying to reach the relative security of a side street when she noticed that in the excitement she had lost the paper bag with her children's lunch. So irreplaceable were the sandwiches, she left the children alone and returned through the line of fire to retrieve them. During the war without my father by her side, she learned to fend for herself and had become strong and self-sufficient.

Apart from a few books, documents and a clothes brush, I have only yellowed photographs to show for my eighteen German years. One of these, well preserved in spite of Papa having carried it for a long time in the breast pocket of his uniform, shows my sister and brother praying for him. Two handsome Jewish children with upturned eyes and piously folded hands in the manner of Christians at prayer, beseeching the ceiling of the most fashionable photographic studio of Alt-Moabit in the center of Berlin. Had my father not volunteered at the outbreak of the war, someone in his situation with two small children might have been spared the trenches. As an obvious patriot he was put into the First Prussian Guard Grenadier Regiment Alexander where, even after being shot through both thighs, he would return to the thick of things. Was it the indisputable love of his country that prompted him to follow the Kaiser's call to arms so quickly, or did the vulture of bankruptcy have something to do with it? After seven years of comfortable married life, the ugly bird was already pecking at our window, timidly at first. By the time I saw the light of this world, inflation had firmly nested in our midst.

Even though Papa was sick of war, he would have liked to continue seeing his chronic money troubles in the purer light of patriotism. "While I was stuck in mud up to my hips at the battle of the Marne, my brothers-in-law at home transferred their capital safely to Switzerland," he said. "At Verdun I had to drink from a puddle with a dead cat in it, and in the meantime Max built up his cigar import business."

Notwithstanding the Fatherland-loving circumstances, my mother felt swamped by the burden of growing debts. She was able to put up with street fights, though not with the increasingly tighter household money and a cuckoo under our dining table. (The cuckoo bird is Berlin slang for the Prussian eagle on the bailiff's seal.) This was not what she expected from a love-match. She and her younger sister, Aunt Toote, listened mainly to their beating hearts in the choice of two young merchants from respectable Jewish families who were pursuing them. On the other hand, their older sister, Aunt Hanna, had hesitated before giving her hand to a man who, though a doctor, was neither young nor dashing. Putting their dark heads together, the three sisters agreed to leave the decision to their lapdog Puppchen who had a keen flair for character. Afterwards, when Uncle Albert asked Aunt Hanna in marriage, the little dog was said to have jumped up at him, licked his hand and barked "Yes!" with enthusiasm. These are some of the family stories I grew up with.

Aunt Hanna's wedding, which followed soon afterwards, was one of those made in heaven, something one could hardly say of Aunt Toote's or my parents' union. True, Aunt Toote's husband quickly became rich, but it was rumored that he spent his money more easily on pretty secretaries than on his wife, while my father, loyal husband, hardworking and keeper of orderly accounts, oversaw the disappearance of my mother's dowry. Although his wedding gift to my mother was a series of music books bound in green leather with gold lettering, he would fall asleep at the opera even during the most passionate arias. Whoever might have come into possession of those song books after our flight from Germany must have wondered about a Margarete Spicker whose name shone under those of Johannes Brahms and Robert Schumann. During her pregnancy with me, my mother's moods were so blue that they led to the third of my given names, Dolorosa, the sorrowful Mother of God — me of all people.

For the nine months before my birth, my mother visited all the museums in Berlin — in those days, many pregnant women believed that absorption in great works of art could in some mysterious way transmit their beauty to the unborn. Apparently during her school years, my mother had never been accused by her classmates of being responsible for the crucifixion of Christ, at least not to her face, for she fell so in love with the painting of a Spanish Madonna, that she bought a framed reproduction. My father, brought up in an Orthodox Jewish family, must have been quite shocked, though in light of my mother's delicate condition he could not protest too loudly. Later he must have grown accustomed to the stranger in the bedroom, for I remember well the Mater Dolorosa on my mother's toilette table, the tears rolling over olive-green cheeks down to her pointed little chin, and I kept trying to wipe them off from under the glass.

With pre-war social conventions, a married woman such as my mother could only dream of a career as a singer or performer, and so she transferred her hopes to me. I would become a tragic actress, a new Pavlova or a bosomy Wagner heroine. With the exception of the bosom I did not fulfill any of those hopes; even the pompous name Dolorosa did not stick, though a few of my uncles and cousins would occasionally call me "Dolle Rosa" (Mad Rosa). I always liked the name Irene. A post-war child, I liked to identify with the Greek goddess of peace, and during my later wanderings "Irene" let itself adapt to foreign languages with only minor changes. My second name, Paula, in Yiddish Feigele, which is a translation from the Hebrew. Zipporah, meaning bird, was one of my father's sisters who died at an early age.

As if Dolorosa was not sufficient for a theatrical finale, the Nazis later forced me to add a Hebrew name, Sara, making me Irene Paula Dolorosa Sara — and so I entered the world with the names of a Greek goddess, a deceased aunt from Krojanke in Posen, a Spanish Madonna and a biblical Mother of Mothers.

First scene: a family idyll, Sunday in the Grunewald, a general name for the forests surrounding Berlin. To the basket full of mushrooms which my older siblings collected, I proudly added lustrous dung-beetles. "Blueberries," I babbled, running in my Sunday dress and white shoes straight into a lake. In the meantime my wet nurse, wearing the Slavic costume, wide skirts and the winged bonnet of the Spreewald region, a marshy area east of Berlin, was off in the background kissing some young man — until my father chased everyone off stage. Milk from an immoral source could in later years have had a bad influence on me, he feared, and so he fired one after another of my nurses. In the end my parents understood that the good old pre-war days were gone, that even in the Spreewald only the famous pickles were still untouched by rot, and that their youngest had to drink from a bottle.

My mother was always open to the new ideas flooding Berlin at the beginning of the twenties and supplemented my nutrition with vegetables, much to my father's horror. So swallowing a good portion of Prussian discipline together with North German carrots and the milk of Brandenburgian cows, I grew into an easy child who asked few questions, ate fast and did as she was told. Even when fed spinach I would obediently open my mouth, spitting it out again only after my plate was clean.

Thriving on this regimen my days were passing in orderly fashion. I spent a good part of my time on walks in the Tiergarten looking for "little people" among the tree-roots. On Friday evenings our family would go to services at the synagogue on Levetzow Street; on Sundays we went by train into the woods, in winter sleigh-riding, in summer mushroom picking. One of my first memories is an Easter Sunday in the forest carrying a little back-basket and seeking the chocolate eggs the Easter Bunny had laid for me. I found no end of them, for the treasures I stowed away in the basket behind me were being hidden again and again in the bushes in front of me. But Jewish holidays were the most important. One week before Easter we celebrated Passover with matzah and a roast goose. To pass the time during the long seder, I made use of the rotating illustrations in my children's' Haggadah to let Pharaoh and the Egyptians drown in its cardboard waves.

Still another memory glimmers through the mist of my early childhood, my mother singing a sad song about a flower that is in love with the moon but is afraid of the sun. "Of lo-ove and lo-over's pain, of lo-ove and lo-over's pain," the song goes. Her chin cupped in one hand, her elbow resting on the keys, my mother is sitting there staring at the piano as if she were able to see through it.

"Please, Mama, let me see them once more, please, just once more." With blurred contours softened by time the figure rises slowly, takes my hand and draws me with her up the three flights of steps to our attic in the apartment house on Tiele Wardenberg Street. It is gloomy under the rafters. By and by my eyes get used to the twilight, and from a dust-covered jumble of discarded furniture and knick-knacks a trunk emerges covered in faded fabric, the magic trunk. The lid creaks, I smell mothballs, then six pairs of glass-eyes with painted lashes stare up into the dim attic light. A peasant woman in Alsatian costume and a German soldier with his nurse lie beside elegantly clad Trude, Herta and Lotte, my big sister's old-fashioned dolls, all in an orderly row resting here undisturbed. A wave that welled up from a faraway country called "Before the War" had swept them into our attic. Before my birth, when my family still had money, there had been this other world where little girls with long, open hair and lace dresses with sashes sipped lemonade from great-grandmother Treumann's crystal glasses, where my brother Werner wore a soldier's cap and boots with a long row of buttons. I had come too late to remember this. Only up here in the attic was it still possible to catch a corner of Before the War.

For my fourth birthday I wished for a big garlic sausage. No more sausage ends on my plate, no more. "Here Irene, the end is for you because you are the youngest." A four-year old was due a whole sausage for herself. When the great day dawned I found no sausage — instead I found the doll named Lotte sitting in an armchair in the liv-

My brother Werner and sister Gerda praying for father, a photograph he carried with him during World War I.

My father was awarded the Iron Cross for his service in World War I.

My mother's famiy. Upper row, from left: Uncle Richard, Uncle Albert, my mother, my father, Uncle Max; second row: Aunt Hanna with Karl, Grandmother and Grandfather Zoegall, Aunt Toote with Lilo. Below: my sister Gerda and my cousin Lilli. Heringsdorf on the Baltic Sea, 1911.

Grandfather Spicker. Farecard identification card for using the Berlin tramway, 1911.

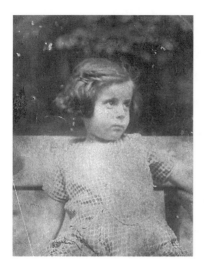

Above: age 4, a photograph my brother took of me with a box camera that he made. At right: age 5, at the time of my short movie career. Below: my first day of school.

ing room, who in order to serve as my birthday present had given up her world in the enchanted trunk. I almost did not recognize her in that sobering new dress. Also in place of garlic sausage, my mother had ordered ballet shoes made to measure for me, not the pink ones I had dreamed of, but practical black ones that do not soil easily. I can only add here that the black ballet shoes did not kindle the kind of enthusiasm in me that is indispensable to a life on the stage.

In any event, my lessons with Papa Gronsky, a White-Russian ballet master of Bülow Street, were soon interrupted when I fell sick with double pneumonia. I owe the continuation of my story to the devoted care of my parents and to the experience and common sense of Doctor Kalmus, our family doctor. I still see the green silk scarf shielding my feverish eyes from the glare of the electric lamp on the night table. They are so hot, they keep on burning even after I have been plunged into a cool bath to bring down my fever. Kerchiefs and linen steeped in turpentine drip from the railing of my bed. Doctor Kalmus arrives in the middle of the night, and in the triple mirror over my mother's toilet table I can see myself in his lap in my long flannel nightshirt, fighting for breath. All around I see me sitting in the wings of the mirror gasping for air; then Doctor Kalmus presses something glittering and hard so deep down my throat that vomit and mucus bespatter the image of the Mater Dolorosa.

Feeling weak and tired can be a very pleasant experience. Especially when I am served consommé, veal brains, roasted pigeon and lady fingers in bed, when brand-new storybooks are read to me, and when my aunts come with big sheets of paper dolls and their wardrobe to be cut out. In order to bring back my hearty appetite my mother plied me so successfully with "biomalt" and cod-liver-oil that by then I already disliked stepping onto a scale. To regain a figure, I had to wait until the second World War — the only period in my life when I had a waist was my year-and-a-half in the Gestapo camp in Mechelen, Belgium.

As a four-year old, however, I obediently swallowed tablespoons of cod-liver oil baited with candy swimming in the middle. Twice a week my mother would again bring me to Papa Gronsky's ballet studio. It was the time between the great inflation and the great depression, a period of feverish activity in the arts and sciences. In Berlin's coffee-houses intellectuals sat discussing literature and politics, people queued up for blocks to see the newest avant garde play or some futuristic silent movie, and heated controversies arose over expressionistic art shows, Bauhaus architecture and atonal music. "Hindemith, her damit, weg damit" (Hindemith, here with it, away with it), sneered my father, as my mother saved money from her small household allowance to take me to the theater or the ballet, still hoping her youngest would conquer the stage.

Indeed some froth from the tossed-up waves of Berlin's art world wetted the feet now taking their first hesitant dance steps. On the worn-out stair leading up to the ballet studio my mother would give me a last critical glance, spit into her handkerchief and wipe the corners of my mouth clean of the sticky, red memento of some candy.

"Now you look decent again. Don't forget, Reni, you have to make a better impression than those little shiksas up there."

A year later my father and Gerda would plant on my mother's grave a wild rose and snowdrops, her favorite flowers. For me there would be no more quick fix with a drop of spittle, no more little taps of encouragement. She would not see me grow up, nor would she be there when it finally became clear that neither cleanliness nor a passion for order, no amount of politeness and not even true patriotism would help me, my family or any other Jew in Germany.

At this moment, however, my mother was first and foremost intent on assuring a career on the stage for me, and up here on the fourth floor of the old building on Bülow Street, on parquet boards spotted with colophonium, Papa Gronsky was working hard to transform a chubby duckling into a swan. In unison with a dozen other aspiring ballerinas I grabbed the bar, flung my short legs upwards and backwards, the black ballet shoes hopping again and again from the first into the second position where I tiptoed and then tripped. Just like Anna Pavlova, I thought, whose passionate and feathery demise I had admired from the third tier through our opera glasses.

In the train on our way home my mother let me sit by the window. The tiny pointed face of her fox fur-piece hooked to its own tail was looking down on me from her shoulder. It smelled of puppies. My mother had gone off into her private world — Papa would say she was staring holes into the air. And where was she supposed to look, she would ask pointedly on such occasions? At all the unpaid bills on his desk perhaps? Mostly, however, she would sit for hours at the piano and sing, or she would retire with the heating-pad, for my mother suffered from gallstones.

The train accelerated. Wiping a big flower out of the condensation covering the window pane, I pressed my cheek to the wet glass and tried to see what was going on behind all those other brightly lit windows flitting quickly by. Here and there I caught a glimpse of little people sitting around their kitchen table — as in a doll-house. Aunt Jenny, Aunt Alice and Uncle Isidore must be somewhere among them for the rails pass near their apartment, each train thundering by and making the furniture rattle as though there was an earthquake. I liked visiting Aunt Jenny who was nice and filled her cookies with jelly. Uncle Isidore, her son, rarely talked. Papa said he was an eccentric. He had guinea pigs and hamsters. Aunt Alice was his sister. She was heavy, not married and always crocheting. For every birthday she brought us presents, handkerchiefs bordered with crocheted lace. She was always around when someone was sick or something else in the family was happening. Her heart was sadly dried up — she needed the joys and pains of others for it to beat more excitedly.

I do not know what became of Aunt Jenny and her children after our flight to Belgium in 1939. At that time there were still tens of thousands like them living in Berlin, maybe not the most efficient among the "German citizens of the Mosaic faith," but decent people asking not much more of life than to look from their window at a lilac bush blooming by the trash cans in the backyard. When their fellow-believers from the apartments with the front windows, more affluent and better connected than they, found ways to slip through the mesh of the Nazi net, they would be left behind. In vain they stood in line in the corridors of foreign consulates, hoping someone from somewhere would stamp an entry-visa into their German passports marked with a big red "J." Then they ran from one barely functioning office of the Jewish community to the next, begging advice from those who were just as helpless. It was the last flutter before the Nazi vultures took them into their claws. People like Aunt Jenny with her home-baked cookies, Uncle Isidore with his guinea pigs, Aunt Alice with her crocheted borders, like so many others, disappeared without leaving a trace, barely a memory.

As usual I was unable to make out Aunt Jenny's apartment — the train raced by too fast. We had the compartment all to ourselves and so my mother made me rehearse the song I was supposed to sing the next morning for an impresario:

> "The likes of me you've never seen,
> I'm made of Meissen porcelain.
> A China doll I'm for a fee
> For who knows how to handle me?"

To the rhythm of the little minuet I danced down the steps of the station. My mother heaved a hopeful sigh. "If you get the role of the Marquise we will finally be able to pay the gas bill," she said more in the direction of her fox than in mine. Mirrored in the black water of the Spree River, the light of the gas lantern looked oily, like oily eels, and up on the Hansa Bridge we encountered the wind.

"Stop the babble, Reni, close your mouth. It's windy, you'll catch a cold again. What nonsense, golden eels in the Spree in February. Children who talk too much have no more words left when they grow old," and mother's leather gloved hand got a firm grip on my mouth. In autumn when the temperatures were still warmer, I liked to rustle through the fallen leaves in the wind, but it is winter now — whistling, the wind pulled at the bag with my ballet shoes in it, bringing tears to my eyes and pinching my nose.

The wind passes its time on the Hansa Bridge, but in the Tiergarten lives the liebe Gott (German for the Good Lord). Whenever our path crossed the Landwehr Canal, it was impossible to budge me from the small bridge until at least one barge had passed. A wooden shed with checkered curtains and geraniums in its small windows would glide past below me, wash fluttered, a dog barked at me and was gone. There in the lock house by the canal lived the liebe Gott. I had seen Him from afar more than once turning His wheels mightily to open and close the lock gates for the barges. If I squeezed my eyes shut when I prayed in bed at night, He would appear again in his blue denim shift, big tufts of silver hair and white beard.

"Dear God, make me meek, so I shall enter Heaven," I would murmur, but only with the "Shema Yisrael," which I used to recite in Hebrew without understanding a word, would the old man in his blue shift crank the wheels. Gates opened, whirling waters rushed out, and I fell asleep.

I did not get the part of the rococo marquise. Holding a little boy by the hand, I danced the next morning as gracefully as I could, knew my lines and sang in tune. Alas, a little girl on the pudgy side with straight, dark bangs was no ideal choice for a porcelain figurine.

On my fifth birthday I wished for Tilsit cheese. What I received was a doll's pram and permission to push it back and forth in front of our house with Lotte tucked into it. My brother Werner went still farther.

"If you promise to stay on the sidewalk, you may walk once around the block. Just don't talk to Gypsies!" he insisted before taking off in the direction of the Spree, holding his handmade kite high over his head. "Once around the block, you hear, Reni, till you get back to our entrance!" he warned once more as if I did not know that one can get run over in the street and that Gypsies steal children. (A five-year old can be forgiven the prejudices which later in the concentration camps contributed to the sometimes more inhumane treatment of Gypsies than of Jews.)

Lotte's glass eyes staring trustfully into mine, I started pushing the pram. At the end of Tiele Wardenberg Street our grocer leaned on the door to his shop.

"You did not wash your eyes again today," he teased me, "black as can be. Cute little Jew-girl," he said sideways to his wife, thinking I would not hear.

My feelings for the grocer were a mixture of fear and greed, somewhat like the feeling I had for Uncle Max, who with every one of our greetings would swing me upon his arm and pinch my cheek and my behind with his free hand. First shrieking with pleasure, then with pain, I would wait for one silver mark for chocolate to emerge finally from his pocket. I feared the grocer even more than Uncle Max, but I liked candy on a stick. Whenever the man caught me sucking my thumb, he would pull me over to his smelly barrel full of herring. "If I catch you once more at it, I'll put your thumb into the brine!" Threatening me with this most awful of all punishments, he would push a little stick with candy into my other hand. Of course, in order to accept candy I had to be accompanied by someone, and so I paused this time only for a second, greeted curtly and continued around the corner. At this same instant our house and our street disappeared and Alraune, Uncle Max and Aunt Toote's terrier pursuing some spitz in the distance, was a welcome sight. Unfamiliar children played "Heaven and Earth" on the pavement, and strange windows stared at me from both sides of the street. I had no idea where I was and ran almost around the next corner — if only I could once more make out the shop with the herring barrel.

"The-end-of-the-world, the-end-of-the-world" rattle and squeak from the wheels of the pram — before the war the pram had been for my sister. Another corner, and one more, and in my panic I almost passed the entrance to our house. It had to be sorcery. All the time I had been running away from our house, how could I then have ended up in front of the entrance? No matter how often I repeated the trick, the inner workings of "once around the block" remained a mystery; nor has my spatial thinking developed far beyond this early stage.

In March, Purim — the festival celebrating the Biblical Queen Esther's saving the Jews from the villainy of Haman — came around again, one of the rare joyous Jewish holidays. We should rejoice, Rabbi Levkovitz enjoined us in his sermon, for rarely in the course of our history had Jews escaped pogroms and the threat of destruction. I paraded with the other children of the congregation through the corridors of the synagogue, with one hand shaking a wooden noise maker and the other waving a colorfully printed paper flag while candy rained down upon us from the gallery. "People like Haman and his ten sons, those who incited the Persians against us, are called anti-Semites," my father explained on the way home. "They have always existed, and they still exist today. Now it is Hitler who is doing the same. Turn your noise maker, Reni, we'll show them!"

My mother had prepared kreplach soup, meat-filled dumplings in bouillon, which she served only once a year, on Purim. The three-pointed dumplings swimming in my plate were supposed to represent Haman's ears. They tasted heavenly. Besides kreplach soup the best part of Purim was the yearly costume party at Aunt Toote's. The whole family showed up, Aunt Luise as a Biedermeier lady, and my cousin Karl, dressed as a pirate, teased me with his usual greeting: "Irene, Irene, yikes, your feet are not clean."

Was this a way to address an elf with gossamer wings? Bursting with indignation I was nevertheless delighted by my big cousin's attention. And who would have guessed that the chimney sweep was in reality Uncle Richard and the two babies with bonnets, bibs and pacifiers, Grandfather and Grandmother Zoegall? In order to pass as a Berlin shoemaker's apprentice, my brother Werner is behaving with all the cheekiness he can muster, while my sister as a Gypsy reads everybody's palms, predicting a rosy future for family and friends. Chatter and laughter, then a bejeweled Aunt Toote, glittering Queen of the Night, invites her guests to dance. As my aunt sits down at the grand piano in the drawing room, Great-grandmother Treumann used this opportunity for her big entrance scene. Emerging from behind the tiled stove, she wielded one index finger with dignity and proclaimed with a voice coming from a toothless mouth that was still surprisingly biting, "Pigsty!" Her bony finger smudged with soot pointed accusingly at Aunt Toote and her maid of many years, Anna, blushing with embarrassment as she passed a silver tray with hors d'oeuvres.

"Pigsty!" I knew my mother and her sisters feared their grandmother's sharp tongue. "The old lady with the asphalt gullet," they called her when she was out of earshot, mainly because her coffee always had to be boiling hot. Nobody dared talk back to her. The respect shown her had not come easy. Seventy years earlier my great-grandmother had a husband registered in the annals of the family as

Eduard Treumann from Berlin — then he vanished. Maybe he went to America and found himself a softer mate — no one ever knew. With four daughters and penniless, Nanette Treumann was not one to raise her hands in despair; instead she and her daughters learned how to sew brassieres, then still called bodices. They sold them in the market, and with the marriage of my grandparents in 1878, their manufacturing business grew into a well-known lingerie and linen firm that became the financial backbone of my mother's family. Still operating many years after the death of my grandparents, it remained in the hands of the Zoegalls until the beginning of the Second World War because of the role of Aryan-born Aunt Luise.

Purim 1926 was to be the last celebration in which nearly all members of the family participated. The exception was Uncle Albert who, in the words of my parents, had worked himself to death for his patients in the slums around the Kreuzberg. One year later my grandfather, my great-grandmother, my grandmother and my mother would also lie in Weissensee, the big cemetery for the Jews of Berlin.

Tw o

———

WHEN GROWN-UPS WOULD WHISPER in my presence and my mother was dressed in black, I knew without asking that another member of the family had vanished. 1927. The first to go was my fun-loving Grandfather Zoegall. Soon after his laughter had died, my Great-grandmother Treumann and her croaked commands were gone as well. Her room stood empty, and only her sharp smell of old age continued to cling to the green plush upholstery. When my grandmother lay dying, my dutiful mother wanted to let her see her youngest grandchild one last time. Though I was unable to understand the gravity and meaning of her dying, I have never forgotten the sickroom and its misery. I was wholly unprepared for the old woman with waxen, contorted features who had once been Grandma Fränze. Thrashing about amid strands of gray hair and crumpled sheets, she now lay groaning in the grandparental bedroom. I have been unable to erase that scene from my memory.

Deprived of its main pillars, the family continued to hold together. Aunt Luise and Uncle Richard took over the linen and lingerie shop on König Street. As in previous summers, my uncles, aunts and cousins would take the train to the shores of the Baltic Sea to meet in Heringsdorf. We had the poorest accommodations there, for Papa had slipped another rung down the social ladder. After a long and unsuccessful struggle to remain independent, he had to close his housewares shop and take a position as a traveling salesman. Who still needed brushes, brooms and baskets of pre-war quality, German handiwork that would last forever? I still have an old clothes brush from his stock.

If post-war Berliners believed in anything at all, it was in the present, in cheap mass production and in department stores with escalators.

For weeks on end my father was absent on business trips, and more and more often my mother was not feeling well. It fell to my older sister to drag me along on all her outings. "The child needs a breath of fresh air," my mother said. Like many an eighteen-year-old of the period, Gerda, spirited, with racy Semitic features, gleaming white teeth and a beautiful singing voice, would have loved to become a film star. With me in tow, she made the tour of the studios. But there was no lack of young ladies of piquant appearance — and singing voices were not needed for silent films. In one of the smoke-filled offices an impresario, jabbing a finger under my chin, turned my head from side to side.

"Whose boy is that here? What's your name, little man?" asked a fat, deep voice.

"My name is I-re-ne," I drew out the three German syllables, offended that I had been taken for a boy because of my jump-suit and the fact that I was wearing my brother's visored high school cap over short bangs.

"Okay then, I-re-ne," the agent laughed, with one hand redistributing the thin hair on his head, the other removing a cigar from his mouth, "Boy or girl, I-re-ne, you are the answer to my prayers." I was given the part of a boy I vaguely resembled but who had fallen sick. After he was well again, I changed into his twin sister. In the film I sat with my twin in a wooden tub full of suds, and Lil Dagover, the leading diva, was our mother, washing us, a pleasant memory.

The Weimar Republic already had a child labor law and while I sat splashing in the warm suds, a social worker waited for me in the wings with outspread towel, dry clothes and hot noodle-soup. If this was work, then I liked working. The only drawback was the mascara on my lashes and the constant admonition to stare straight into blinding reflectors. Playing the part of a boy was fun — every part was fun. And on the set of the studio at least, I had as yet no inhibitions. I laughed or cried with abandon, feigned toothache, fear, the sorrow of farewell or the joy of reunion just as needed. Whatever the director asked of me I carried out enthusiastically.

After my debut as Lil Dagover' son, I was given several more boy's parts to play, among them a little Tyrolian in leather pants living with his mother in a chalet high up in the Alps. A dark child was not a good match with a flaxen shepherdess, and since the remnants of her false tresses were not enough to hide my hair, I had to become a little Tyrolian with a toothache. Only a few strands of blond hair were now needed to show under a big shawl wound around my head and face.

On winter mornings we had to walk to the Tiergarten Station in the dark. Seated on the wooden bench of a third class compartment on my way toward a new role, the window slowly filled with dawn. Trees that looked like my father's brushwood brooms raced over a sky brimming with icy tangerine juice. The film I was to be in, and where I was for once a girl, is *The Silent Nun*. I was the nun's daughter, alone at home, frightened out of sleep by a thunderstorm in the middle of the night. Magnesium lightning flashed, buckets full of water whipped the window, thunder growled and clapped each time someone in the wings shook a big metal sheet. Although the film was silent, the director was trying to frighten me out of my wits with all the racket, hoping to imprint the scene with a seal of authenticity. If that made him happy, it was fine with me. Pretending to be terrified I romped all over the mattress, cried, screamed for my mother and put on fearful grimaces until she at last came home, and took me into her arms. I never learned what "my mother" did at night, for my parents thought it improper to take a five-year-old to the cinema. Probably because all my film mothers were entangled in complicated marital situations, I never got to see the results of my dramatic activity on screen.

About this time I discovered an art form that did not require me to get up before daybreak to catch the train. Nobody smeared black makeup on my eyelashes; neither did I have to trip over my feet at Papa Gronsky's ballet school. My friend Ilse Ackermann, a first-grader who lived in the back of our building, taught me how easy it was to conjure up faces laughing or crying on command. All that was needed was paper and a pencil — with this discovery of the endless combinations that I could make, I decided to become a painter.

Notwithstanding the smell of boiled cabbage pervading Ilse's home, I liked to visit there because Ilse's parents were more permissive. For example, she was allowed to cut bread by herself, smear it with lard and let me have some too. In our household lard was forbidden — it would give me a rash, said my mother. Though she had long ago given up on keeping a kosher kitchen (we even ate ham) the thought of eating pig's lard was beyond even my parents' otherwise considerable power of assimilation. Consequently, I ate my lard sandwiches at Ilse's. Only when she became cranky, saying that it was because of Jews her uncle was out of work and reproaching me for what we had done to Jesus, would I return to our second floor apartment, perplexed and hurt. Yes, we were Jews. Our religion, my father said, is simply, "Do not do unto others what you would not have them do unto you." Two thousand years ago, a wise Jew named Hillel said this to someone standing on one leg.* Jews and Christians had the same "liebe Gott," it seemed, but Ilse Ackermann had Jesus and a Christmas tree besides!

What did she mean by saying her uncle was out of work because of us? With the exception of Aunt Hanna, who had remained loyal to the Kaiser, all my relatives had black, red and gold flags blowing from their windows at election time. Trying to keep step with my father in the torchlight parade of the Social Democrats, I had shouted "For work and bread!" as loud as all the others. Fluttering with the colors of the various parties, Tiele Wardenberg Street looked very festive indeed with the black, white and red flags of those who still hoped for the return of the Kaiser and the black, red and gold flags of the Social Democrats like us. We sneered at the plain red of the Communists with their hammers and sickles, though only the increasing number of red and white flags with hooked black crosses so upset my parents. Going with them to the Tiergarten to help distribute handbills, I was dressed in a red sweater; each time I met people with a bill printed in the wrong colors or wearing the wrong kind of badge in their lapels, I stopped them to point out their error. Most were friendly and laughed when I tried to push one of my flyers into their hands. When

---

*Rabbi Hillel, a contemporary of Jesus when mocked and asked to explain Judaism in the time he could stand on one leg replied, "What is hateful to you do not unto your neighbor. This is the entire Torah, all the rest is commentary."

no more flyers were left to distribute, I found a twig and drew laughing and crying faces in the sandy paths of the park.

"Duty comes before pleasure," my father always drummed into my head. So what did my friend Ilse want from me? While I had been handing out handbills that pleaded for work and bread, she had been at the Lunapark.

On Sundays Ilse's hair was done up in corkscrews by her mother. Leaving with her parents for an outing she would then dangle her little red patent-leather purse.

"I am off to the Lunapark," she called to me. For a brief moment my father would lift his eyes from the Sunday edition of the *Berliner Tageblatt*, the liberal daily newspaper, to gaze through the window — "goyim naches," his lips just barely moved. Yet those two little words were enough to take out of reach all that my heart most deeply desired. (Though no one in my family knew Yiddish anymore, such irreplaceable expressions as goyim naches, a term designating the kind of amusement beneath the likes of us, still remained in use.) Alas, all that was garish, so deliciously sweet and gooey, all that shone and glittered was goyim naches. The green and pink spun sugar sold at the entrance to circus tents, the heart-shaped earrings, the lacquered garden dwarfs, the colored glass spheres and the silvery angel's hair glimmering on Christmas trees, and naturally the Lunapark with its wheel of fortune — all these belonged to a long list of temptations I found it difficult to simply shrug off.

"Reni, stop pestering me, the circus is pure goyim naches — and elephants you can see at the zoo." In this respect my mother always agreed with my father. Since the time a monkey had bit my finger for feeding it a peel after I had run out of peanuts, and especially after I had heard that the animal had been shot for being aggressive, I was not so eager to go see the animals. That is, until the ghost of the slain monkey faded into the background before an Indian exhibition opening at the zoo. Inexplicably and luckily for me, anything Indian seemed not to be on a level with goyim naches. Neither elephants hung with carpets and jewels, nor brown-skinned men sporting earrings, decorated turbans and embroidered vests, nor women with gold in their nostrils, belonged to this inferior category. My mother even bought me a ticket for an elephant ride.

The giant animal swayed back and forth as we passed the cages of the lions and the tigers. I held on for dear life to the passenger in front of me, loving the view from above especially when looking straight into the goggle-eyes of the giraffe. Too soon the mountain settled to its knees. Two arms smelling of ginger-cake and sweat brought me back to earth, a young Indian woman in a saffron-colored sari pressing me to her bosom and kissing me.

"My boy, my boy!" she called out to my mother in a language which I took to be Indian, then pulled a photograph from the silken depths of her sari. It was a little boy that could have been me, the child she had to leave behind in India, her gestures were explaining. Tears welling up in her eyes she stroked my hair, trying to teach me a few words of her language. She looked at me so lovingly, my heart went out to her, so beautiful with her long, silky eyelashes, smiling lips and the drop of gold in one nostril. And what was the mysterious round, red dot in the middle of her forehead?

"Illepen, illepen," I said after her, pointing to an elephant and elated in the belief that I was speaking Indian. When my mother wanted to move on, the young woman lifted a strand of silvery beads over her head and put them around my neck as a parting gift.

No Maharajah ever possessed jewels as precious as my mercury-coated glass beads. But invariably, removed from saffron silk and ginger skin to be worn with my wardrobe, the necklace reverted into garishly glittering goyim naches, and as such had to be kept in a little box with velvet lining for the more exotic existence I hoped for in a far away future.

In the following year, when we moved to the suburbs after my mother's death, I sometimes would take the beads out of their box. Using a three-legged table, Lotte's pre-war high chair and some discarded knickknacks, I improvised a special corner for myself in the attic of our row house. In this privacy I could unashamedly adorn myself with my glass beads. No one saw me there apart from my balding Lotte.

As the years went by, the beads began to crack and burst. In the end, when I had to flee Germany, forced to leave any kind of jewelry behind, there was little more than a bare thread, fine glass shards and silver dust remaining at the bottom of the box.

In that winter of my film activity, I asked for a pink marzipan piglet for my birthday present. That kind of thing was goyim naches par excellence; I received instead a blackboard on an easel, colored chalks and a sponge. Though less intensive a pleasure than marzipan, it provided for more durable entertainment. I was happy at best that my present was not another doll from the old trunk. I was tired of dolls, mostly because of an incident that occurred shortly before my birthday on the set where I had been acting. In a crowd of children I had been bustling about a Christmas fair movie stage made of cardboard and artificial snow, where only the toys in the stalls were real. When the screening finished, the director grouped all the children in a half circle around the heaped up toys and invited each of us to choose one. I did not have to think twice. Like nails to a magnet, my eyes fixed on a red, white and green tin drum with wooden drumsticks and leather tongs to hang the marvelous drum around one's neck. As each child was called up to choose a toy, my heart missed a beat, but my luck held. When my turn came the drum was still available. Flushed with anticipation I lifted my hand to choose the drum when suddenly, like a balloon pricked by a needle, I pointed limply to a doll, not even a pretty one. At the deciding moment, I had lost heart because of a red signal blinking in my mind. Jews must not attract attention! To play a boy's role might still pass as make believe, but what would people think of a girl banging the drums?

Carrying the doll, deeply disappointed and without a word, I followed my mother home. Emotions had to be locked inside, especially painful ones. Songs full of feeling could be sung, the stage was there to vent them but in everyday life, in real life, you were not supposed to show them.

Such restraint though did not mean that our home was a quiet one; this was especially true of my brother Werner. On my father's orders, the door to his room had to be closed at all times. Nevertheless, horrible squeaks, screeches and howls escaping from a wooden box inside could still be heard around the apartment. Werner said he was catching sound waves with the wires, tiny lamps and screws called a radio, a contraption he had built himself. Hidden in a cloud hissing from his steam engine, my brother stood singing arias against the noise. With his newly deepened voice he was earning pocket-money as an extra at the opera. He had won the steam engine as a first prize for his entry in a young peoples' building block competition. Not only was the engine running — the whole room was covered with intricate tracks and tunnels propelling Werner's marbles, clay and glass. Opening the door a crack, I caught snippets of some hit songs piercing the static of the radio: "Who was it that rolled the cheese to the station?" Then my favorite hit rang out: "What does Meyer do by the Himalaya?" Still humming, I shut the door because of the smell coming from the lizards he kept in a terrarium.

The room I shared with my sister smelled of the violet perfume she was given by an admirer, though that was a secret I was not supposed to tell my father. Accompanying herself on a guitar with ribbons embroidered in all colors, she liked to sing nostalgic songs by Hermann Loens. Her other songbook, the Zupfgeigenhansel, lay on the table, opened to one of the old German folksongs I still know by heart.

Between the double windows of the living room stood tall glasses with hyacinth bulbs protected from the light by funny, little pointed paper hats. Sunrays that filtered through their tangled roots touched my mother's hands as she played the piano. She sang a long song about gray hours lit up by the muses, then a gayer one of a brook cascading down the valley from its mountain spring, songs of a world without debts or bailiffs. Giving in to my pleading she next sang my own song for me, about the moon peeping through my window. "He tells the blooms in the flowerbed that He saw your naked little leg."

The next noisiest place after Werner's room, and also the most cheerful, was the kitchen. There our underpaid household help, a

miner's daughter from Silesia, was busying herself clinking and clattering, trilling Slavic melodies with deep feeling and little ear. She was
not the only one to do so. Many of the kitchen windows overlooking
the backyaplyrd were ringing with laments, refrains like, "The oil lamp
flickers sadly, it's running low on fat — the girl I'm in love with, is
sleeping fast in bed," or "Your father wallows in plenty, has forgotten
about you and me." These and other such melancholy songs may not
have prepared me for life, but nevertheless they left a lasting imprint on
me.

To complete these musical matinées, all kinds of wandering song-
sters and organ grinders plied their trade under our kitchen window,
more and more of them. Laid-off heads of family, disabled ex-service-
men and ordinary beggars used the trash can area as a stage to present
in song and prose their accounts of undeserved and unbelievable blows
of fate, trying to move the kitchen auditorium into giving them alms.
At the start of any of these presentations, I ran to get my mother.

"Does the man look clean?" After I reassured her that his coat was
not torn at the elbows, she would follow me into the kitchen to convince herself that the poor devil would not spend our pfennigs on
drink. Most of the time, however, she let me throw a well-wrapped
sandwich from the window in place of coins.

Apart from a blackboard, I also received a book for my birthday, a
present from Aunt Hanna who naturally had chosen stories of an educational nature. Although they made me afraid, I would often ask my
mother or Gerda to read one of the tales, though not in the evening.
The stories were of dolls, teddy bears and stuffed animals who in the
dark of night spoke to each other of their misfortunes and how they
had landed in the clinic of a doll doctor. One doll told how her
owner's brother had banged her porcelain head against a wall until it
broke. Another had a face, but both her arms had been pulled out to
punish her for saying "mama" but not "papa." All the stories were sad,
but even though the book had no images, I was unable to keep them
at bay at night in my bed — the sailor boy with empty sockets needing new glass eyes, the baby doll smeared all over with red after a game
of "operation."

If I was superstitious I would say those stories were a foreshadowing that pointed eerily to my future. The author's and Aunt Hanna's intention had evidently been a very different one, namely to teach children from early on to love their fellow creatures, taking good care even of their pseudo-human friends. If the book did not make me a better mother to my dolls, it did give me a bad conscience. Still, long after I was able to read the stories by myself and knew very well that beings made from celluloid and porcelain had no souls, I would be plagued by a sense of guilt. The thought of Lotte's unkempt hair stuck together with jam, her scratched cheeks and broken-off thumbs would pursue me sometimes even in broad daylight.

A few weeks after my sixth birthday, my mother came down with the flu. My father was away on business, so Aunt Hanna came to pack the book about the doll doctor next to my nightgown in a small suitcase. She would read the rest of the stories to me in my mother's place, she promised.

I would have preferred to go to Aunt Toote's who lived only ten houses farther down our street. Absentminded but friendly, she left me in peace, and on my visits occasionally took one of her music books out of their glass case. My cousins Lilo and Ursula long outgrew childrens' songs framed in pretty vignettes. It was now my turn to lean against the grand piano and sing to accompaniment like an old pro. No song would be left out, except for the lament of a young soldier about to be executed in the redoubt of Strasbourg because he attempted to swim from the French to the German side of the Rhine. This page would be automatically turned over before the bugle call from German shores brought tears to the eyes of the girls in the family.

Aunt Hanna, on the other hand, felt such heavy responsibility for my safety that I was not even allowed to go to her balcony alone. To prevent me from falling out of bed at night, she bundled me up in blankets and placed a bulwark of chairs and settees around the couch. Doing so she would tell me in detail about all the accidents she had witnessed in Uncle Albert's clinic, all the broken arms and legs that were the result of jumping on mattresses; there was also the case of a little boy with a chamber-pot so firmly clinging to his head that a plumber had to be called in to cut the pot off.

Aunt Hanna believed that the earlier a girl learned to cook, the better. One morning she wrapped me in one of her aprons with ceremony and then, to help me look into the pots on the range, had me
stand up on an inverted wash basin. I was allowed to help her cook!
Eagerly I stirred red tomato soup with a big wooden spoon when suddenly the bell rang. It was the aunt who had trains rattling through her
place, Aunt Alice. I recognized her voice. She always spoke loudly, so
why was she out of breath and whispering? And why did she remain
standing with Aunt Hanna in the hall in darkness?

"Grete is dead," I heard her stammer. What did she mean? Dead
people disappeared, but my mother was at home in bed. Still holding
the dripping spoon I stood there on the inverted basin listening to
Aunt Hanna's suppressed sobs. Something awful must have happened,
grown-ups only cry on Yom Kippur at the synagogue. I was angry at
Aunt Hanna for crying and at Aunt Alice because she had to stick her
nose into everything — if only she had not come.

Many years had to pass, more than twenty, until one day I suddenly
realized why I could not eat tomato soup.

⟶

Sitting opposite each other at our kitchen table, Mrs. Hecht and Mrs.
Hammer drank coffee from our big stoneware cups and rubbed their
eyes. Just like the two cats in my Struwelpeter book, a popular illus-
trated book from the 19th century, they sat there, wiping away the tears
rolling down their face with their paws. The cats looked so tearfully at
little Pauline, reduced to a small heap of ash in the middle of the page,
whereas sad-eyed Mrs. Hecht and Mrs. Hammer were contemplating
my new dress spread out between them. Much as I wanted to persuade
myself that the black taffeta was making them moody I knew better. I
know only too well why their eyes were red.

My father and my brother and sister were sitting on the floor of the
living-room on pillows — Papa and Werner with black mourning
bands around their sleeves, Gerda in black from head to foot. Visitors
were coming and going from morning to late at night. They talked in
muffled voices; not even Else, our maid from Upper Silesia, sang. On

my father's instructions, I had to stay with her in the kitchen, but Else, who kept moving all day long between trays, coffee cups, visitors and sandwiches, had little time for me.

Mrs. Hecht, more wrinkled and careworn than ever, had finished her coffee. Going into the adjoining room she returned with a handful of colored cotton thread from mama's sewing-table.

"The child's all in black, it's too much to take," she sighed, and bending over the taffeta dress began embroidering the hem with little flowers. Mrs. Hecht and Mrs. Hammer had been part of our household for as long as I could remember. Mrs. Hecht, a seamstress, would come now and then pedaling our Singer machine, turning threadbare collars and cuffs, transforming my mother's old dresses into new ones for my sister. What Gerda had outgrown would, in turn, make rompers and ballet clothes for me.

Mrs. Hammer, as imposing as Mrs. Hecht was short and bent, earned her living as a shampoo woman. Visiting the various families of our clan at regular intervals, she shampooed everybody's hair with tar soap and bony fingers.

"This is in her memory," said Mrs. Hecht as she planted a tiny red flower with green leaves on the black taffeta, then bit off the thread. "Did they take the poor little mite with them to the churchyard?" Else stopped grinding coffee. She cut the seamstress short: "Don't you know, Reni's mother's gone on a trip?" She stressed every syllable, speaking so loudly as if Mrs. Hecht was hard of hearing. Not wanting them to see me so upset, I turned my back to the three women and gazed at the gray sky. They all take me for stupid, I thought. Churchyard! Churchyards were for "them."

I would not ask anything more of anyone. Not even my father was telling me the truth. One thing was sure, Mama was dead, and dead people do not travel. The same as my grandmother and great-grandmother Treumann before her, she was brought to the Jewish cemetery. What they had done with her I did not know nor did I want to think about it.

Three

M Y MOTHER CAME TO ME IN DREAMS, blurred like a poorly exposed photograph, without ever smiling. Nevertheless, I loved those dreams, waking up with the warm feeling that Mutti maybe was still somewhere. My father had always been the one to romp and play with me rather than my more reserved, careful and pensive mother, so that I suffered less from the separation than one might have expected. What I could not bear was to be treated by family friends and even strangers like a sick puppy — eyes full of pity made me feel like an animal whose fur was being stroked against the grain. To be handled by people I barely knew like a raw egg, because I had no mother, was humiliating, unjust and none of their business.

At the end of sitting shiva — the prescribed seven days of mourning in the home of the deceased — I was sent on rotating visits to relatives still wearing my new black taffeta dress. Emerging from the gloomy week of mourning, I felt as if I was setting out on an adventure with little room for homesickness and longing, like being handed a ticket to see "Little Peter's Trip to the Moon." My first stop was Aunt Toote's at the other end of Tiele Wardenberg Street.

Considered old-fashioned and therefore disdained by other relatives, Great-grandmother Treumann's carved chairs were now standing in front of Aunt Toote's bay window. Occupying such a prominent place, they had turned into "museum pieces," at least in the eyes of the other inheritors. Whenever I was tired of Aunt Toote's children's songs, I would climb onto one of these heirlooms — standing on the seat and circumventing a carved lion's head, I could look through the bay window at the Spree River.

"Reni, quickly . . . you may lick the stirring ladle . . . sweet shortcake dough," Anna called from the kitchen.

"Reni, hop, hop. . .into the bathtub!" called my Cousin Lilo with the almond eyes. She told a story of the fairy Melusine while I was soaking. Then, sponged down, I floated to the faraway forest where the blue flower of magic grew. Until the prince on his white steed finally approached, I was sitting in cold bath water. Behind the door, Uncle Max was laid up in his bedroom with an attack of gout: he abused in turn the masseuse and Aunt Toote. Served him right, instead of pinching my behind it was his big toe that was being pinched! After my bath I caught tiny, colored cardboard fish out of an imaginary lake with a little fishing rod and line that was capped by a magnet — the game had once belonged to my cousin Ursula. Though Uncle Max's cries of pain and curses rang out from behind the bedroom door, they did not bother me in the slightest.

Delivered to my next destination, I found in Aunt Hanna's less varied household a pastime harmless enough to be left alone even by her watchful eyes. Lying on the carpet for hours, I leafed through thick tomes of Flemish, Italian and German masters (a wedding present seldom opened, but regularly dusted). In there were princesses with their lapdogs, severe gentlemen stuck into huge, frilly collars, ladies either loaded with furs and feather hats or else not dressed at all. Velvet and silk looked as if you could touch them, not to mention fruit and flowers: peaches that made your mouth water, wine glasses more transparent than the rummers on Aunt Hanna's sideboard, grapes shimmering with dew. In each book there were plenty of Ilse's Jesuses, often as a baby with his mother, but also as a man hanging on the cross all naked and so pitiful it was hard to look at him.

"Irene, Irene, your feet are never clean." I was glad my cousin Karl came in, pulling my leg in the usual fashion. Good-natured as he was, he would perhaps let himself be coaxed to the piano to sing my favorite song: "There once was a king, He had a flea so fat, He loved it as a son, He spoiled it as a pet. . . ." Rendered in his full, warm baritone, Goethe's "Song of the Flea" to Mussorgsky's music sounded so beautiful that the chromatic tones gave me goose pimples.

Aunt Hanna's idea of a little girl's education, fortunately not limited to the art of cooking, also meant encouraging my interest in painting. Since the old masters could not affect me adversely, I entered a museum for the first time in my life holding her hand. I was flabbergasted. On the walls, a hundred-fold in size and in gilded frames, I met my acquaintances from Aunt Hanna's books: the fat little angels floating on pink clouds, the gentlemen in buckled shoes, ironclad breast and silk sashes haughtily looking down on me. Each hall had at least one painting of Jesus with a circle around his head, because he was a saint, said Aunt Hanna. Best of all I liked the picture of a laughing old Dutch woman with a raven on her shoulder.

Paintings were fine, but the history of Prussia was more important. For this reason we took the way back from the museum through the Siegesallee, where I repeated parrot-fashion, even before knowing how to recite the ABC's, all the names of margraves and electors of the Hohenzollern monarchy whose busts then flanked the promenade. My aunt's pedagogic zeal did not end with what Berliners used to call "Doll's Avenue." The next morning we went on a patriotic excursion to Potsdam, to Sans Souci and then to the tomb of Frederick the Great and his dogs, where I at last understood what is done with the dead. Dragging me energetically from palace to palace, from the likeness of one Frederick or Wilhelm, or Frederick-Wilhelm, to the next, she bounced ahead, a short lady on high heels, a ball of patriotic duty and Prussian loyalty. Aunt Hanna had gotten hold of herself again. No one would have guessed that in despair after the death of her husband, she had jumped from the second floor window of a sanatorium. Later she would steadfastly and without complaint live through the degradation of the Hitler regime, the loss of her considerable assets and the flight to America.

At the time of my long stay in 1927, however, she was still Frau Doktor, owner of the apartment house on Passauer Street where she lived. A bright blue convertible, with its horn blowing, had stopped in front. Uncle Richard in his "Wanderer," pride of the Zoegall clan, had come to collect me. With one hand he set my small suitcase and me on the front seat, passing me an ice cream cone, with the other he cranked up the motor. Turning the corner of the KaDeWe, a well-known department store, into Tauentzien Street, I kept waving to Aunt Hanna on her balcony.

In the eyes of my family, toy cars with pedals were only for the off-spring of millionaires; I did not have the nerve to ask for such an extravagant birthday present. Not only was I driving down Potsdamer Strasse and Unter den Linden in a real car, I was also licking an ice-cream cone. The sun was shining, the cone was big enough to last through the Brandenburg Gate, and it was a marvelous morning.

Uncle Richard, my mother's younger brother, and Aunt Luise were a graceful couple who talked in hushed voices, and were most at ease in the subdued light of their "peasant room." Gold-green light filtering through windows of bull's-eye glass flowed over the hand-painted tiles of a Bavarian stove and left the rest of the room in gloom, especially the painting of a terribly sad Hagar with Ishmael in the desert, which they had discovered in the cellar of some provincial museum. By compari-son, the inflated fish with a mustache was quite funny. Hanging from a ceiling beam and grinning with a hundred pointed little teeth, it observed me trying to eat my bread and butter, called a sandwich, with knife and fork. It was just as well that the peasant's room did not have more light. In the snow-white bedroom with a pink baby lying amidst a tulle creation, my black dress made me feel even more out of place. Fortunately Uncle Richard and Aunt Luise had a little black poodle, so that I was not the only spot on the virginal snowscape.

When at last Papa came to get me, he was received rather coolly. Not by me though, joyfully jumping up at him like a young dog. Much later I understood why relations between my father and Uncle Richard were so pointedly polite.

My maternal grandparents had worked their way up from modest beginnings and wanted to give their children, in particular their only son, the kind of education they themselves had missed. Was it Uncle Richard's fault that he looked like a Spanish Grande, that women rarely could resist his melancholy brown eyes smoldering with an indefinable something?

A young man whom nature had destined for the part of a romantic lover, he evidently preferred bars, coffee houses and such to lecture halls. What? Their son Richard was squandering their hard-earned money on shiksas? For Sally and Fränze Zoegall, there was not much time to lose. So they charged my father, at the time still a promising new son-in-law, with accompanying their free-spending young son to Hamburg, seeing to it that he indeed left on a Hapag ship for America. His parents hoped that Uncle Richard would learn to stand on his own two feet, to make something of himself and to take my father as his model.

As for my father, the irony of fate would turn everything upside down. In Berlin Uncle Richard had been preoccupied with the ladies; in America he threw himself into his work on inventions. The German army used one of his patents, a precursor of the flashlight, during the First World War. My father claimed that in critical moments in the trenches it never functioned; but since he had lost my mother's entire dowry, in contrast to Uncle Richard who had returned from America with plenty of money, he may not have been impartial in the matter.

Returning from the New World in straw-hat and knickerbockers, Uncle Richard took a job with the German company Bing and married Aunt Luise, a daughter of Rothenburg, in some way related to nobility. For the sake of the Zoegalls she had converted to Judaism. The partnership of a womanizing Prussian Jew with a passion for electrodynamics and a Catholic Rothenburg lady with a penchant for religious mysticism seemed to fit the young couple's home I was now visiting. A mix of Bavarian peasant furniture, white art deco and the latest achievements of American technology were not without charm. Their partnership would last through the most devastating times, surviving the Nuremberg laws, a long separation dictated by the Nazis, the Second World War, emigration, Uncle Richard's escapades and Aunt Luise's joining the Seventh Day Adventists. Even after all other members of the family had fled Germany, sat in camps or perished, Aryan Aunt Luise was for a while able to keep the linen and lingerie shop on König Street going. After the war her marriage to Uncle Richard, which I shall return to, continued in California.

My sojourn with my mother's relatives had lasted long enough. My father's older brother's turn had come, my little Uncle David with the funny, bald pink head. My cousin Karl would welcome me with "Irene, Irene, your legs are never clean!" But Uncle David and I also had our private greeting ritual.

"Hi, what's for dinner today?" I would ask standing at the door, Uncle David would promptly lead me into the kitchen to sniff at the pots on the range.

"L'ho daudis (Hebrew for the first two words of the prayer inviting the Sabbath) with puppies," he answered without moving a muscle. Only his sharp blue eyes behind equally sharp glasses gave the tiniest wink.

⁓

My father was born in Posen, a region that at the time of his birth was German, but became part of Poland after the First World War. For this reason, and even though he was only three years old when his family moved to Berlin, the Zoegalls thought of him and all Spickers as unequal. I concluded from my father's stories that the Spickers from Krojanke, glaziers and horse-breeders for the Prussian army until the first part of the nineteenth century, had not been Spickers at all, but Cohns. However, when the emancipation and equality of rights had blown into the easternmost provinces of Prussia, the Jews of Posen had been given German-sounding names together with German nationality. Maybe there were no spittoons in magistrates' offices, maybe ordinary Jews at that time had no handkerchiefs and were compelled to spit on the floor while facing the great name-giving deputy of the reigning authorities. Since that day we were called Spicker, similar to the German for "spitter." My ancestor from Krojanke must have been poor. Had he been a man of means, he could have chosen a more elegant name evoking the perfume of flowers or the glittering of gems, in which case I might have been born as Irene Silberschatz, Edelstein, Veilchenfeld or Rosenthal.

According to Aunts Hanna and Toote, my vivacious sister Gerda was a true Zoegall, while I with my straight hair, insignificant nose and chubby figure was counted as a member of the Spicker tribe. My brother was considered a borderline case depending on his conduct of the moment. Not me. Neither the piles of egg warmers I crocheted for my aunts, nor the doilies I laboriously edged with drawn-thread work could change the fact that I was a little Spicker and would remain so.

And now I was with my less refined relatives in Friedenau, where you might sometimes shriek with laughter and cut boiled potatoes with your knife. The extensive proportions of Uncle David's villa made him seem even shorter than he was. Swallowed up by the huge red leather armchairs of the salon, he looked even more out of place on the spindly golden chairs in the music room. Whenever he wanted to be by himself, he retired into a corner behind a potted palm. There he put on his black yarmulke or scullcap, wrapped two leather straps around his arm, and a black small box (in Hebrew, tefillin) on his forehead, and began swaying back and forth. He was praying, Aunt Johanna Spicker intimated, putting a finger over her lips, and was not to be spoken to.

I was not the only one to run after him. Everybody — his wife, his children, my father, the indigent belonging to his congregation and the people he employed in his readymade ladies clothes manufacturing business — constantly sought his advice. . His insight coupled with a dry sense of humor, his helpfulness and his staunch belief in the magnanimity and justice of the God of his forefathers, made my little uncle the hub around whom all Spickers turned. Since his youth, Uncle David had assumed an immense responsibility. As the oldest son of a mother who died soon after my father's birth (he was the sixth child), Uncle David thrived on hard work. Marrying a resourceful woman, his house had become fertile, his vine producing more fruit than he had ever dreamed.

When he had finished his prayers, Uncle David carefully put his tefillin back into the embroidered bag. He glanced disapprovingly at the gilded mermaids that embellished the mantle clock and wandered through an all-glass folding door to the bust of Beethoven on the piano. Among what strange fruits of wealth had he landed? Would the golden coach, as in the fairytale, transform itself back into a pumpkin the moment that clock with the fishtailed shiksas rings midnight? And so it happened. When one year later Uncle David declared bankruptcy, his house and all his possessions went under the hammer of the auctioneer. There were, however, twelve more months to go until that time, a whole year when it was always five minutes to midnight. You could sit trembling with cold in the unheated conservatory, drink tea from a samovar in the Turkish room and let the green felt on the billiard table go fallow.

Aunt Johanna, on the other hand, grand dame to the bitter end — not just her financial ruin but her family's fate during Hitler's time — harbored no doubts about the tangibility of Persian carpets. She strode them with confidence. Working as her husband's business partner, managing the education of her children, making her own Passover wine from fermented raisins or teaching Gentile kitchen help how to keep a kosher household, she rose in full-bosomed stateliness over her domain and over Uncle David, always showing him the respect a good Jewish wife owes her spouse, never making decisions without first consulting him.

"The soul of the enterprise!" Jews from the Berlin neighborhood of ready-to-wear wholesale businesses used to admiringly call a woman of Aunt Johanna's cut. Trying to hold off bankruptcy, Uncle David, she, their sons and my cousin Hilde, all worked hand in hand with the employees at a workshop on Kommandanten Street, a kind of beehive that I preferred to the grand villa in Friedenau. That place would have been all right except for the prohibition on using the dumbwaiter for me to go up and down between the kitchen and the dining room. Nor did I feel like playing with my Cousin Hilde's huge, graying dollhouse. I much preferred sitting cross-legged on a work table of the Kommandanten Street, designing dresses with their flounces, valences and bows on large sheets of brown wrapping paper. In passing all my relatives, the seamstresses and cutters felt compelled to "ah" and "oh" at my creations, pretending they were soon to hang from the racks. Naturally, their reactions strengthened my ambition to become an artist.

⌒

Under these circumstances the date for my starting school came at the right time. Not only would I soon be able to read stories by myself, I would be taught the same drawing tricks as Ilse Ackermann. At school the children made pictures out of colored paper and glue — arithmetic was of minor importance. With the school situated in proximity to Aunt Toote's place, that is where my weeks of wandering came full circle. She hurried me first to Lindemann's department store on Turm Street and bought me a burgundy-colored corduroy outfit hemmed in silver and a hat to match. A leather schoolbag of my sister's of pre-war quality — indestructible and often serving me as a sled on the way back from school — completed my schoolgirl attire. And so I entered Mrs. Herring's class with confidence to begin my formal schooling. Like all children I was accompanied by a family member, in my case my father, and like other children I was given a huge cardboard horn of plenty heaped with sweets. Until I found out that under the candy the bottom of the pointed cardboard bag was filled with oranges, I could not count my blessings. Though it would not last for long, at last I was like other children.

Class began with our teacher, a motherly woman with a crown of blond braids, asking us to fold our hands as for prayer, which seemed simple enough. But when I put my left thumb on top of my right, as I always do, I was trapped, having to sit in the back rows of the class with those who had not done it correctly. This disgrace was nothing in comparison with what was to follow.

"Irene Spicker!" called Frau Herring, forty pairs of eyes staring at me as I got up. "Is it true, my child? I heard that your mother died?" Mute and red to the roots of my hair I stood there nodding, wanting to run. It became even worse. "Poor child, so young and without a mother. We will all be especially nice to you, won't we, children?"

"Yes, Frau Herring!" shouted the class. I will never forget the hot shame and mortification I felt at that moment — I had not yet grown the thick skin I would one day need. Mrs. Herring's well-meant public compassion wounded me more deeply than coarse anti-Semitic insults ever could. Not even the mocking, curious eyes of the Gestapo on my naked body years later in Mechelen would be so hurtful.

Fortunately we moved soon after this incident to a new housing development, Uncle Tom's Cabin (in German Onkel Tom's Hütte) in the Zehlendorf district of Berlin. In Miss Flachshaar's class in the Zinnowald school, I would no longer have to fear pity — nothing I did would ever please Miss Flachshaar. Not even in drawing class did I do well. My brushwork was not clean, my paper collage was smeared with glue, and worse, my gothic letters, Miss Flachshaar's passion, were not of an even up-and-down stroke. I tried to make good on my shortcomings, eagerly raising my hand to answer questions.

"Lothar Bauke has cut his mountains out of blue paper . . . what color should he have taken instead?" Miss Flachshaar held up a landscape that showed signs of imagination.

"Brown!" the class shouted in unison. I raised my hand.

"Both," I said. "Mountains in front are brown, farther away they are blue." Miss Flachshaar belabored her desk with the pointer.

"Quiet, quiet! Brown. Quiet! Of course they are brown. Sit down, Irene. You think you are so smart, but I say you are stupid." That oral slap in the face was much easier to bear than being handed over to my classmates to be pitied. With all that, Miss Flachshaar's remark made me think. Was she right? Maybe I was not all that clever. Perhaps all mountains were brown, and the painters at the museum had not done it right? It would not have entered my mind that I could never do or say anything right because I was Jewish. Until then my only contact with anti-Semitism had been through the story of Purim and the villainous Haman.

Nevertheless I liked school, so much so that I did not want to stay home even when I had a cold or a sore throat. Since we were a family again, though without my mother, my sister Gerda in such cases treated me with wet compresses, aspirin and a thermometer, taking my temperature three times a day. Refusing to be sick, I would pull the thermometer out the moment my sister left the room after covering me with my blanket. I would put it back only when her steps were once more approaching. In this fashion, free of fever, I was allowed to return to school the next day.

Uncle Tom's Cabin, a development designed in the Bauhaus style by the famous architect Bruno Taut, was a paradise for children and for grownups, a verdant relief after a day's work in the city. Gehag, a union construction company, built the development as well as a park (called Fischtal Park, or in German Fischtalgrund) for the working class. Never before having had a garden, my father so loved the sight of the pines, the gooseberry bushes and the lawn that in his free time he started painting everything in green. Walls, the verandah furniture, shelves in the cellar, even the hot water stove in the bathroom shone in lime-green enamel. Here he wanted to start a new life; he spoke enthusiastically about our row house and wanted to stay to the end of his days.

Uncle Tom's Cabin offered affordable rentals. In the summer of 1927, when construction was still unfinished, we were among the first to move in. On the day of our arrival the rain was relentless. The street was not yet paved, and since the horses were unable to pull the heavy moving van through the mud, planks had to be pushed under the wheels. It was late at night when finally, after great difficulty and much shouting, the last of our belongings was accounted for in the limited space of our new home. The rooms were designed for the light fittings of Bauhaus New Realism, not our heavy oak furniture that required much shoving and pulling to get into place.

Our small house would have burst at the seams had the bailiff not seized some of the furniture before we moved. However, with carpets inherited from Grandmother Zoegall, our Delft porcelain and the heather landscape with its purple dots, our refuge here turned out to be cozy. From the doorway, visitors could see how patriotic we were: my father's etchings of the uniforms of all Prussian regiments hung in the stairwell, one etching above each stair. You can be a peaceful Social Democrat and still value order the etchings seemed to imply, though my father's dream of a quiet, orderly existence would hardly materialize. For this reason I could name the period of my life that followed as "Disorder and Early Freedom" (a distortion of Thomas Mann's *Disorder and Early Sorrow*).

"Heini, look, a fire!" All excited, I turned to my little guest and pointed to a house at the other end of Fischtal Park, its windows ablaze in the glow of the evening sun. I did not notice that there was no smoke. "I have never been near a big fire." I said expectantly. "Wouldn't it be something to see a house really burn?" Though we ran across the park as fast as our feet would carry us and until we were breathless, the orange and pink glow remained. Heini kneeled on the grass and I was beside him:

"Baruch ato adonoi elohenu" (the beginning of the Hebrew prayer, "Blessed art thou our Lord God") — please, dear God, let the house burn!" we prayed with folded hands. Heini was orthodox. He visited often, because his big brother was my sister's favored suitor, one of those beleaguering our home when Papa was away. In order for my prayer to be heard I had put my right thumb on top of the left, yet the fiery shine in the windowpanes faded, the sun went down. Disappointed and hungry we returned home — a little later, a little earlier, mealtime was anytime when my father was absent as he usually was. When the cat's away (from Eisvogelweg number fifteen) the mice will play. With the help of a young maid and a skimpy allowance, it fell upon my nineteen-year old sister Gerda to keep house, look after my fifteen-year old brother and be a second mother to me. There never was enough money to pay the bills and maids gave notice after a few months. My brother, who missed our mother at the most difficult age, refused to accept authority. I, however, thrived in this free and easy household, happy to be left alone to explore my new surroundings.

On one side the Gehag settlement was bordered by the Fischtal Park with a pond and a sledding run, on the other by a forest full of mushrooms leading down to a lake, the Krumme Lanke. Splashing and swimming in its dark brown waters I would spend a good part of my summers there from then on. I preferred a place the children called "Sand Desert," a vast construction site for the future underground, to the three sport areas nearby. Excavators had thrown up high slopes of sand there that served us as slides. In comparison my sandbox at the end of our garden was just good enough for cats. Building fortifications in the cool soil of our "desert," we armed ourselves with clubs to play "war of the cavemen."

Yearly parade at Uncle Tom's Cabin. I am on the top in the middle of a big fish. Part of the area was called Fischtalgrund (Valley of the Fish).

"Olle Rene, Olle Rene . . . come and get me if ye are afraid." Why the children in the next cave were my enemies is unimportant — in a war one needs enemies and has to hate them. And when on the way back some chieftain in a warlike mood stole an empty milk bottle from a porch, smashing it on the pavement, at home I would listen for the siren all evening. Were the police coming for me?

Not all our games were that wild. At the crossroads of the narrow concrete paths running behind everyone's gardens stood the "refuse-house," a small brick construction for trash cans and social meeting-place for the neighborhood children. In its smelly shadow, within earshot of one's parents, we played hide and seek, catch, marbles, and rode up and down on scooters. That year I went around all summer with a bruised knee. Every time it was half healed I would take another turn too close to the corner of the refuse house, the bricks shaving off the crust.

I never lacked playmates, girls or boys. Whether their parents worked in a factory or at a college, and no matter what color the flags fluttering from the windows at election time, no one asked for my mother or for my religion. All children simply wanted to play. All of them except for two little girls who were too well brought up to play in the street — after much prodding, they shyly whispered their names, Maya and Anna. Wearing freshly starched summer dresses of the most delicate lilac, they stood for hours behind their wire fence, their big eyes longing for the world of the children on the other side. All I ever knew of Maya and Anna were their names. I had almost forgotten them until many years later in Mechelen when I saw the big sad eyes of so many children that brought them back to me.

If I was not playing outside or, in bad weather, in a neighbor's house, then I too got my share of education. In addition to Miss Flachshaar's severe lessons, my sister taught me good manners and etiquette from a tractate translated from English into German.

"If you want a second helping you don't just trumpet the fact — you lay knife and fork on your plate crosswise, like this." Before serving me more cauliflower, Gerda gave me a lesson on my dish. "Don't be such a glutton, Irene. And when you have finally had enough you put them this way"; she rested my flatware parallel and sideways in the gravy. "What on earth are you doing now? Never touch an egg sunny side up with your knife!"

When we were eating in company, at one of my aunts for example, then my manners were adjusted by little kicks under the table. Fresh from the hairdresser and in one of the pretty dresses my sister had made for me, I could be taken for the best brought up eight-year old from Zehlendorf.

Order was not Gerda's forte, but she was talented in other respects. She was musical, uncommonly adroit and inventive, and with our chronic shortage of money her talent for improvisation in the kitchen and the garden was a godsend. She always took a shovel with her when we went for a walk. In a nearby fen she dug out elderberry bushes, in the woods wild roses and raspberries, in the fields and meadows we found pretty flowers to transplant into our garden. All these, together with the shoots she received from neighbors, and fruit trees and petunias that my father contributed, made not only for a varied garden, but at the same time triggered my interest in the characteristics and names of plants. It was from listening to my sister that I learned so many German songs.

When my father returned from a trip, he would invite Sunday guests to our verandah for coffee and cake. He prepared a special treat for Aunt Jenny and Aunt Alice, city dwellers so used to the trains rattling through their apartment that they did not hear the ear-splitting noise anymore. He hung the young apple tree with radishes, tying cucumbers to the branches of the stronger pear tree. If Aunt Alice inspected the strange crop with suspicion, Aunt Jenny was full of admiration. The trees looked very pretty.

My father had put an end to my film career before I enrolled in school, and for a while I enjoyed being like other children. With snow and ice covering the Fischtal during the coldest North German winter in memory, I had a wonderful time, especially when my brother Werner took me sleigh riding. Sundays, a day of dense traffic on the icy runs, an ambulance at the foot of the hill would await accident victims. I would lay on my belly, my brother sitting on top of me and steering as we raced down the run until the sled, slowing to maneuver a curve, came to a stop on a frozen pond. Stomping up through the snow to start all over my brother shouted at me, "Down on your belly, Irene — here, hold the string for a moment and don't be squeamish. On your mark, ready, go!" Instead of sitting on top of me, my brother gave the sled a kick. Desperately trying to brake with my feet and feeling as if dragged along by wild horses, I landed safely on the pond.

The two best days of that winter came at the end of January, the first when a pipe burst on Eisvogelweg that enabled the neighborhood children to skate in the street. The second was my birthday. I had asked for a bag full of goose crackling, but Gerda had not been able to find any at the settlement's cooperative grocery; instead she baked me a cake rimmed with marzipan. In the afternoon, children and Aunt Toote came to visit. She had taken the bus all the way from Moabit to bring me a big wooden box with a croquet set. Afterwards my cousin Karl with his friend Leonhard, Gerda's latest admirer, arrived for dinner. A law student like Karl, Leonhard wore horn-rimmed glasses, had the biggest Adam's apple I had ever seen and could play the piano with or without looking at sheet music. Luckily my father was away, for otherwise there would have been trouble. Papa had once grumbled that Karl's friend played so loudly he was ruining the piano. In love with Gerda, Leonhard played that evening with such passion that the thin Gehag dining room walls shook. Jochen Kaps, our next-door neighbor, protested the noise by practicing his violin behind the wall where our piano stood. The combination of his fiddling and the sound of our piano was awful!

After dinner the grown-ups turned romantic, singing Heine's "A Poet's Love," soon moving to the "Three Penny Opera," which I liked better. Karl and Gerda sang, Leonhard accompanied them with abandon, and Werner and I kept time, making wine and water glasses tinkle with our forks and knives.

"Soldiers are living . . . on their canons . . ." jingle, jingle, ding-dong with the forks, "From the Cape to Cooch Behar," a place hard to pronounce, followed by my favorite refrain, "When it rained someplace, and we'd meet an unknown race . . . a brown one, a pale one, no matter. . . beefsteak tartar on our platter!" Great drum-roll with flatware and feet. Kitchen towel in hand, Gerda sang the aria of the pirate's bride and the ship with eight sails. "Gentlemen, today you see me drying glasses and making the beds for you all. . . ." She seemed to feel deeply for poor Jenny, waiting for her pirate, but finally the ship with the fifty canons sailed into port. "And then, when the head falls, I say . . . hoppla!" sang sweet Jenny. I knew what was coming with that "hoppla!" — I was sent to bed.

This day had been a beautiful thirtieth of January, and I was the first person on Eisvogelweg to own a croquet game. Putting on my nightgown I read the rules. Falling asleep I visualized behind closed eyes all the January snow melting. Spring brought the grass back and I could invite my friends to play croquet.

F o u r

COMING HOME FROM SCHOOL one noon, I was dumbfounded when I walked into the house. What happened? Where were the etchings of the Prussian uniforms? Where did this ugly hallstand come from? Suddenly I grasped I had taken the wrong entrance path and had rung the wrong bell. I apologized to Mrs. Pohl.

"Liberté, egalité, fraternité!" The cry of the socialists had been condensed into one word by the builders of the settlement — uniformity. In every street, houses resembled each other like eggs in a basket. Topped by the flat roof of the new functionalism, they all were three stories high, they all had the same small square windows, the same tiny front yards and the same square-cut hedges. Since more than street names were needed to find one's way through all that fraternal resemblance, the architects had hit upon color. The Auerhahnbalz had blue-green balconies over white walls. The more expensive properties on Reiherbeize were graded in discreet shades of brown, while our street was painted yellow from end to end. For eleven years I lived in mustard sauce, a color that pursued me into Belgium, where dirty yellow prison walls stared down at me for another year and a half.

Nevertheless, after a period of yellow tedium, Eisvogelweg was planted in all its length with mountain ash. The leaves and berries of the growing trees helped for a while to resolve deepening political differences among the inhabitants into a seemingly harmonious triad of green, red and yellow. Throughout Germany the economy was going downhill, and the families in Uncle Tom's Cabin were not exempt. When flags were hung, a few swastikas appeared in attic windows. The barely visible fissures in the idyll of our settlement were developing into open cracks, and along with them my childish innocence was also getting knocked about.

"Is our Ulla here? Ulla, come home." Little Christoph from the house opposite ours stood in the door, snot hanging from his nose. His nose was always running; every time his sister came to play with me he cried until his mother sent him over to bring his Ulla back. But on this afternoon, with screams coming through an open window, something at the Prietschkes' seemed to be amiss.

"My own wife is Red...better dead than Red!" roared Mr. Prietschke. But Ulla's mother's voice was shriller and louder.

"You can choose him or me. I'm not staying under the same roof with that scum. Cook yourself, clean up your own dirt — you can have him, your Adolf!" With that a picture frame came flying out of the second floor window shattering on the red bricks in front of the entrance. Mr. Prietschke stormed out of the house, the door shutting behind him with a bang — taking long strides, he headed towards the metro station and disappeared.

"Mom has thrown dad's Hitler out," said Christoph with unusual composure. Wiping his nose with dignity on his sleeve, he repeated, "Our Ulla must come home."

The fight between Communism and Fascism in the house opposite ours continued until Hitler came to power. After that, Mrs. Prietschke had to shut up if she loved her children and her freedom. Meanwhile, Ulla would not visit anymore.

"Careful, Irene! That Klatschkowski woman says Mr. Hirt has consumption. That's why he coughs so much and he gives children candy so they will catch it too," whispered our neighbor's son as we stood in line by the milk van holding our empty bottles. Mrs. Platschkowski, nicknamed Klatschkowski (Klatsch is German for gossip), despite having more children than anybody else on the block, found plenty of time to stand in the street talking. And woe to whomever got into her mouth. Since her eldest was strutting around wearing a brown uniform, we avoided the family — they did likewise because we were Jews. Mr. Hirt was probably coughing from old age and regrettably never gave me candy.

Once a week I walked to the center of Zehlendorf to receive religious instruction and learn Hebrew. Since I liked the Biblical stories, I went willingly. Besides, it made me feel important to be the only one in my regular class who was learning to write the square Hebrew letters from right to left. It was like being initiated into a secret language. Miss Flachshaar would have had a fit if she had seen the thick horizontal and thin vertical strokes! I liked it less when we were each given a round piece of brown-red felt with a chalked design of a lion to embroider in gold-colored thread — this was the Lion of Judah and was to become a table mat, a present for my father. Despite the mane, the lion's face came out looking like a dog's; and though I had not yet finished the paws and claws when we went on summer vacation, my father could not have been more pleased if the thread had been real gold. I was puzzled. Which one was more important to us, I asked him, the Prussian eagle, the bear of Brandenburg or the Lion of Judah? What tasted better, an apple or an orange? A dumb question, grumbled my father.

I didn't think much about the Lion of Judah. It was simply one more image in my menagerie of heraldic animals, though soon afterwards, having to write one of my first compositions, I became truly confused. Miss Flachshaar was teaching my class about the Germans of antiquity.

"Our ancestors lived in forests and went hunting. They slept on bearskins and drank mead from horns," I began, satisfied with the opening and the chic word "ancestors." Stop! I said to myself. What nonsense was I writing? My ancestors were not hunters roaming forests and drinking fermented honey — they had crossed the desert on camels, grateful to have water for their thirst. In place of Odin and Freya in Valhalla, they had only one God, invisible, whose name was so holy you were forbidden to pronounce it. And where in this muddle was I? How was I now to start my composition? I had no choice but to change "our ancestors" to "the ancient Germans," resigning myself once more to the fact that I did not belong.

Sometimes, though, it is satisfying not to be like everybody else. As a nine-year-old, I had started making a name for myself among my classmates by drawing their portraits, though for three years my report cards had been disfigured by "C's" in art. They did not care if the small drawings I gave them were not the cleanest. What mattered to them was resemblance, and strangely enough, my drawings looked like them. Though I did not understand how this came about, I was happy to have found a means of becoming popular. I even was invited to Dorothy Dofifat's costume party with carnival fritters.

For my birthday a few weeks earlier I had asked for a pineapple, not canned, but a real one like the pineapple in the still-life painting in our dining room. But fresh pineapples were both hard to find and very expensive; instead, my father's gift was two Bleyle school dresses, one gray and one brown. They didn't need much care and yet looked respectable. For years they grew together with me. They did not easily show spots — they were indestructible.

The highlight of 1930 was the summer day when crossing our front-yard with my friend Irmchen Liebeskind, I found the local paper lying on the stoop. This monthly had previously announced a short story competition for children of the settlement, with a camera for first prize. Weeks earlier I had sent in a story. Turning the pages, I could not believe my eyes — there I was smiling at myself from a photograph. My story of a husband and wife team of squirrels had won! I was in heaven until the slap. Unexpectedly, with no warning like a sharp bolt of lightning, Irmchen slapped my face. We had had occasional quarrels, but we never fought — why this slap now? For a long time it was a riddle that I could not solve. Years went by until I understood that jealousy was the sting in what may have been for her a congratulatory slap.

Discord had been developing in our house. On each return from one of his long business trips, my father grew more and more angry at the goings-on in our household. He thought that the new maid was sloppy. Meanwhile my brother was getting more intractable by the day. My sister had not paid the bills and I was permitted to run wild. Worst of all, what decent young lady received male visitors in the absence of her father?

I had not tattled. With Günter Wasservogel, Gerda's suitor before last, there was nothing to tattle about. He had honorable intentions and money; returning from a trip he brought a porcelain sparrow for Gerda and marzipan potatoes for me. Regrettably, he was short and had thick lips. In contrast, Gerda's fencing teacher at the sports club was six-foot-two and had hair slicked down like an American film star. With a ready smile he would agree, "like Robert Montgomery, no doubt."

Except for an indecent song that naughty boys used to tease girls with on the way home from school, no one had spoken to me about sex, let alone the birds and the bees. However, together with some Shakespeare, Goethe, Schiller and Meyer's *Conversational Encyclopedia*, I had read the remaining books in our library. Leaving for school in the morning, with my sister still in bed, I would open the door to her room to say goodbye.

"Will Karl-Friedrich sleep here again tonight?" I tried to sound natural. Although experience had taught me to ignore delicate situations pretending I had neither eyes nor ears, on this morning I could not resist the temptation to ask this not-so-innocent question. Silly Gerda tried to hide her fencing teacher under the bedcovers. How dumb did she think I was? I had not tattled, less out of loyalty to my sister than because speaking to my father about something so delicate would have been embarrassing.

During his next homecoming, after the usual recriminations, Papa threw Gerda's cigarette box and lipstick into the trash. It proved too much for her. She had found a job as a saleslady in a department store and moved out. Werner also spent less and less time at home. While doing a technical apprenticeship and going to evening school, he also belonged to the Social Democratic Reichsbanner Youth. He trained for street fights against the Nazis and then participated in them — he had no time for mischief. But what was my father to do with me, the baby of the family? The maid was unreliable, and he could not afford a governess nor did he want to remarry, having himself grown up with a stepmother. It seemed the only solution was to find a hard-working housekeeper who contented herself with a modest salary and was fond of children, three qualities rarely found in one widow. The first to be hired was one Frau Frischauf, followed by one Frau Frühauf — I am not making up their names.

I was glad they left me alone — that our carpets became ever dustier and our sheets ever grayer did not bother me. When it was too cold to go swimming in the Krumme Lanke or too warm for sledding in winter, and I did not feel like company, I went up to the attic. There in my small world of discarded pedestals and a rickety chair, beside the disheveled old doll Lotte and between a photograph of my mother and the necklace of the just-as-unreachable Indian woman, I would sit drawing or crocheting egg-warmers for my aunts. One day I made a new dress for myself. Fabric of the cheap kind used for flags was left over from a demonstration of the Reichsbanner. I had participated, holding my torch high and singing with the grownups as loud as I could, "Brothers, toward the sun, toward freedom!" For whom does the "future shine brightly out of a dark past?" For all Germans, including those with the swastikas, or only for those with the black, red, and yellow flags? The meaning was not only "sunny" but somewhat nebulous, especially for Jews whose future could hardly be imagined at this moment of patriotic ardor.

To make a dress out of the red fabric, I double folded it and pedaling on our old Singer, I sewed it together on three sides, then cut out a half circle to make an opening for my head. As a result of my museum visits with Aunt Hanna, and influenced by Rembrandt and Frans Hals, I had to have a ruff around my neck, which I pieced together from an old pillowcase. When Frau Frühauf called me to come down from the attic to buy bread, I proudly walked the streets in the colors of Brandenburg.

Even though I obeyed our housekeeper, I disliked her, the more so since she had taken me to church with her. How gloomy and oppressive it was, much darker than any synagogue, a huge cross with Jesus looming at the end of the aisle. I stopped short. I simply would not go any farther. Let Frau Frühauf sit or kneel there by herself to pray or do whatever else Christians did in their church — she would not get me nearer to that Jesus. But she did not loosen her grip on me. Sprinkling and crossing herself, she bent one knee before the crucifix. In a low, sharp voice she ordered me to bow.

The main thing was not to attract attention. Uncle David's urging came to my mind. If only we did not arouse anti-Jewish feelings, those hoodlums in the brown shirts would disappear back into the gutters they had come from. (My little uncle now lived in an ordinary apartment without golden chairs and red ottomans.) Should I then be pigheaded and balk, attracting attention in a church of all places? Plenty of brown shirts were walking the streets, organizing parades. So I bowed stiffly without looking at Jesus, deeply ashamed at my treason. Was my aversion to crosses conditioned by my upbringing or had two thousand years of persecution so gotten in my bones that I had a natural antipathy? Christian crosses, swastikas, they all rubbed me the wrong way.

Although I resented the visit to the church deeply, this incident was of the kind I was ashamed to mention to my father. In this case anyway, it was unnecessary. Frau Frühauf's days in our household were over. Coming home, my father brought a Mrs. Lange with him from Thuringia, presenting her not as the new housekeeper, but as the lady who would take care of our household and me. She would stay with us for eight years, until the day when as Jews we had to leave Uncle Tom's Cabin. It was she who after years of a "Gypsy ménage," as my aunts referred to our household, slowly got the gray out of our wash, scrubbed the kitchen, served me regular lunches and dinners, and on Saturdays heated water for a hot bath. Still, instead of appreciating my being like other children, living in an orderly house, going to school in a freshly ironed summer dress, I missed the old "Gypsy ménage," the loosely structured days, Gerda's songs, the laughter of young guests and my unrestrained movements. Mrs. Lange, a childless war widow in her middle forties, would have loved to take my mother's place, had I let her. For reasons that are still unclear to me, mainly because she did not have a very sensitive nature, I could not even bring myself to call her "Aunt Martha." I circumvented her pleas and my father's admonishments by not speaking to her directly, which in the long run was not easy.

The change to a peaceful but more boring life on Eisvogelweg was less significant than my simultaneous passage from elementary school to an all girls high school in Dahlem, new teachers, new friends, new courses. At last I was studying French!

"Que, que, que. . . ." Miss Kleckel, our energetic little teacher of French and gymnastics, was intent on exorcising our guttural German accent once and for all. Though a German accent in French was anathema to Miss Kleckel, it would not prevent her from developing into an enthusiastic follower of Adolf Hitler. A classmate in the last year of high school, when I already was a refugee in Belgium, related an anecdote that illustrates her transformation. In the summer of 1939, two rowing teams from my school were training on the Kleine Wannsee when they saw a large yacht approaching from the direction of Schwanenwerder, the site of Goebbel's manor. On deck stood none other than Hitler himself in a brown S.A. (Sturmabteilung)* uniform. Goebbels and the captain were by his side.

"Children, our Führer, our Führer! Heil Hitler, Heil Hitler!" screamed Miss Kleckel, in her excitement jumping up from the seat she used to steer the boat — she could not, after all, greet the Führer sitting down! The boat swayed heavily from side to side, and Miss Kleckel fell into the lake, giving rise to loud laughter. The girls refused an offer of help for the little teacher now gurgling "Heil Hitler!" in the water. They pulled her back into the boat dripping in green duck scum.

During my time with Miss Kleckel she still abhorred a German accent, and for hours and hours we repeated "mon, ton, son," holding our noses tightly shut. We had to bring tissue paper torn into little pieces to our first French lesson, putting them on the back of one hand to hold to our mouths. If we pronounced "ke, ke, ke," instead of the softer "que, que, que," we had to practice until the pieces of paper would not fly off anymore. I thought anything French was marvelous and fas-

---

*The S.A., also known as storm troopers or brownshirts, was first led by Ernst Röhm. The S.A. began as Hitler's personal army and under Röhm's direciton, it expanded to more than 4½ million men — the S.A. played a significant role in destroying opposition to the Nazis in the 1932 and 1933 elections. Röhm's growing influence was his death knell: on June 29, 1934, Hitler arrested him and during the next day more than 200 S.A. officers were killed. Hitler referred to the purge as the "Night of the Long Knives" (from a popular Nazi song); in a speech on July 13th, he said, "In this hour I was responsible for the fate of the German people, and thereby I became the supreme judge of the German people. I gave the order to shoot the ringleaders in this treason." The S.A. gradually lost its power and was replaced by the Schutzstaffel (S.S.) under Heinrich Himmler.

cinating, up to the irregular verbs. Meanwhile I excelled in art class and continued not to understand the first thing about mathematics.

These first years at the Gertraudenschule were perhaps the most peaceful of my life. While the seeds of Nazism had probably started to germinate even in upper middle class Dahlem, I had as yet seen little growth in my contacts with classmates or teachers. My moments of tension occurred in the morning. Because I was not an early riser, I would try to cover the distance from Eisvogelweg to the Gertrauden-schule in ten minutes on a bicycle left to me by my cousin Lilo, Aunt Toote's daughter. The bike was old, and the faster and more desperately I pedaled in my race against being late, the more often the chain jumped off the frame.

My brother followed Gerda in leaving home as soon as he turned eighteen, the legal age. He and my sister first bought themselves a canoe, then a sailboat, spending weekends on the lakes around Berlin without ever inviting me. Mesmerized by water and by boats at an early age, my favorite dream was to live on a houseboat. I turned to do-it-yourself help. I was going to build a raft like one my heroes Tom Sawyer and Huck Finn had. Wherever I could find a thick broken branch, I would haul it into a hideout under some bushes in the Riemeister Fen near the waters of the Krumme Lanke. Fearing that other children with the same idea might come upon my treasure, I had to keep my eyes open. When I had enough wood for a raft, I appropriated all the string my father kept rolled up in the cellar to tie my branches together. The thought of navigating the Krumme Lanke gave me strength to pull the raft into the water. As I put out to sea, standing proudly upright, my feet began getting wet — my ship and I were sinking. The raft was too light and I was too heavy. Never mind that the school physician called me "well developed."

From the time Mrs. Lange came to us, I was enticed to do household chores and perform well in school by a system of rewards. If I polished the brass bell, the name plate and mail-flap on our door once a week, or if I helped Mrs. Lange with the dishes or brought home an

"A" in spelling three times in a row, I was rewarded with money for either a cinema ticket or an ice cream cone. I was so impressed by *Ben Hur* that with the money I had left over, I bought pictures of Ramon Novarro. My friends had crushes on more Nordic types like Hans Albers, while I, in the privacy of my attic, looked with rapture into the black-painted eyes of my movie idol, the portrayer of a Jewish prince in Roman times. The awakening pride in my Jewish identity would penetrate deeper into my consciousness with a discovery at the cemetery in Weissensee. On one of our yearly visits to my mother's grave, Gerda tied the climbing rose to the stone; afterwards, as always, we continued to the grave of Papa's father. For the first time I noticed the two hands engraved above his name. "What does it mean, these funny fingers so oddly spread apart?" I asked. Gerda and my father looked at each other in a way that seemed to ask, "should we tell her or is she still too young?"

"If we explain, then you must promise not to talk about it, especially in school," Gerda said with a mysterious air. My father interrupted her.

"These hands are anything but funny," he looked very earnestly at me. "They are symbolic of our family being descended from the Kohanim, the high priests of Israel. Two thousand years ago they conducted sacrifices in the Temple and bestowed blessings on the people until the Romans defeated the nation and destroyed Jerusalem along with the Temple. My father forced the third and fourth fingers of both hands apart. "This is how they gave the blessing, you see? Don't ever brag about this. It's getting worse and worse with Jew haters." On the return journey, a long trip with several buses, Gerda tried to break the solemn mood.

"Irene, Paula, dull Rosa," she teased me, "who would think that you are of more ancient nobility than that Erika von Voss and Brigitta von Zitzewitz in your class? But for God's sake, don't get puffed up like a balloon!" What did she imagine? To whom would I report our strange conversation at the cemetery to? To Mrs. Lange? Completely ignorant about things Jewish, she would feel my forehead. Irmchen Liebeskind? She would die laughing if she did not slap my face again. Nevertheless, the discovery about our origins heightened my self-esteem. Once a year at the Gertraudenschule, students had to answer questions about their fathers' professions and religion that were then registered in the classbook. The room resounded with "Protestant," "engineer," "officer," "manufacturer," "high school teacher" — I did not call out "Mosaic" and "merchant," as I had before, but simply "Jewish" and "salesman." Slowly, tapping in the dark, I was becoming aware of the thousands of years of weight my family was pulling along.

Though my father had done little to foster love of Judaism in my brother and sister, he was nevertheless upset over their indifference to our heritage. When Gerda told him of her intention to marry her Karl-Friedrich, a Protestant, she was not allowed to set foot in our house anymore. My brother also had a Christian girl friend and did not come home on his own accord. That left only me. Repeatedly I heard from my aunts, from Mrs. Lange and from my father that at least I had to be a good daughter. Part of being a good daughter was to do my homework and to belong to a girls club where once a week we played educational games and ate cookies. My classmates wrote dedications in my autograph album, for example, "Be as a violet in the moss: humble, modest and pure." Drawing and painting were second nature for me, though they were not enough to complete my education. While my aunts and Mrs. Lange were delighted by my progress at becoming well brought up, they also prescribed piano lessons.

I was more than agreeable and thought that being able to play music as well as Aunt Toote would be wonderful. But I had not foreseen there would be an obstacle race of finger exercises and lots of C-sharps and B-flats. Mrs. Lange tried to coax me into preparing my lessons, but I would usually sit down to practice half an hour before the arrival of my teacher Miss Becker, who I was afraid of. Too late. Rapping my hands with her bony fingers, she brought "Clementi's Sonatina" to a resounding halt. Her reaction, though understandable, did not endear her to me. After an unsuccessful hour of trying to coordinate my hands on the keys with my feet on the pedals, Miss Becker accepted Mrs. Lange's offer of a cup of coffee on the verandah.

"Why don't you show me your gooseberry bushes, Irene," she said as she drew me into the garden. "Is it really true what I have been told?

Did you call me an old goat?" I don't think I have ever blushed deeper in all my life, redder than Miss Becker's hair. (Mrs. Lange said it was a wig.) Miss Becker's allegation was true, but how could I tell her, "yes, I did," to her face? Her frayed hairdo, shabby suit and stilted Hanoverian accent should have made me feel sorry for her. There was no way out — to deny the insult made things only worse. It was that ugly Jutta from Reiherbeize, another one of Miss Becker's students, who told on me. I started to cry, feeling sorry for myself and for my teacher. Altogether, it had been an unpleasant afternoon to remember.

Despite the headlines about political intrigues and attempted coups, about Schleicher, Hugenberg and Hitler, about the Communists, the Nazis and the Stahlhelm, my days passed quietly. What were newspapers for if not for that kind of a racket? They were none of my business. Killings, bloodshed — for me they were headlines in large print under blurred snapshots of street fighters with clenched fists. They were happening far away at the other end of Berlin, in places like the blue collar area of the Wedding. They did not happen in neighborhoods like ours, in Zehlendorf and Dahlem. When the Reichsbanner organized a great meeting and lodged three men in our house, I was glad for a change in the order of our days. My father hung a red flag with the three white darts of the workers' front; and from then on, it fluttered beside the black, red and yellow striped flag in our attic window. Publicly underlining our views in red, I could not help wondering at Papa's growing nervousness and how jumpy he was, running at each noise into the hallway to see if our morning newspaper, the *Berliner Tageblatt*, had been delivered. In the evening, he left more and more often to see the Königs, the nicest, blondest family on Eisvogelweg. Playing cards with Mr. König, they discussed the latest events over a glass of beer.

Herr König worked for the unions and was knowledgeable about politics. He was as dead certain as my father that the Nazis were going to lose the elections. As a German and as a Protestant, he was ashamed of their anti-Semitic propaganda, Mr. König shouted, throwing his cards on the table. Those lying rowdies in their disgusting brown uniforms would promise the masses anything — even the blue out of the sky. Most Germans were decent people. They would not be taken in by the likes of an Adolf Hitler, he told us with conviction.

In her effort to get me accustomed to housework, Mrs. Lange would send me to empty the trash can after I came home from school. Chalked all over the wall of the trash house, with a swastika for good measure were two short sentences:

"Germany awake, Judah perish! The Jews are our misfortune!"

I shuddered in my woolen sweater. For a moment I experienced a repulsive, clammy feeling that foreshadowed something awful, inescapable. No one had seen me. It was winter and anyhow, my former playmates from the neighborhood were by now too big to play hide-and-seek. I emptied my trash can. Returning home, I did not say a word about what I had seen.

F i v e

PUTTING ONE FOOT OUT from under the quilted bed cover, I quickly pulled it back. Overnight the window had become overgrown with ice flowers, though for my father it was not yet sufficiently cold to justify heating my bedroom. Still, I would not get out of my warm bed a minute earlier than necessary to make it to Miss Vogel's class in time. Then I remembered that it was the thirtieth of January! I ran downstairs. Papa was already waiting with a kiss and a birthday present, a pair of skis with poles he had bought for me on his last trip to Bavaria. What I had really wanted was an ice bombe, though I did not exactly know what it was. In novels, daughters of millionaires on the Riviera were spooning them up. Of course we had no refrigerator to keep an ice bombe which was a kind of huge torte made of ice cream, so the pair of skis was naturally a better gift.

1933. I was now twelve years old. Two more years and the teachers at the Gertraudenschule would have to address me as "Fräulein Spicker," or so I daydreamed in class. That is, until Miss Vogel, pointer in hand, sharply tapped at a location on the map of Yugoslavia.

"What is the name of this mountain?" Silence. "Inge-Maria?" My neighbor remained mute. "Irene?" A brainstorm mixed mountains with islands.

"The Canarian Mountains."

"Maybe you are the canary," said Miss Vogel to the enjoyment of the class, apparently unaware of the synonym with her name. "Dinaric, Irene . . . the Dinaric Mountains."

After school I had to set the table for my guests. In the sideboard was my mother's collection of mocha cups — twelve small cups that I was allowed to use once a year on my birthday. I had invited eleven friends for coffee and cake. Once more everything seemed to be on track. On Eisvogelweg, with the excitement about the elections having died down, our flags stood rolled up in a corner of the attic. Herr König and my father had been right about Hitler's party, which had lost by two million votes. This did not mean that the Nazis had given up on seizing power. Judging from what I overheard of Papa's telephone conversations with Uncle David, old Hindenburg, the victor of Tannenberg with his stand-up collar and sagging jowls, had a hard time keeping the Reichstag in working order. With a clique of schemers maneuvering to be Chancellor (Kanzler in German), we had a new government every few weeks. First von Papen, then Schleicher, then von Papen again, and just for my birthday there was talk it might be Hitler's turn.

But having to set the coffee table, I had more immediate problems than stuffy old politicians. Who was my best friend, the one I would serve hot chocolate to in the rococo cup bearing the picture of a shepherdess? Who would get the one with the bouquets set in medallions, who the bellied little cup on three legs? I was just putting the white and gold birthday cup inscribed with "the good child's" at the head of the table for myself, when the first guests in their Sunday-best arrived. Why could I not look as well groomed as my girl friends, at least on this day, with their precisely braided blond tresses and white knee-high socks that never slid down? Despite Mrs. Lange's efforts, I, the honored birthday girl, kept tugging at my panties — my elastics always lost their stretch; meanwhile, the hem of my skirt had opened and I had to keep myself together with the help of safety pins.

Perhaps there was some truth to Nazi propaganda that Jews were inferior. Climbing rope in Miss Kleckel's gymnastics class, I hung there like a sack of flour. Instead of descending from high priests, I would have preferred to swing svelte hips over the parallel bars and play volleyball as aggressively as Anneliese Eschtrut — I could only duck to avoid being hit.

I felt hopeless. Not even the cake I made turned out right — I hid the icing, which turned out to be sticky, under a colorful design of sugar beads. I did not account for its being almost impossible to cut. My classmates spent more time sucking than chewing. With their mouths full of hard little beads it was difficult to speak. But, well brought up, they finished eating and were finally able to sing "Happy birthday!" We played party games, among them naturally, "The Jew has slaughtered a pig, which part do you want?" "It's left, crippled molar!" I had answered, having Margot König and Irmchen Liebeskind eliminated for giggling. It would not have occurred to anyone, including me, that the game might be an anti-Semitic caricature. On the other hand, the threat on the wall of the trash house was not a game and I had not forgotten it.

When the last of my friends had left, Mrs. Lange did the dishes by herself. She stroked my hair and excused me from helping. In an elated mood I looked at my presents, a sketchbook, watercolors, Heine's *Book of Songs*, Möricke's *Mozart on the Journey to Prague*, poems by Konrad Ferdinand Meyer and chocolates of all kinds. I had no inkling that the date of my birthday was just then taking on historical significance, that from now on it would be a day of celebration with no school. At this instant I had been fingered as a parasite to be removed from the green foliage of Miss Vogel's class. While my friends and I had been drinking hot chocolate from my mother's mocha cups, the sun over the Third Reich had risen. The threat on the trash house wall had been but a fleeting shadow of the storm clouds that from this day forward would inexorably gather over German skies.

When my father came home, he told us that at this hour great assemblies and parades were taking place in the city. What he had heard was not to be believed, he added, switching on the radio.

"Sieg Heil, Sieg Heil, Sieg Heil!" the sound waves carried over static screeching, the announcer confirming what my father did not want to believe: Hindenburg had named Hitler as Chancellor of the Reich.

"How is this possible? They were gone. . . they lost the elections," he raised his hands to his head, "The Nazis have bamboozled old Hindenburg! A joke, but not for long. Schleicher held fast two months in the saddle. . . I don't give Hitler more than two weeks before the German people recognize him for the madman that he is."

Going to bed with a book of poems and a big piece of chocolate, I put Hitler out of my mind. "Feet in the Fire. . . Feet in the Fire, by Konrad Ferdinand Meyer," I hummed, falling asleep.

Several weeks passed. The Reichstag burned down and Hitler, Goering and Goebbels staged a big hunt for Communists. Hitler not only remained Chancellor, he managed to get his hands on more and more positions of power in order to destroy the Weimar Republic. It was rumored that prominent adversaries of the Nazis, mainly Jews, Communists and Social Democrats, were taken from their homes and sent to Oranienburg, a peaceful little town near Berlin. Some were returned to their widows as ashes in small boxes, while those who came out alive would not tell where they had been or what had been done to them. A new word came into use, concentration camp. Since we did not move in circles of prominent Jews and since we knew no unmistakable Communists with the exception of Mrs. Prietschke, I became aware of these events through the ever-softer conversations of grown-ups and through my father's dark jokes. Clinging to his optimism and to his belief in law and order, he tried to illustrate the absurdity of the new regime.

"Father," a little boy asks at dinner, "who set the Reichstag on fire?"

"Ess, ess man, and don't talk so loud." (A double meaning in spoken German: "Eat, eat man" and S.S.) It was clear as day that Germany had been overwhelmed by a band of arsonists, criminals and murderers, Papa and Mr. König agreed. Now, finally, Hindenburg and everyone else could see whom they were dealing with.

⁓

After the government's overthrow, the first perceptible change on Eisvogelweg was the great silence in the Prietschkes' house. The Prietschkes seemed to have stopped fighting, while Ulla greeted me only from afar. On the other side, Mrs. Platschkowski went about wearing a swastika pin, talking more than ever behind her neighbors' backs. At the Königs, things were no longer the same. The unions having been dissolved, Mr. König who was now jobless installed a presser in his house and took in laundry.

The changes in our house had largely to do with my father's increasing moodiness. He continued traveling through southern Germany selling men's hats and exchanging political jokes with his clients, who told him how much they liked their Mr. Spicker even though he was Jewish. Mrs. Lange went on doing the housework, while I drew and painted but neglected to prepare for my piano lessons. At school during needlework lessons, I was sewing a baby shirt with uncommon assiduity. Whether or not they had sewing machines, the future mothers of Germany had to be prepared. With these words our teacher had spurred the class on to learn the rudiments of cutting, hemming and step-stitching.

In this fashion it had become clear to most of us how to make little shirts, less so how the babies who were to wear them were made. For the lower classes of the Gertraudenschule, sex and the male high-school students at the other end of König in Luise Street were not yet a theme of conversation. I had a more practical reason to hurry with my needlework — my sister Gerda, now Mrs. Schmidt, was expecting, and I wanted by all means to have the shirt ready before the baby's birth. I almost made it in time for the arrival of a little boy and was proud to be an aunt at the age of twelve.

My new station did not keep my aunts from embellishing my education with fine brush strokes outside Mrs. Lange's domain, for example, in how to bake an authentic Rothenburg bund cake. The dough had to be stirred in one direction for three-quarters of an hour exactly, using in turn the right hand and then the left. The way to a good marriage led through the stomach, repeated Aunt Luise, who also warned me never again to line my closet with newspaper if I wanted to find a husband. When I spent a weekend at Aunt Hanna's, I had to wash my panties under her watchful eye, then rinse them seven times. She too was trying to scare me into paroxysms of cleanliness, warning that gray soap scum swimming on my rinse water predestined me to a life of spinsterhood. In 1933, these were the only calamities my aunts saw hanging over our well-combed heads.

"Now look here Irene, and pay attention." With these words Aunt

Hanna plucked one of her dark, long hairs and, drawing a needle from under her lapel, threaded it with the hair. Descending from the tramway on our way to the Pergamon Museum, a button had come off her coat. "You see," she said: holding the button between the thumb and index finger of her left hand, she began to sew it back on. "The damage has been taken care of. That will hold until we get home — no goy can find anything objectionable. Remember, you should always keep a needle under your lapel."

On this my first visit to the Pergamon Museum, standing on white marble steps among colossal white bas reliefs, I had a strange experience. While the temple and its sculptures appeared to me as truly divine creations, the visitors going up and down its steps seemed to be caricatures — dark figures contorting on high heels and wearing ridiculous hats stood confronting goddesses and giants. To view my racially pure fellow citizens as caricatures stalking by on two legs gave me great satisfaction, a kind of counterweight for the "Stürmer Jews," lately grinning at me from each newspaper display.

Aunt Hanna thought my happy face reflected only my joy about the sculptures. Taking seriously my unwavering resolve to become a painter, she decided I should become acquainted with the world of art, not just the artists. Her niece Else, red-haired daughter of a distant relative of mine, a district attorney nick-named the "black Heinrich," had married the painter Ludwig Meidner. So my aunt took me on a visit to the young couple's studio apartment, the threshold of which I crossed full of expectation. But where were the huge easels and plaster Aphrodites, my idea of an artist's studio, the requisite skeleton, the crystal bowl with grapes and peaches gracefully tumbling over an old trunk draped with oriental carpets? Old stuff galore was lying around, but not of the kind I had imagined. Where were the sideboard and buffet that belonged in every respectable home? Without the conventional furniture I was used to, the attic apartment looked empty and poor to me; it even smelled poorly, of dust and fried potatoes. While I was disappointed with the two painters, the Meidners didn't know what to do with a twelve-year old art enthusiast. Did Bohemians and the union of two artists signify smudgy smocks, a painter with thick red, unkempt hair, a husband with a bald spot? Aunt Hanna called the drawings and paintings on the wall Expressionism, but was unable to explain to me what that meant. Although I thought the paintings with their distorted proportions and topsy-turvy perspective anything but beautiful, I could not deny that the tortured landscapes and their scary figures were impressive.

The experience of that afternoon reinforced my suspicion that the way to art was not strewn with roses. I already knew plenty of examples. While Rembrandt's wife and son had died of consumption, he himself had struggled in a morass of debts. Beethoven had become too deaf to hear his own music. Bach, with his twenty-one children and no money left for candles, had so strained his eyes that he became blind. After each blow of fate, however, the work of those geniuses had become more brilliant. The meaning was self-evident — without suffering, I could not be a great artist.

As soon as the winter ice on the Krumme Lanke was thick enough to carry me, I set out for the lake with a small painting pad, a box of watercolors, a bottle of water and stoic determination to paint a winter landscape. Low over the snowy pine trees, the sun was mirrored on the icily glittering surface, and for the first time in my life I experienced an aspect of nature so intensively that I simply had to translate my feelings into color.

To handle the brush with mittens was not easy, though without them my fingers stiffened. Besides, any color I tried to mix with water froze instantly to my metal box. Only with constant spitting was it possible to dissolve the colors sufficiently to brush them on the paper. It was a technical tour-de-force to finish the small painting, but I did it. In order to make my fingers move once more, I forced myself to hold my hands under cold water as soon as I arrived home — and that hurt badly. Notwithstanding all this trouble, the satisfaction I felt was compensation enough — even more so when Aunt Toote paid me three marks for my aquarelle. I had sold my first painting!

Shortly afterwards, at Aunt Toote's yearly Hanukah party, I found my framed painting hanging on her wall, where it was admired by the assembled family. Mrs. Buchsbaum and the old Schlesinger, two widows I was somehow related to, smilingly examined the aquarelle, then me. But instead of saying something flattering about my picture, the old Schlesinger said in an aside to Mrs. Lange, "How charming, these little breasts."

Turning beet-red with embarrassment and fury, I was glad to see at the same instant the door to the salon opening its wings. At one end of the darkened room stood a large table filled with gifts and sweets for every participant in the celebration; at the other end, Uncle Max stood by the Hanukah menorah, ready to bless and light the candles. Aunt Toote played the first chords of the Hanukah song, everybody joining in, except for Mrs. Lange. Invited along to every family affair, her Hebrew consisted of two words only, "Amen" and "Hallelujah."

The German translation of the first verse of the Hanukah song we then sang seemed less pompous to me than it had in previous years. With all the public incitement against Jews it sounded like a prayer.

> Our shield and shelter in storm and dread,
> We sing Thee a song of joy.
> Protect, Oh Lord, Thine holy house,
> Where praise and thanks mount up to you.
> But when one day our enemies fall silent,
> Those who make a mockery of your people,
> May then resound from all over
> The song, oh Lord, uniting us.

All my aunts and uncles and first, second and other cousins sang the verse with an ardor that these rather bombastic words had never evoked before Hitler's rise. "Shield and shelter in storm and dread?" Were the brown storm troopers in the streets that dread? Having saved us at Hanukah thousands of years ago from the onslaught of the pagan Greeks, would He also save us from the Nazis?

I saw my cousin Lilo, Aunt Toote and Uncle Max's daughter, for the last time on that evening in December 1933. I am going to leave you my art books, she whispered to me, drawing me aside. Just having finished her medical studies and not sharing the family's optimism about

Hitler's imminent fall, she had decided to emigrate to Palestine. Uncle Max and Aunt Toote were upset at the very idea; my father and Aunt Hanna were flustered and agreed wholeheartedly with them. Who but the Zionists were provoking the most anti-Semitism, giving credit to the Nazis' crazy ideas about race? We were of the Jewish religion, but just as German as the next. By tearing ourselves loose from our homeland to build a state in the middle of a desert and swamps, we justified all those who shouted, "Jews, go to Palestine!"

Lilo went to Palestine anyhow and lived and worked on a kibbutz. However, Uncle Max would not help finance what he called his daughter's Zionist aberrations. Furthermore, there was already an overabundance of physicians.

So many German academics had left for Palestine that jokes about the difficult existence awaiting them there circulated among the Jews of Berlin. "Please, Herr Doctor... thank you, Herr Doctor," you could hear the waves in the Port of Jaffa murmur. They had learned those words from the Jewish stevedores standing day in and day out in the water, passing along bricks that they were unloading from a ship.

To some extent, my cousin's ideals about Zionism came from her books, many of which were about the pioneers, especially the women among them, who had built collective settlements in Palestine under incredible hardships. Proudly speaking only Hebrew, they had dried malaria swamps, paved roads and planted trees. They survived deadly epidemics, attacks by Arabs, fieldwork under a pitiless sun, while eating little besides bread, onions and oranges — with all that, they would dance the horah under the starry skies of Eretz Israel, singing songs of the freedom, love and beauty they had found in their new and yet old homeland.

After Lilo, the next one to leave Germany was my friend Lotti Rosenberg and her family. Lotti's father had been fired from his position as lecturer in political science shortly after the change of regime, and he was taking the family to England. I will get back to Lotti, since a few years later I was invited to spend my summer vacation with her in Liverpool.

Starting with the "Deutsche Gruss" at school, the demands of dictatorship were making themselves felt in my daily life. On entering class all teachers had to raise their right arm and say, "Heil Hitler!" All forty students had to stand and return the same greeting. Teachers who in the beginning were still rebellious came through the door mumbling; barely lifting their right arms, they instantly began to teach their class. Tamer ones raised their right arms indifferently, as if those arms did not belong to them. Only Doctor Kadner, who now often arrived at school in his brown S.A. uniform, pulled himself into position on the rostrum and greeted us snappily. Through a mute mutual understanding, my two Jewish classmates and I were permitted to stand up with the others, remain silent and let our arms hang by our sides. The daily, rather hourly humiliation to stand in the midst of a "Heil Hitler!" chorus was only the first of a long chain of indignities.

No classes on my thirteenth birthday, on which the whole school had to assemble in the auditorium to celebrate the first anniversary of the birth of the Third Reich. Having been subjected to Hitler's promises and threats, we Jews were described as a cancerous growth on the body of Germany. Still, more than half of my friends came to my party in the afternoon. To have enough guests for my twelve mocha cups, I needed to invite my younger cousin Jolanthe and two teen-aged girls from the city who were in some way related to me. Forced to mutter something about hostess gifts over the phone, I would still not admit that this year's birthday was a flop.

My main wish was to give up piano lessons, a wish that was accepted by all concerned, including Miss Becker. While my father had brought me a pair of ski trousers from Bavaria, there was a problem with the extra fine green peas I had requested for my birthday dinner. Costing twice as much as regular peas at the cooperative grocery, the can of extra fines had waited so long for a buyer that it finally spoiled. Though the peas had a strange taste, I did not want to find fault with such an expensive present so I finished them, but also got jaundice. With brown skin and yellow eyes, I started my fourteenth year in bed.

Whenever I could, I would go up to the attic to speak with my neighbor Jochen Kaps. Boring a hole through our respective attic walls with long nails, we had met in the middle. Passing a string through the tiny opening and tying the ends to empty toilet paper rolls, we had a Morse Code device that enabled us to converse in secret. Apart from Jochen entertaining me, and despite all the Nazi propaganda and more and more swastika flags emerging from the windows of Eisvogelweg, my old friends Margot König and Gerda Struck came to visit when I was getting better.

Our flags stood rolled up in a corner of the attic — we were not allowed to display them anymore.

〜

"For sixteen years I have subscribed to the *Berliner Tageblatt*, but now I am canceling it," Papa complained to Mr. König. "It's incredible how that paper has been changing from one day to the next. They have fired all the Jews and all the journalists with liberal opinions. Who remains? Turncoats and cowards," he added bitterly. "Support that rag with my money? Never. They won't soon forget the letter I wrote them today!"

The realization that we were now living under a dictatorship and the free press was gone was difficult for my father to accept. Nearly every day, he went to the Königs, where the master of the house would crank up his optimism together with his laundry presser. Even though a Nazi official had warned the former union employee to shut up if he valued his freedom, Mr. König could not do it. Each time his invective about the Nazis forced its way through the thin walls, his wife pleaded with him to think of his three children if not of her.

My father, Uncle David, Aunt Hanna — most of the family's older generation — could not imagine that in the not so distant future they might be uprooted from Germany. Young as I was, I was slowly beginning to see the light. More and more of my classmates were coming to school in the smart clothes of the Hitler Youth. Though they conducted themselves correctly and politely with me, I had at last understood that no matter how exemplary I was, I would never belong. My brother and sister with their non-Jewish partners had to let their dark heads bob up and down with all the others in the waves of the great Aryan sea. In order to blend in and come nearer the ideal picture of a young German mother, Gerda had her hair dyed blond. Her blond locks, her dark brown eyes and brows, flashing teeth and curved nose really attracted attention. Did I have to change myself into something I wasn't because I was vermin in the eyes of murderers who had just assassinated their own comrades Röhm, Strasser and hundreds of others? And if Germany did not want us — tant pis — an old French expression of defiance I had recently learned was a fitting answer. I was proud to be Jewish and would remain so.

S i x

HOW DOES A THIRTEEN-YEAR OLD show that she is proud of her religion, even if mainly out of defiance? She becomes devout. For the first time I fasted the full twenty-four hours on Yom Kippur, accompanying Aunt Hanna to the women's separate gallery at the synagogue on Fasanen Street. Disconcerted, I stood by her side when during the remembrance of dead souls she and all the other grown-ups started weeping terribly. I was trying once more to find the lost liebe Gott of my childhood. On Fridays, all by myself, I rode into town by metro to listen to the sermons by Dr. Prinz or Dr. Nussbaum, both of whom I had a crush on. Singing the Hebrew prayers together with the choir, I made every effort to feel a religious ardor. What exactly I was striving for I did not know, but they were values other than ice bombes, Tilsit cheese and goose greaves.

In a transport of sturm und drang I danced during a cloudburst in our garden in my swimsuit, later painting the scene from memory complete with lightning and a first self-portrait. Another first was reading a French novel, Anatole France's *Amethyst Ring*, in the privacy of my attic corner. The book had belonged to Lilo. To this day I have no idea what it was about. With my three years of French, I was at best able to translate half of each sentence, being too lazy to constantly leaf through the dictionary; nevertheless, I read on and on hoping to finally get an inkling of the story. I didn't, though I really read the entire book, proud that I had mastered a French novel! From the time when I no longer had to prepare lessons, I sat more often at the piano with my mother's music books playing songs by Schubert, Schumann and

Loewe with one finger. I sang the words to those songs and also "composed" my own melodies to poems by the Romantics, still with one finger and preferably on the black keys.

The more dashingly the Hitler Youth marched by outside, the louder the voices of my classmates resounded — with their flags and fanfares, I felt more and more isolated. My former friends were enthusiastic with their new marching songs, "with the Führer through night and through dread, with the banner of youth for freedom and bread." Meanwhile, signs of "Jews undesirable" were posted in windows and entrances. I retreated, searching for keys to a private ivory tower. My friend and classmate Tutti Mahlow was a great help, more than a replacement for Irmchen Liebeskind. Unlike Irmchen, Tutti had not yet been swept up by the Hitler Youth. She did not care that I was Jewish and would come all the way from Schöneberg to Uncle Tom's Cabin to visit me. Disliking mathematics and gymnastics on the apparatus as much as I, we both aspired to something better than the volleyball corner in our schoolyard. We met twice weekly to recite any plays that we could find in our parents' bookcases — classics, of course. Who had ever heard of anything else? Assigning major and minor parts in sisterly fairness, I cursed as Götz von Berlichingen; she was a virtuous Kätchen von Heibronn. In this fashion we felt intellectually mile-high above those Hitler Youth girls in their enviably pretty Berchtesgaden blazers.

Otherwise, I have little to say about the state of mind of a thirteen-year old on the road to puberty, a criss-cross path under the best of circumstances, if not that my class had begun to study Latin. Having to teach forty teenage girls Latin declensions, Dr. Barth knew he needed methods out of the ordinary. Therefore, he made up examples so striking that I have not forgotten any of them. For instance, a sentence demonstrating the use or non-use of the ablative: "The young man thrashes the bride with the table" versus "The young man thrashes the table with the bride," a clever combination of our restricted vocabulary.

The year 1934 seems as foggy and muddled as my head was at the time. Little of it has stayed in my memory apart from a visit to Mrs.

My class at the Gertraudenschule with the Latin teacher. I am in the middle, upper right; Tutti Mallow is to my left.

Lange's relatives in Eisenach, Turinghian bratwurst, of course, and a donkey ride up to the Wartburg. Unaware that Martin Luther probably perceived little difference between a Jew and the devil, I admired the famous ink stain resulting from his battle with temptation.

Mrs. Lange's family were employees of the railway and postal system. They never before had contact with Jews and treated me, a rare bird, kindly. Like Berliners, Thuringians were glad Hitler had freed them from the Versailles treaty. Finally Germany had a government, one that appeared (for the time being) to be stable. Listening to the conversations of Mrs. Lange's relatives, however, I asked myself where Papa found those clients who reassured him they were not Nazis and held him in high esteem despite his religion?

With Latin vocables, French irregular verbs and the many parts I play-acted with Tutti Mahlow, the year passed quickly. Once more on January 30th, the second anniversary of the dictatorship, I had to sit in the school auditorium and endure Hitler's outbursts of rage coming over the air. I did not invite any friends to celebrate my birthday. Birthday parties were childish, I told myself — let the mocha cups remain in the sideboard until they rot. The paint-box with oil colors, brushes and a palette my father had given me were proof that I was now too grown-up for birthday sprees. And since secret longing for the traditional birthday party with my old friends was below the desires of a burgeoning artist, that same afternoon I began to paint a self-portrait.

Wearing a broad Basque beret, I stared into the mirror until Rembrandt himself stared back at me out of my own eyes. My nose gave me the most trouble: to my astonishment, it seemed to be pointed from the profile, rounded and a little like a potato in front. After an encouraging result I asked others to sit for me, beginning with flaxen-haired little Uwe, the Königs' youngest, so lovable and pretty that I gave him the picture. Many years later I learned that shortly after the end of the war he had been killed playing with a leftover explosive.

In spring, we had two family festivities, the last ones before the curtain came down. Lilo's younger sister Ursula, the more spoiled of the two, became engaged to Dr. Fritz Rosenthal, a young physician. Ursula threatened that she would kill herself if Doctor Rosenthal walked out on her because of her father's refusal to buy him the necessary outfit for an X-ray laboratory. The suitor got his clinic, a rabbi was asked to come to Uncle Max and Aunt Toote's home and a huppa, a bridal canopy, was erected in the salon where I had once sung children's songs to my aunt's accompaniment.

Because Aunt Toote was too excited to sit by her grand piano, my cousin Karl began playing the first bars of Mendelssohn's wedding march. Uncle Max led Ursula, all wrapped in white, into the room. Cooped up with Mrs. Buchsbaum, the old Schlesinger and Aunt Alice, the three family gossips, I barely heard someone speak of a certain kind of bosom and a dowry consisting of brassieres. After a prayer, the bride and groom walked seven times around the huppa; he placed a ring on her finger, and they were married. Only when Fritz shattered a wine glass under his patent-leather shoe were they truly wed. Shattering the wine glass has been said to symbolize the irrevocable loss of virginity; more often, it has been interpreted as symbolic of the destruction of the Temple in Jerusalem in 70 A.D., presumably the saddest event in Jewish history. When the young husband crushes the glass, it is to remind him, even in his moment of joy, not to forget his origins and his obligations to future generations.

The rabbi alluded briefly to a ship in stormy seas — as I understood it, the young couple was meant to be the ship, the stormy sea the Third Reich; otherwise there was no talk of politics that afternoon. Of course the rabbi enjoined Fritz and Ursula to transmit their Jewish heritage to their children as they had received it from their parents. Half a year later Fritz and Ursula indeed left the ever-stormier seas of their homeland, taking the X-ray equipment to California. Was it because of those X-rays, at the time still handled with little precaution, that the marriage remained childless? Who can say. To the end of their lives, Fritz and Ursula had only well brought up poodles sitting at their table.

Then came the great finale of Tiele Wardenberg Street, Aunt Toote and Uncle Max's silver wedding anniversary in early summer, 1935. She gave me the gift of a dark blue velvet suit for the occasion, an outfit I took with me on my escape to Belgium several years later and that I held onto and treasured for a very long time. As if sensing this was to be the last family celebration before our separation, all but one of the relatives on my mother's side was present. The exception was Lilo, who sent a telegram of congratulations from her kibbutz in Palestine.

More interested in the menu than in talk about Hitler breaking the Locarno pact and his military occupation of the Rhineland, I sneaked into Anna's kitchen. "Ah, this heavenly asparagus," Anna was sighing, swallowing one and putting another into my mouth. My younger cousin Jolanthe, always following me, nibbled at a tiny carrot, poked her little finger into the trembling aspic of a big veal roast and sniffed the lemon crème. A feast for the gods stood waiting on the range and the kitchen table; even the windowsill was occupied with platters of Olympic dimensions.

My cousin Karl had dedicated a poem to Uncle Max and Aunt Toote, which he recited between the remaining asparagus and parsleyed potatoes. It abounded with Greek and Roman gods and goddesses, my uncle and aunt striding hand-in-hand through the verses, here Philemon and Baucis, there Venus Anadyomene with

Apollo. Grasping that Philemon and Baucis were an allusion to Aunt Toote's hospitality, I applauded enthusiastically. I did not know, nor would I have understood, that the diamond jardinière glittering beside Aunt Toote's wedding band was Uncle Max's compensation for all his affairs. He had stopped pinching my cheeks and my behind years before, and so I raised my glass, the first champagne I ever tasted, with true emotion and good wishes. Aunt Alice had the last of the lemon crème before it was my turn for a second helping, so I indemnified myself with Lübecker marzipan, chocolate truffles and Schiller locks. A new relative, Ewald, sat down by the piano. It was said that Uncle Max's niece Ruth had married him solely to get away from her mother. "I love you as you do me, evenings and mornings. There was no day when you and I would not share our worries," he sang. Had Karl sung Beethoven's beautiful song in his baritone, I would have had goose bumps, but Ewald's tenor fluted somewhat thinly through his nose. Then, for some reason, I had unpleasant memories from my childhood of Uncle Max shouting at Aunt Toote.

"So they were borne more easily by you and by me both," Ewald continued, "You were soothing my sorrows, I cried over your woes." Many eyes were wet, and always when I think of Lilo's death a year-and-a-half later, her parents' silver anniversary and the image of the family grouped around the piano come to mind. The new and soon-to-disappear cousin Ewald accompanied himself; at his side stood Uncle Max with a carnation in his lapel and one arm around Aunt Toote's shoulders. Aunt Hanna dabbed her eyes with a handkerchief artfully hemmed by Aunt Alice. Aunt Hanna's daughter Lilli (named for Goethe's Lilli), a classic beauty with raven hair, smilingly whispered something into her brother Karl's ear. In the light of things to come, Ewald could have dispensed with the last verse, "God's blessing on you, joy of my heart." If only we had known what awaited us, the whole family would have packed their valises the next morning to leave Germany forever.

For an encore Ewald sang Schumann's "Dedication." We then dispersed, the men retiring to the smoking room. I remained with Papa, listening to Uncle Hans talking politics.

"Now he is fortifying the west side of the Rhine — has Germany totally forgotten 1914-1918?" his bass resounding high over my head (the "he" of course was Hitler). "All at once cannons are more important than butter to Germany. Hard to believe how people swallow these slogans." Only a few of those in the room knew that Uncle Max and his two brothers, owners of a cigar import business, were quietly preparing for their emigration to America. The youngest, Uncle Willi, also expressed his opinions.

"Hitler is rearming and where are the French and the British? Sleeping. Only now, with the German army already on the French border, they suddenly get scared. So scared they won't even honor their pact with Poland and Czechoslovakia. How can the German Jews believe anybody will help them out of this mess? Ridiculous! Our only help is self-help — we should know that by now," he growled, sucking on a cigar with a golden bellyband. When the discussion shifted to foreign currency, the less wealthy of my relatives grouped around my father. Lacking money that could be transferred to a foreign country, they were not interested in the direction the conversation was taking. Instead my father told one of his war adventures.

"That's the only time I knowingly killed an enemy, a Sudanese, on the Somme. He was lying there, seriously wounded, with a wedding ring on his finger. I felt sorry for the black fellow. But as I bent down to give him a sip of water he tried to stab me — so I had to shoot him." Since I had heard the story before and did not like it, I went back to the salon to try the funny things offered to the ladies there on a silver plate — crystallized violets and mimosas imported from the south of France. Tasting less interesting than they looked, the tiny blooms made the roof of my mouth tickle. True elegance apparently had to be a little bland.

The men in the next room reached their last subject, losses. Anyone wanting to emigrate was getting but a pittance for his property. Jewish houses were snapped up for next to nothing, voices cracked with indignation. Only my father's disclosure that he would let me go to England for summer vacation caused his corner to fall silent.

"Did you hear that, Toote?" Uncle Max called over to my aunt.

"Mohr is letting Irene go to Liverpool all by herself!" My aunt's gestures made short change of this piece of news.

"How will she cross the channel? And how will she change trains in London? She hasn't yet learned any English. Nonsense, even Mohr cannot be that irresponsible."

I myself had a hard time believing that my father had accepted an invitation from my friend Lotti Rosenberg and her parents, mostly because my ticket would cost a fortune. But since, at his urging, I had been taking an English course for beginners at Uncle Tom's Cabin, the plan for my trip was going ahead. Aunt Alice could not help meddling. Grete would turn in her grave, I heard her say to Aunt Luise when we were already putting on our coats.

Once more we congratulated my uncle and aunt on their silver anniversary and expressed our thanks — with that, the curtain came down on our family celebrations, on calf roast in aspic, on Schiller locks and on crystallized violets, and on Aunt Toote's gracious last bow. That summer marked a time of separation for our family in general. Even my father saw that with the exception of Jews, people were better off than before; he no longer counted on an early fall of Hitler's regime, though he could not persuade himself that it would continue indefinitely If not the German people, then the great powers would one day put that megalomaniac corporal in his place. Like so many generations of Jews before us, we must adapt to the situation, making ourselves as invisible as possible, he said. Emigrate? Where to? With what money? And what could we do there? Apart from the youngest among us, nobody knew more than the rudiments of any foreign language, if one did not count some Hebrew from the prayer book and the Haggadah.

⌒

The curriculum at school became more and more warlike. We learned a song about Death "beating a drum stretched with the skin of cadavers, riding through Flanders on a black steed," a somber, very ancient song from the Thirty Years War. Afterwards we were cheered by a merrier song: "How good it was to be slain by the enemy, how much better to be cut down as grass in May, in a field out in the open rather than all alone in a narrow bed; and how beautiful red blood looked in a green meadow." Those songs were an integral part of our music lessons; in literature classes we were also fed stories of heroism, for instance, an account of the valiant resistance of the town of Stolberg against I don't recall what attackers. I do remember, however, Miss Vogel choosing an excerpt from my composition on the subject to demonstrate incorrect style. "There was famine, they had no water and bullets were flying through town," I had written.

"Bullets do not fly, Irene, they flit or whiz . . . birds. . . ." Here Miss Vogel (her name meaning bird) cleared her throat, "chickens fly through town." It was hard not to burst out laughing, but on the whole I was in no mood for fun. With the intensifying incitement against Jews, poets like Heine and Mendelssohn ceased to exist, even in my school. Since German art and literature had to be of pure lineage, deeply rooted in German soil, Jews with their soulless, cosmopolitan intellect were incapable of true creativity. I myself was beginning to believe that I would never become an artist worthy of the word. Where was I to take my roots? Steal them? I could not even go to the cinema anymore. Jews were undesirable there and someone from the neighborhood could recognize me. All my classmates had gone to see *Hitler Youth Boy Quex*, a Nazi propaganda film, apparently so enchanting that even Tutti Mahlow went to see it, refusing to tell me the content, however. I knew why, of course. Even though I understood that the film had to be rife with anti-Semitic propaganda, I still wanted to see it. With a last feeble effort, I pushed against the door that had slammed shut, closed my eyes to the sign, "You do not belong here anymore." What was better, to wallow in my own humiliation or hide my head in the sand? In the end I did not go to see either *Hitler Youth Boy Quex* nor *Jud Süss*, which the newspapers called, a powerful drama depicting the Jew in all his cruelty and lust. Much as I dreaded the whole thing, I still wanted to eavesdrop at that door. Such morbid weekday ruminations were soon pushed into the background by my approaching departure for England. Mrs. Lange helped me pack my suitcase.

At age fourteen, equipped with a passport (for the time being still without the red J stamp for Jewish), tickets, pocket money and a list of telephone numbers for an emergency, I traveled to London via Hook van Holland and Dover. For me, who had seen nothing of the world apart from Eisenach, Heringsdorf and the immediate surroundings of Berlin, this trip was an exciting adventure. The Channel crossing went well. After reaching my first destination, a boarding house for ladies in the center of London became my springboard for a hurried tour of the British capital. As though it was a miracle, I would find my way back to my address on Russell Square, each time panicking and believing myself lost in the maze of London's streets. With my very limited vocabulary I made it to Buckingham Palace, the sights on the Thames, the Tower of London and the most famous of the museums. The man who taught English in Uncle Tom's Cabin had written down a sentence for me to take on my trip, "Where there is a will, there is a way."

What of London remained unforgettable? Yorkshire pudding with roast-beef, buttered toast and Turner's paintings in the Tate Gallery — all three of these buoyed me up in times of dearth with a Fata Morgana of delights. The day would come when I thirsted for the colors in Turner's aquarelles like a dog panting for water. In Berlin I was born too late to see the impressionists, expressionists and post-impressionists, since all "degenerate" art and works created by Jews had been removed, stowed away in cellars or sold abroad. Just when I was old enough to visit Berlin's museums by myself, the only paintings left on the walls were sentimental and tame realism I took to be modern art. William Turner, though he had lived much earlier, showed me how mistaken I was: almost without contours, using movement and color in their place, he conjured up air and light, water and clouds. His paintings were magic.

But I had to shut my mouth gaping in amazement and continue to Liverpool. Lotti and her new friends were awaiting me in surroundings better fitting a teenager. Here in an atmosphere of warmth and openness, I was invited to garden parties, innocent pleasures where I ate the thinnest of sandwiches with watercress, and drank lemonade. Instead of songs glorifying dead warriors, we lamented the last rose of summer and sang about a lady with green sleeves. I went on an excursion to Chester and Wales with Lotti's class, then on a bicycling tour along the coast until my buttocks hurt so I did not dare sit down. Bathing hurt me less — I swam into the sea until I was out of earshot from the shore and shouted over and over as loudly as I could into the roaring waves, "Nieder mit Hitler! Down with Hitler!"

It felt so good I screamed until my voice cracked and I became hoarse. Looking back at the beach after a while, I was astonished to see how small the people had become. They were waving at me to turn back, which was easier said than done. There I was in the Atlantic Ocean and the ebb tide, which I knew nothing about, had pulled me far out into the sea. Urged on by worried bystanders on the beach, I needed all my strength to swim against the current back to shore.

Of course I did not tell either Lotti's parents or my family about such episodes. After three train transfers to get back to Berlin, I made my appearance as a pseudo grown-up who had visited the British Empire all by herself and had come back in one piece. In my absence Aunt Toote and Uncle Max, Uncle Richard, Fritz and Ursula had all emigrated to California. Thanks to being racially Aryan, Aunt Luise was permitted by law to keep my grandparents' shop on König Street open until further notice. She remained behind with Jolanthe. On the other hand, my sister opened a small shop on her own in her Aryan husband's name. "From Old Make New! Owner, Karl-Friedrich Schmidt," the shop sign said. Gerda sat inside cutting up old stockings, tattered curtains, dresses and tablecloths into long strips, which she wove on a small loom into pretty runners or rugs for the amazed proprietors of former rags. She filled the shop with her own needle-work, such as knitted and crocheted children's outfits, bed-covers and wall-hangings; by special order she even made leather gloves. Letting himself be mollified by the birth of his first grandson, my father, for whom Gerda was as good as dead because of her marriage to a non-Jew, had become a proud grandfather.

Who knows if in the grip of ever sharper anti-Jewish measures, my father still considered little Peter not growing up as a Jew all that terrible. Grief about the injustice of our situation had embittered him and made him tolerant enough to let me join a Zionist youth organization. Though I continued to go to synagogue on Friday evenings, the sermons were too light a counterweight to keep my wobbly self-esteem balanced. I needed friends in my age group and ideals I could identify with.

Shortly after returning from my vacation trip, the Nuremberg Laws were published, making mixed marriages unlawful and punishing sexual intercourse between Jews and Aryans with hard labor. At the same time we were demoted from citizens to subjects. To top it all, my friend Tutti Mahlow dropped me like the proverbial hot potato. I should try to understand, she said, sounding very considerate — her father was a magistrate, her sister had to think of her fiancée's career. In the space of a day, we went from being good friends to classmates who politely greeted each other from a distance. It was more humiliating than having to sit through one of Doctor Kadner's ethnology courses. Though he was a good teacher of French and geography, and had a doctorate from the Sorbonne, the Nazi bacillus seemed to have softened his brain. More and more often he arrived in class wearing his brown S.A. uniform, giving the "Heil Hitler!" salute as if from a grandstand and proclaiming the planned geography lesson had been changed to ethnology. For forty-five minutes I would try to concentrate on a drawing so as not to have to listen to Doctor Kadner's description of the characteristics of sub-species such as Negroes and Jews, mainly of Jews. On the blackboard, he wrote in neat rows: "kinky hair," "flat feet," "receding forehead," "obesity." Then he strode to my bench at the back of the class, praising my drawing. My teacher's conduct toward me remained correct and friendly, the unspoken agreement of my dispensation from the "German greeting" extending to ethnology. While he taught his revolting anti-Semitic drivel, I continued to sit in the back of the class drawing.

As the only non-Aryan student remaining in class after the departure of Hanna Frenkel, I felt I had to hold on to any last shred of Jewish honor. This meant that when changing clothes for gymnastics, I could not allow myself even one safety pin in the hem of my skirt, nor the smallest hole in my socks. Not to have it said that Jews are cowards, I climbed to the top of the ladder and like the rest of the class jumped from a height of three meters to a leather pad on the floor. This senseless, bone-rattling exercise, designed to make German girls courageous, made me, one of the race of sub-humans, feel rebellious. Meanwhile, the smell of the leather pads was nauseating.

In the Zionist youth organization of the Werkleute (Working People) that I now joined, boys and girls were placed in separate groups under their own group leaders and gathered together at meetings or on excursions. Now I was among my own kind. No need to be clean as a pin or show death defying courage. After completing school and a short agricultural apprenticeship, the members intended to emigrate to Palestine, there to join the kibbutz of the movement and help build our own state.

I was at ease in the Werkleute and became inspired with the idealism of my new environment. I dreamed of Eretz Yisrael, seeing as my highest goal the planting of tomatoes in HaZorea, my comrades' recent settlement at the foot of Mount Carmel, eating my meals in a communal dining hall, and eventually having babies who would grow up at the communal children's house. It was less clear to me how I would combine these activities with my painting, but for the moment I used my talents mainly to compose photographic layouts of pioneers carrying sheaves of wheat, Yemenite singers and Jewish watchmen with rifles on horseback.

Before putting up my collages in our meeting room, I volunteered to give the walls a fresh layer of paint. The next Sunday I arrived early with buckets, a thick brush and my father's instructions on how to mix his favorite linden-green. Four walls needed two coats of paint — my arms began to hurt already after the first one. How could I leave a room in this smeared state when the leadership was to meet there on the following afternoon? The one electric bulb hanging from the ceiling was burnt out, and it was almost dark in the room when at last I finished. My ten hours of work was a disaster, I thought — dotted with spots and smears of all shades, from poisonous dark green to tones of garish grass, the walls looked much worse than before I began. I had not stirred the color long enough I thought, but was too tired and discouraged for a third coat. Let them sneer or make fun of me — I went home. With a newly developed sense of responsibility, I returned the following morning to the third coat. But a wonder had occurred overnight. The dried walls were beaming in even, light linden-green. Compliments came raining on me from all sides.

I now had many girl friends, nicer and more sincere than Tutti Mahlow, even male friends. Instead of classic plays I read Theodore Herzl's *Jewish State* and sang Hebrew songs in the choir. If I had any problems I could go to my group leader, a young woman with the kind of sympathetic understanding that until then I had only found with my cousin Lilo. Inside my group we gave each other presents of small books with dedications such as, "To you, Irene!" Reproductions of sculptures by Barlach and Kolbe, woodcuts by Masereel and poems by Rainer Maria Rilke. Rilke and more Rilke. To avoid the hostility on the outside, the rowdy brown columns and the revolting caricatures of *The Stürmer*, we looked to each other.

Some members no longer had a place to return to, so the movement rented an apartment for those whose parents had lost their jobs and their homes. Everyone living in this rather Spartan refuge contributed what he or she could toward the upkeep. The so-called "home mother," a young woman a few years older than the rest of us, did the cooking and made sure that all these teen-agers behaved. They did. Most of my new friends came from the eastern and northern parts of Berlin, working class neighborhoods where Jews had been handled more roughly than I had in the western part of the city. Because of their own experiences and the worries of their families, these young people had matured earlier and were much more serious and purposeful than the girls of the same age I knew at school. My classmates, if I can call them that, at the Getraudenschule only thought of pranks to play on an unfortunate young teacher who was doing his teacher-in-training year at a girls' school. Irmgard Brecht had been first to come to class in the brown monkey-blazer of the Hitler Youth. She would not figure in the class book as "Protestant" any longer. She now was to be registered as a "German, believing in God," she said to Miss Vogel, thereby defining a new religion that had gotten rid of the Jew-loaded Old and New testaments.

Despite being undesirable in many shops, despite the banners in the streets and their thick exclamation marks for Germany to wake up and Jews to drop dead, I never experienced a direct insult from my classmates or my teachers. There were still girls at school who on Sundays went with their parents to the Annenkirche, which bordered our schoolyard, the domain of Pastor Niemöller. A Protestant, he enjoined his flock to listen to their conscience first and foremost and did not give in to the Nazis. In some kind of powerless protest against the regime, they sat there listening to his sermons about conscience and individual responsibility before God. Not everyone was softened up by the Nazis — though a good word from that side would have been so welcome and encouraging, it seldom came. An exception was my art teacher at the Gertraudenschule, Professor Eberhardt. She went so far as to invite me to her home. Saying it was time I tried to draw from nude models, she sat her five-year old son in bathing trunks in front of me on the living room carpet and gave me free lessons, with tea and cookies to boot! I remain grateful for her generosity.

1936. My fifteenth birthday was uneventful if I discount Hitler's usual speech threatening international Jewry for intriguing against Germany. No lessons that day; instead we all had to report to the school auditorium to listen to the Führer on the radio. Mrs. Lange baked a Thuringian stollen, friends from my Zionist group gave me a book with Rembrandt drawings and my father sent a sweater from Hessen. The same mail included a letter from Switzerland — Lilo had contracted tuberculosis and her parents brought her from Palestine to Vevey.

In March, my brother's wife gave birth to a daughter; this moved my father to finally lift their long banishment. He invited them all for coffee. Mrs. Lange, perhaps with the presentiment that our days on Eisvogelweg were numbered, contributed much to the somewhat tepid reconciliation. That same month new elections took place. The results ended my father's optimism that the German people were too smart to vote for a madman, or that the great powers would intervene. With the streets covered in swastika flags, Goebbels jubilantly announced that ninety-nine percent of all Germans had given a resounding "Yes" to the Führer. No longer a German citizen, my father was not allowed to vote. Mr. König's voice, much to his wife's desperate worry that the whole family was at risk for the concentration camp, was one of the one percent of naysayers. Those so-called elections were but falsehood and deceit, shreds of paper from Goebbels' propaganda machine, Mr. König shouted in the presence of his few clients who still dared to come in broad daylight to use his laundry service. Mr. König's business had fallen on hard times — his steadfastness was costing him dearly.

From the outside, Eisvogelweg number fifteen may have looked unchanged. Gerda Struck, a teacher's daughter and a girl from the other end of the street, still came to visit me from time-to-time; and we naturally continued to see the Königs. Though there were no more festivities, the family — or what remained of it — regularly gathered on Jewish holidays. We celebrated the first seder of Passover in the modest home of Uncle David and Aunt Johanna Spicker. Only their oldest son Kurt was missing in the family circle that assembled around the drop-leaf table, which was saved from the debacle of the Friedenau villa. He had gone to South America with his forbidden Aryan fiancée. As a seventeen-year-old volunteer, he had survived cholera and the Russians at the German front in Gallipoli. A clever man with a doctorate in economics, he always knew which side his bread was buttered on. Turning his back on Germany in time, and running far enough away to Uruguay, he was one of only two from this branch of the family to see the fall of the Nazis — his youngest brother Viktor survived the camps and returned a lonely and broken man.

We celebrated the second seder at Aunt Hanna's. To her apparent surprise, Karl had brought a young woman with cheerful eyes and silky lashes who turned out not to be intimidated by my aunt's dignified airs. Nor did she behave bashfully at the table, throwing her head back with laughter. I liked her at once. She was Suse, captain of a Jewish volleyball team. My cousin called her in turn Sue, Suse and Suzanne all evening and could not get enough of her name. He remained deeply in love with her to the end of her life in America many years later. I will come back to their near miraculous escape from the Nazi machine.

German schools were being cleansed of Jews. Nevertheless, as the daughter of a war volunteer I was still tolerated, for the time being at least. At the start of the school year, I was in the eighth grade and a rarity. My heart was not in my studies anymore and I kept up with schoolwork indifferently. From Cato's Punic wars and Hannibal's elephants freezing in the Alps, my thoughts would wander off to thirsty camels swaying in the desert, and more often to myself picking oranges under a burning sun. The Nazis certainly would not let me stay four more years to finish school. By then I would have long been in Palestine, I told myself, framing the border of my copybook with the profiles of my fellow students. Forced to abandon my dream of studying at the Berlin Academy of the Arts, I had heard of an art school by the strange name of Bezalel in Jerusalem. Would my aunts be willing to pay the three thousand English pounds to send me there for a three-year program?

But this dream would not materialize. We received the news of Lilo's death in Vevey. She was twenty-six. A leaf fell out of the envelope with Aunt Toote's letter from Switzerland, a short poem: "Barbed Wire Around Vevey." Lilo, as a physician, was surely aware of her own condition and had written those verses in a light vein to conceal the truth from her parents. Seeing how fond she had been of her comrades in the orange groves, Uncle Max, who had refused her any help to go to Palestine, now gave her dowry to the kibbutz.

Seven

IN THE YOUTH MOVEMENT we were trying to prepare ourselves for the rigors of pioneer life in Palestine. Groups of us marched many miles in the summer heat on country roads and through woods, most of the time with blisters on our feet. To drink water on those marches was considered a weakness, to be a sissy; to quit was out of the question. Though this discipline was surely not good for one's kidneys, it toughened us and helped me stand more firmly. I was cautiously beginning to grow new roots — rather than singing the ancient Hebrew during Friday night prayers, I began learning Hebrew as an everyday language.

When a popular Hebrew teacher was preparing to depart for Palestine, he was given the customary Jewish send-off, much tea and long speeches. I was given the honor of expressing the students' thanks, which was to be in Hebrew. Though I as yet had no understanding of the language, I memorized the short speech that was written for me. In parrot fashion I had learned it by heart so thoroughly that even if awakened in the night I could have recited it. Nevertheless, when I stood on the rostrum and looked into the multitude of eyes expectantly fixed on me, I could not bring more than two or three words from my lips. I stood there like a robot put together the wrong way, opening my mouth mechanically without a sound coming out. How did the free and easy film acting of my childhood suddenly disappear? Only half a year earlier in our living room, I had play-acted so effusively with Tutti Mahlow; but now, even with clearly audible prompting, I was paralyzed with stage fright and returned to my seat. Despite all the compassionate clapping, I was crushed. It was a disgrace I have never forgotten.

In July we were able to take a breather. First the anti-Semitic streamers disappeared from the streets; then, insofar as I still wanted to, I could enter shops and restaurants where previously I was an "undesirable." The radio and the newspapers calmed down and even Goebbels dribbled less of his poison. Suddenly I was once more able to go to the movies. With diligent dish washing I earned the money for tickets, and could feast my eyes on such darlings of the regime as Marika Rökk, Zara Leander and Anni Ondra.

The reason for this temporary tolerance was the 1936 Olympic games. At that time the Third Reich was trying to project a positive impression on foreign powers and for a while we Jews were simmered on a lower flame. Though a beautiful city at anytime, Berlin was now dressed up. Great festivities were organized for the masses of visitors coming from all over the world. Hitler wanted to show off Germany's new prosperity, the country's well-nourished and well-dressed citizens, and its athletic youth. They were to serve as the ambassadors of goodwill towards foreigners. The proverbial wolf clad in sheep's skin, he intended to lull his future victims, to appear as a father of his people who had turned gentler under the load of his responsibilities. All those newspaper articles about the persecution of the Jews were obviously exaggerated, empty talk not to be taken seriously. Was it Hitler's fault that Mussolini had attacked Ethiopia? Why would Germany not meddle in Austrian politics and help the Spanish Fascists when half the world was meddling there? The foreign press was welcomed with great flourishes of trumpets, and it reciprocated by polishing the nice dictator's tarnished image.

This year, with no money for vacation trips, my father was happy to still have his job. I spent the summer at the Krumme Lanke and with my friends in the Zionist youth movement. When the Olympic games began in August, I sat at home on pins and needles. What a pity I was not present when Jesse Owens, a member of a race as despised as the Jews, triumphed over the German athletes. My father was not much interested in sports and was traveling besides; Mrs. Lange's tight household money would not be spent, she said, for watching yellow, black and white people running and jumping. Meanwhile, nearly everyone I knew had been to at least one event.

With the games nearing their end, I could no longer sit quietly in Uncle Tom's Cabin just listening to the games on the radio. I had enough money for a bus ticket. So I went straight to the stadium. What did I really want there? To find a ticket lying on the ground waiting just for me? To listen to those inside cheering? At this stage of my life, the idea that I could possibly sneak in without a ticket would not have crossed my mind — not so much because of moral scruples but out of my still deeply rooted Prussian fear of the law. However, finding the entrance indescribably crowded, I was pushed and pulled into the stadium whether or not I wanted to go in. Nobody showed any interest in a ticket. Easily finding a seat, I had landed at the women's diving competition. I watched female figures spiraling one after the other from great heights into the swimming pool. They all rotated clockwise, one jump looking like the next. Was that all? It was less exciting than I had imagined, until I heard voices rising, "The Führer, our Führer is coming." Arms all around me shot up to a rhythmic "Sieg Heil" roar, the whole stadium swaying like a field of wheat. Hitler and his retinue made their entrance, striding to the tiers of honor not far from where I was seated. In flesh and blood, the lowbrow face with the little mustache appeared just as cold and impenetrable as on the thousands of photos, posters and pictures I could not avoid everywhere I went. I tried not to attract attention by my lack of enthusiasm. The women continued diving, the "Sieg Heils" died down, then changed into hand clapping when the three victorious ones were awarded their medals. Then, making their way to buses, the crowds pushed toward the exits without paying further attention to the Führer. This was the only time I saw the man who was to become world enemy number one of the twentieth century. "A glick hot dir getroffen" is Yiddish for, "You met with a real stroke of luck there." I would be made fun of later on when I told the story of my "encounter" with Hitler.

Did Hitler attend the diving competition because all of the divers were white? It is a strong possibility. After Jesse Owens won his track and field events, Hitler had refused to shake his hand. He was rankled that what for him was a justified refusal offended the world press at a moment when acceptance of his regime seemed at hand.

The games were over in September. The welcome banners were rolled up and replaced by the anti-Semitic slogans that swelled in the early fall breeze. "Don't trust a Jew on his oath, and not a fox in the green moss!" (Trau keinem Fuchs auf grüner Heid, und keinem Jud bei seinem Eid!) was not the worst among them. I abhorred this rhyme over others because the inane singsong hummed in my brain for hours at a time. "Undesirable" once again, as before the games, I shuttled on my old bicycle every morning and noon between Uncle Tom's Cabin and the Gertraudenschule, still doing some homework despite the knowledge that my school days were numbered.

In October the peaceful dictator showed his mettle, sending planes and pilots to Franco to test his new bombs; at the same time he formed an alliance with Mussolini. In November Hitler signed a pact with Japan, and on January 30, 1937, my sixteenth birthday, he made a long speech that enumerated all he had accomplished in four years. Though he was proudly ruffling his feathers, he was not exaggerating — what he said was correct. There were almost no more jobless citizens, trade was flourishing, the treaty of Versailles was in the wastebasket, and the Rhineland was reoccupied. Thanks to him, Adolf Hitler, he boasted, Germany once more had a strong army and a modern air force and navy. Italy and Japan were now our allies. The voice on the loud-speaker in the Aula of the Gertraudenschule threatened, "International Jewry beware!" It was a very long speech for a school holiday on a birthday of which there is nothing else to relate. Money for presents was scarce. My father, in addition to donating to the Jewish winter assistance whose need for money was so urgent, was also forced to pay a considerable sum to the Nazis' German winter assistance.

⟳

A few weeks into February, riding home from a meeting with my Zionist youth group, I had a strange adventure. At the meeting, our group leader Ilse Meyerhoff had expounded the views of a long-deceased father of Zionism. On the bus drive home, I opened the pamphlet she had given me, Leon Pinsker's *Auto-emancipation*. His essential argument was that two thousand years of refugee life had driven Jews into professions that alienated them from physical trades, including farm work. To help themselves to heal and bring mind and body into harmony, they must build their own state in Zion, a modern, socialist state. As farmers and workers they must give up their current professions, their business suits and stiff white collars. I noticed that a man who had taken the seat beside me was reading the page over my shoulder. I had to read the difficult essay, having promised Ilse to do so — but he?

"Secret police," my neighbor said all of a sudden, turning over the lapel of his winter coat, "please come with me." I felt this could not be real . . . it was like a detective film. I was not afraid — after all, what crime had I committed? At the police station, the man leafed through the booklet; he first questioned me about the movement I belonged to, then about its ideas. What was a secret agent doing with a decent-looking young person who turned out to be Jewish, reading social-philosophical essays and naively expounding her Zionist credo? Since these socialist ideas were not, after all, intended for Germany but for Palestine, he threw the little fish he had hooked back into the water. I took another bus, and back home I immediately telephoned the Werkleute leadership. As far as I remember, they were not bothered.

At the end of the school year a letter was delivered from the Gertraudenschule: new laws forbade all Jews, without exception, from attending classes at German schools. Not hearing an echo of any kind from my former classmates, I concluded then (and now) that I was not missed much in the tenth grade.

My father, Aunt Hanna and my cousin Karl had to decide what to do with me. With some secretiveness, I was told about a small inheritance from my grandmother, which was held in trust for my higher education or for my dowry. In these special circumstances, it would be used for private lessons. I was allowed to study with an artist on the condition that I learn industrial drawing at the same time. In my family's opinion, drawing the cross-section of a ball bearing or drawing a nude, drawing was drawing.

Hurrah! I was on cloud nine at the thought of studying with an artist. Though I had only the foggiest notions of industrial drawing, that was a matter of minor importance. With great enthusiasm I threw myself into my new program. Mornings: private technical school with Drs. Ings. Arthur Werner, father and son. Afternoons: private art school with Eugene Hersch on Hardenberg Street. Its one window, not counting the studio skylight, overlooked the Berlin Academy of the Arts. If I could not be there, the school I had dreamed of, at least I had landed just opposite in a real atelier with a skylight and a skeleton in one corner.

With the time I was spending on trains and buses, and with a very full schedule, I was in the grip of a myriad of new impressions — I had been paying little attention to new anti-Semitic measures and slogans. Having got used to the vile caricatures of *The Stürmer*, which was exhibited at every kiosk, I barely saw them anymore. But I still shuddered in passing the brown columns of S.A. men marching in the streets, hearing them sing, "When Jew blood splutters from the knife, things will go twice as well!"

To my regret Drs. Ings. Arthur Werner, father and son, took great pride in their small technical school. I had jumped out of the frying pan into the fire. Though I no longer had to study chemistry and physics, the blackboard disappeared every morning under a fresh array of mathematical formulas. I conscientiously copied equations and whole forests of "roots" without understanding the first thing about them. Drawing lessons filled one half of the morning, but cross-sections of tools and machine parts had to be done precisely to a millimeter with a drawing-pen. This was torture for me. However, since the course would be over in half a year, I was determined to keep it up, not wanting to disappoint my cousin.

In contrast, at the art school, a fifth floor artist's studio below the beams of a high-class residence built at the turn of the century, I felt like a ship-wrecked mariner who had at last reached her island after a long odyssey. Whole afternoons, until the last glimmer of daylight had left the skylight and the plaster head or still life in front of me had become one with the background, I sat bent over my charcoal drawings. Even though my teacher was not easily satisfied, I understood at least what was being asked of me.

"Construction, Miss Spicker, construction — you are no camera, and you cannot be exact as the liebe Gott anyhow. Do not imitate, but try to build forms that seem organic. The head here in its entirety should sit in one line from forehead to chin." My teacher was an excellent draftsman whose career as an illustrator for a well-known Berliner daily newspaper was cut short by measures against Jews working for the press. He now kept himself, his son and an old German shepherd, above water with an art school. At this time the "school" had only three students: Ruth Klausner, a serious young lady and a much more competent painter than I; a man whose name I have forgotten, a gaunt, uncommunicative bachelor with nothing else to do; and me. We three were the habitués, joined here and there by jobless, art-minded Jews passing through.

On days that we had organically constructed and reconstructed to Mr. Hersch's satisfaction, he would await dusk to tell us stories about his student days at the academy across the street. I liked his story about the genius. Believing himself to be the greatest artist of the century, a young man had run through the wings of the building wailing, "What a shame that I shall die one day! Ach, that I have to die!" he had torn out his hair. But it was Eugene Hersch, and not the genius, who had won the Rome Prize the following year and continued his studies in Italy. A very serious artist, Mr. Hersch taught his students to approach subjects of nature with respect and humility; he venerated German painters like Adolf Menzel and Wilhelm Leibl. To become a good artist nothing was too much, no sacrifice too great. Each time I had a brush or a pencil in my hand, he said I should keep in mind that this drawing or painting might be the last before my sudden and unexpected demise! To freeze one's fingers painting watercolors on an icy lake as I had done was no large sacrifice. Long before my feat, famous artists wearing cut-off gloves had painted winter landscapes at night, mounting candles on their hats that enabled them to see what they were doing.

I was impressed. Reverently, I followed my teacher's progress on a ceiling-high composition of a group of blue Biblical patriarchs clad in loincloths and kneeling before a yellowish sky. I admired his mastery of portraits from nature even more, including a painting of his old shepherd dog bent over his food bowl, posing for his master as if he understood the importance of the moment. We students were not forgotten. An elevator of art-deco splendor past, having surely seen more elegant visitors, also brought models for us to this fifth floor studio. Most frequently it was Mr. Martinelli, a little man with thin hair dyed black and twinkling raisin eyes, a good face for the study of wrinkles. He lived in a home for old actors and he baked delicious cheesecake!

In the fall I received a paper certifying I had visited Dr. Ing. Arthur Werner's private technical institute for six months, though the school was too honest to mark that I had completed the course. Out of hundreds of lessons, two notions stuck in my mind: E stands for energy and the root of nine is three. My cousin Karl, a good person, made no fuss about my somewhat lame certificate. Newly admitted to the bar and administering my small inheritance, he now allowed me enough money to study art in the mornings also. On top of this he paid for my lunches.

Unusual circumstances required out of the ordinary measures. Mr. Hersch was good at improvisations and like many painters he was fond of cooking. For a modest additional monthly sum, he began to prepare midday meals for his students, imaginative dishes like rump steak with sauerkraut and pineapple in white wine, or a mound of thin crepes layered in turn with chopped liver and spinach. Stuffed peppers in tomato sauce, then a rarity in Germany, sent me off dreaming about the Mediterranean. We consumed these culinary works of art in the tiny living room that at night also served Mr. Hersch, his son Wolfgang and the dog Wolfi as their bedroom. The kitchen, where only the cook was allowed, consisted of a rusty range squeezed in a passage between the backside of the painting with the Patriarchs and a wall of the studio. Since this shrine, lit by a naked bulb, was taboo at all times, we did the dishes in the bathroom, the one place with a sink and cold-running water. I felt more at home there than even in my old attic corner on Eisvogelweg. Sitting on beds and chairs around a red and white-checkered tablecloth, Mr. Hersch served spaghetti Bolognese together with stories of the Italian Renaissance, such as one about

Michelangelo. After five years of straining his neck in painting the ceiling of the Sistine Chapel, he wandered the streets of Rome with his nose turned to the sky for all eternity. Finishing the meal with coffee, the conversation turned to anecdotes of Berlin such as how old Max Liebermann had waved his brush, "With this one I can still do it."

In the atelier, we could not hear the voices in the street screaming for our blood. Through the skylight we did not see the kiosk layouts with newspapers calling us vermin. Everyday dirt did not bespatter the fifth floor. If Berlin did not need us anymore, then we did not need Berlin either, Mr. Hersch had decided. Artists were citizens of the world and made their home where the arts flourish. In antiquity that place was Athens, in the Renaissance, Venice and Florence, and now we only had to pick — Paris, London, Switzerland, New York. He made us look at the future through rose-tinted glasses. Though not too sure of myself, I nevertheless interrupted, feeling bound to explain my Zionist views.

"Palestine?" Mr. Hersch made fun of me. "Do you really want to spend your life in a kibbutz kitchen rolling matzoh balls for the collective, Miss Spicker? In the best case you'll sell your paintings to Bedouins, maybe to a camel. But how can you hammer nails into a tent to hang them?" and with that he corrected my construction of a perspective foreshortening of Mr. Martinelli's nose. "Palestine is a cultural desert" and turned to Ruth Klausner's drawing.

"Oh no, you are wrong!" I protested. "There are many beautiful new songs, folk-dances, poems." While Mr. Martinelli took a well-earned rest from posing, I sang the songs I had learned with my group, those melancholy melodies tinged with Russian and Arab music that I loved. One was of Rachel, mother of all mothers, whose blood was running in mine, another of a girl from whom a young man steals kisses as she draws water from the well. A third was about the moon over the dewy valley of Yesreel, "Sleep in peace, precious valley, I will watch you." With great feeling I ended on a heroic note. Mr. Martinelli with his few teeth smiled his friendly smile. Meanwhile, nobody had understood a word. Mr. Hersch asked how I could compare this kind of primitive folklore to a song by Schubert. Though my attempt at saving Eretz Israel's artistic honor failed, something good came of it anyhow. For my seventeenth birthday Mr. Hersch gave me a ticket to a concert with the fabulous pianist Alfred Cortot.

Mr. Hersch had sown the seed of doubt in my garden of Zion. What would a new settlement like Hazorea do with a young artist? The kibbutz needed female workers to milk cows and clean out chicken coops. If for a number of years I met the test as a laborer, then my comrades might give me one day a week off for painting. Still, they would frown at my taking money from the common till for paints and canvasses for such "unproductive" labor.

Despite these considerations, I still met with my friends from the movement, getting into an embarrassing situation when I had to decide what to do about two male admirers. They were my first, if I discounted Karl-Friedrich Schmidt's brother from Stralsund, Pomerania. On a visit to Eisvogelweg fifteen, my brother-in-law's younger sibling chased me around the dining-room table, which led to a hurdle race. Only the abundance of furniture in the narrow room saved me from having to kiss his flabby red mouth. Maybe he wanted a quick little roll in racial dishonor before he joined the Nazi Storm Troops two months later.

⌒

So I was seventeen, still unkissed and curious, when an older comrade from the movement condescended more and more frequently to have conversations with me. He had deep black eyes, wrote beautiful poems that sounded like Rilke's, and his name was Martin Kirschbaum. I was flattered by his attention. All this could have led to a first love affair had not a pine branch come between us. One Sunday we were wandering through the Grunewald absorbed in earnest conversation, when Martin suddenly ducked. A man of medium height ducking a branch two feet above his head made him appear so ludicrous that any seed of budding romance in me was killed off on the spot. The other young man, Erwin Kassierer, nicknamed Kasse, had no chance with me from the start. Though he was a nice boy and probably interesting, he was just another adolescent with a pimply face. The long, passionate but confused message he pressed into my hand disconcerted me, and had me wishing that such fiery feelings would not glow under an exterior which held so little attraction. Continuing to dream of "riper" or mature men, I pretended even to myself that I had never received his letter.

Remaining unkissed, I was busy elsewhere. Mr. Hersch needed more cash and started a course on the craft of restoring old paintings. The buyers for his own paintings were only among Jews, who had worries other than collecting art. While Jewish musicians and actors could still find occasional work with the Association of Jewish Culture, what were painters to do? The work of my distant relative, Ludwig Meidner, had been included in the Munich exhibit of degenerate art. Though Mr. Hersch did not fall into the degenerate artist category, nevertheless as a Jew he forfeited his right to artistic existence. Thus, he had come up with the idea of offering Jews who were facing the uncertainties of emigration, the possibility of acquiring a trade, one that did not require much knowledge of foreign languages. Among those who were now learning how to clean, repair and retouch canvases were a female teacher of German literature, a secretary, housewives, a book-keeper, the owner of a printing press and even a judge. They had come to the conclusion that to escape the debasing rule of the Nazis, they had to leave Germany and plunge into the unknown. In order to have more than one iron in the fire, some of the women took other courses such as manicuring and pedicuring, trades which could help them get work anywhere. My participation in the course would help me, for a time at least, after I escaped Germany and got to Belgium. To come together with so many different people and to measure up to all those middle-aged professionals was challenging. On the other hand, seeing the obtuseness of Herr Kaiser the judge, I forever lost the veneration I had for this exalted profession.

In the mornings, I studied restoration, in the afternoons drawing and painting. During the evenings, I worked on a surprise for Karl and Suse's wedding, copying the story of the Book of Esther in Hebrew calligraphy on parchment-like paper.

Commerce was flourishing, Hitler had boasted in his last speech, but not for Jews. My father was at his wits end. His old clients, who had assured Mr. Spicker how much they esteemed him despite his religion, now bought from other salesmen. What is to be done when there is no money? Buy an old car and hire a chauffeur, my father concluded. He calculated that gasoline was cheaper than train tickets. In addition, a car would get him to out-of-the-way places where trains did not stop, which would enable him to find new clients. He needed a driver because he could not get a driver's license, having recently had cataract surgery on both eyes at the Berlin Jewish Hospital, the only one accessible to us. The Jewish driver he hired was happy to find a job, even one poorly paid. Once again my father miscalculated. Repairs of the old car took more money than railway tickets, and then he lost his job anyway. New decrees excluded him from the company that had employed him for ten years.

At least we had one last fling. My father invited my colleague Ruth Klausner and me to accompany him to Bavaria. After two breakdowns, the car got us to Munich late in the evening just in time for a taste of the local liver cheese and prune dumplings. In the morning at the Pinakothek I indulged even more in Tintoretto's "Susanna," which was on loan there. In Bad Tölz at the foot of the Alps we lodged at a farm with a stinking wooden toilet — a hard-working farmer's daughter with the sourest of faces served us idlers our meals. Provided with much advice from Mr. Hersch, we set out for two weeks of landscape painting.

It was early summer. No meadow could be greener, no brook clearer. How were we to paint these overwhelming riches of greens, blues and yellows? Ruth understood how to interpret colors, while my attempts in spinach and egg yolk proved that more than enthusiasm was needed to make a work of art out of grass and buttercups. Consequently I concentrated on the cows, happy to wander off into the mountains on the last day of our stay. We could not return to Berlin without having seen the Alps. We climbed and climbed. As we did I kept puffing and working up a sweat. When we at last arrived at the peak and there was nothing more to climb, we were enveloped in a rain cloud; I could see nothing at all except Ruth as a specter in the fog. Soaked through, we had a hard time finding our way back to the farm to sleep for the last time under a rustic featherbed and watched over by a crucifix. But Jesus, himself a Jew, was no longer the only God worshipped in Bavaria — Hitler's picture joined many of the crucifixes. Ruth and I talked as little as possible in front of the farmers. Woe to us, had they known whom they were harboring in their midst!

Returning to Berlin we learned that all Jews who ever had a run-in with the law, even a traffic violation, had been arrested. The rest were trying to get out. My sister could no longer hide under the Aryan name she borrowed from her husband and was forced to close shop. That same week we were summoned to present ourselves and receive special identification papers, stamped with the large red "J." I had to sign mine with a new first name, Sara. According to the authorities my other three names did not characterize me as Jewish. I was now officially Irene Dolorosa Paula Sara Spicker. My father, registered in his birth certificate as Moses, was allowed to remain who he was, while all Jewish men without a typically Hebrew first name became Israel.

Decrees followed decrees. I had to say good-bye to Uncle Tom's Cabin, since my father had been given notice to vacate our house at the same time he had been let go from his job. After helping to clean out our home, I came finally to the verandah. Would Papa's linden-green walls be painted over by our successor, I asked myself, unhooking the plate with the flower basket, the weeping hearts and the inscription, "To love and be loved as in this verse, is the greatest joy on earth." I bit into an apple still hanging from the tree, doubting that the new inhabitants would let that many pine trees stand. When I went to say good-bye to the König's, Mr. König looked as if he had no more energy left for either curses or hope. Our other neighbors were so embarrassed and curt that I had no difficulty keeping a stiff upper lip, acting as if I was going on a vacation trip. Only when I came to Gerda Struck's door, a girl who was not even a close friend, was there an unexpected show of emotion. Gerda was not home, said her mother, but I should join her in the kitchen. She was washing dishes, rubbing and rubbing without lifting her face. Then I saw tears dripping into the fatty water — I think she was ashamed. That is when my eyes also teared. Feeling sorry for myself and for Mrs. Struck, I left quickly, telling her to give Gerda my regards. Dear Mrs. Struck. If a God existed, her thick tears would have saved the soul of Zehlendorf.

Of course Mrs. Lange did not take the dissolution of our household easily. Standing beside the furniture van that was to carry a good part of it with her to Thuringia, she cried that she would save all of it for Renchen, the porcelain, the silver and all the volumes of *Meyer's Conversational Encyclopedia*. She would never use the piano, the mocha cups or the large piece of amber my mother had found on the beach in Heringsdorf before I was born. I am sure Mrs. Lange meant what she said. After the war I sent her a care package and wrote her about my father's death and about what had happened to the rest of the family. I had no desire to return to my past or to anything at all that vanished with the furniture van years earlier.

My father sold his car and rented a furnished room in the neighborhood. Seeing no way out, he was dumbfounded by the situation and lived mainly on his social security pension. Uncle David, some cousins, former business friends, and a young protégé would come to visit him in his nearly empty room. Sitting on cardboard boxes packed with the collection of etchings of Prussian uniforms, my mother's music books and family photographs, my father and his visitors kept racking their brains. On one point they all agreed: things could not get any worse than they already were. Starting out with this certitude, was it not best to hold out until the madness passed? Where could they emigrate? Did someone know of a consulate ready to issue a visa to a penniless salesman and his family?

After I took Lilo's books and Goethe's complete writings and temporarily moved in with Aunt Hanna, my father decided I should leave Germany as soon as possible, even without him. He had a photographer take my picture with dramatic lighting to send to Uncle Max and Aunt Toote, so they could see how I had grown up over the last two years. In the accompanying letter, my father asked them to request me as their companion and to vouch for my upkeep. Perhaps the photograph, despite dramatic shadows, made me still appear like a little Spicker; perhaps the idea of replacing their daughter with a niece was

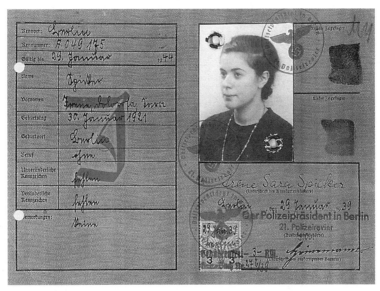

Jewish identity card with my new name, Sara, dated one day before my eighteenth birthday.

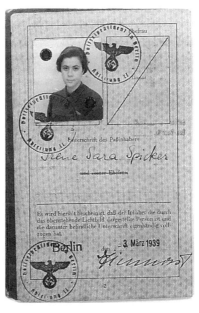

My passport issued in March 1939 (the large "J" is stamped in red).

too unbearable. In any event they declined. In these uncertain times I should remain at my father's side, they wrote back.

⌁

My sojourn with Aunt Hanna was like playing a piano composition where the left hand, unconcerned about the ever more erratically mounting melody of the right, continues clinking its old um-pa-pa. Not only had I taken refuge with Aunt Hanna, but Karl and Suse with their newborn found themselves in a similar situation. I made myself useful as a baby sitter, and at first all went well. As if it was the most normal thing in the world for Jews to go to a public indoor swimming pool, Suse took me there on Sundays as a reward for my services. She also prepared a big bowl of the most delicious mix of sour cherries and macaroons topped with whipped cream that the two of us devoured after swimming. As always, Karl was friendly and in a good mood. With his Suse and their cute little boy, undaunted by decrees, he went on joking and making music. On the Jewish New Year the trio, Karl, Suse and I, took each other's arms and keeping step, we walked together to the synagogue. "The Jews have a holiday, holiday, holiday," we improvised to a little march in turning the corner of Fasanen Street.

In the meantime Aunt Hanna stood with her wooden spoon doggedly stirring her cooking pots. Lately ironing her kitchen towels by herself, she tried to make me believe decent people could not exist without starched, white tablecloths, cutlery benches and napkin rings of freshly polished silver. Since Jews were now forbidden to keep Aryan household help, she, Frau Doctor Meyer, widow of a public health advisor, had to give notice to Agnes, her loyal maid of many years. That was the least of her worries. Her beautiful daughter Lilli had decided to marry a stocky Alsatian cousin, following him to Paris; meanwhile, her son Karl was no longer allowed to work as a lawyer. To top it all, the Nazis were threatening a forced sale of her apartment house on Passauer Street.

As if that was not enough, Aunt Luise's visits every few days were visibly upsetting her. The two would retire to a corner of the living room for hours, excitedly whispering and gesticulating. Until Suse explained the reason of the heated discussions to me, I overheard only snatches of sentences, words like "church, sect, missionaries." Uncle Richard had been in California for quite some time. Lonely Aunt Luise, who had converted to Judaism to marry him, had lately allowed Seventh Day Adventists to turn her head; they were her salvation and Jolanthe's as well, she said. Karl and Suse only shrugged over Aunt Luise's flights into mysticism. Without her husband and under the constant pressure of anti-Semitism, she had become a little crazy. The idea that her only brother's daughter should grow up among Christian missionaries was difficult for Aunt Hanna to bear.

Even though weighed down by worries and balking at the injustice of fate, the old um-pa-pa decorum had to be upheld. With a hat set straight over my bun and wearing finely crocheted white gloves, I accompanied my aunt shopping on Passauer Street. Short as she was, she held her head higher than ever.

"We are not allowed here anymore, Irene, but we can still buy at the Black and White bakery. Until a short time ago the owner was a Jew. Please, go and buy five cinnamon buns and six shoemaker's buns, while I get the cold cuts. Aunt Alice is coming for bridge with Friedchen and her mother." Back in the apartment I had to accomplish the dust ritual. Though I still believed that without my contribution to painting the sun would stop shining, I had to spend my time cleaning imaginary dust. Every second day, mounting a kind of ladder, I would remove all vases, jugs, crystal bowls and porcelain figures from the buffet and the sideboard. Setting them in rows on the dining table, I carefully cleaned each piece before putting it back into its place.

One advantage of living opposite the KaDeWe department store was that in good weather I could walk the distance to the art school. Most of those in the restoration course had now emigrated and the course had fallen apart. Mr. Hersch's studio was very quiet. After the bachelor unexpectedly got a visa, Ruth Klausner and I remained his only students. Then Ruth, too, suddenly disappeared. The colors were drying on her palette, her smock remained hanging on its hook, but there was no news of her, no sign of any kind, nothing. In the end, Mr. Hersch learned from her neighbors that on October 28th she and her family had been deported. The Nazis had shipped thousands of

Jews with Polish nationality by train to the border, chasing them from there into Poland. I never again heard from Ruth.

The quiet under the rafters of the studio was becoming eerie, only old Wolfi was softly whining in a dream. Painting a cyclamen in a flowerpot wrapped in silver foil, I could hear Mr. Hersch puttering at his gas range behind the patriarchs. He emerged to inspect my painting. Only a florid gold frame was missing, he said. A serious artist does not produce pictures, he paints. I should not even think of exhibiting before turning thirty, after having developed a style of my own. I sighed. I would be eighteen in January. Perhaps I had no personality and would never develop a style of my own.

I would certainly not find it wiping dust at Aunt Hanna's where I had to amiably serve, "Tea? Lemon? Coffee with sugar or milk?" to her bridge circle the same afternoon. Questions like, "Irene, dear, could you perhaps paint a sprig of violets on this scarf?" I would decline politely, smiling an awkward smile, though I would have loved to fling the prune pie at Friedchen's mother's head. I felt as if I really was turning into that much-sung violet in the moss, so modest, virtuous and pure. I was so well mannered that I was going to explode.

One evening while baby-sitting little Michael, I was listening to Tannhäuser on the radio. It was just the kind of opera to serve as a springboard back up onto my private Olympus. Not that I liked Wagner that much, but since everybody took him for a genius, and because Tannhäuser was said to be deep, I listened with reverence to the heroic tenor and the metallic vocal chords of his temptress. Unfortunately, Aunt Hanna returned home in the middle of the last act and switched to the news. So, without ceremony, I was chased off Venus' Mountain. I protested, whereupon I was not only chased off Venus' Mountain, but thrown out. I should find a place as soon as possible that was better suited to my spiritual aspirations, said Aunt Hanna.

I found such a place on the other side of the academy and the Tiergarten, a narrow room at Miss Lina Hopp's. A lonely, impoverished Jewish spinster from Kolberg, she needed the rent and left me in peace. But no peaceful corner existed for the likes of us. I learned this in having to register my new address at the local police station, showing my new identity papers with the "J" and the name Sara. In almost five years of official Jew bating, vitriolic speeches, posters, films, banderoles and bellowing, I personally had not yet been reviled by anti-Semites. That was taken care of on this morning. The policeman having to register me in his precinct foamed with rage.

"What? A new Jew sow when we are finally getting rid of them," he screamed, looking me over so disgustedly as if it were not a young lady with a bun, white gloves and powdered nose, but a heap of refuse in front of him. Some people looked at me angrily, others tried to ignore me, some by looking out the window. I had to wait for the policeman to finish his entry in the ledger. His double chin bulging over the collar of his uniform was rosy red with indignation, the face above a loathsome mottle of caput mortuum mixed with Venetian red. Blond bristle glistening with brilliantine stood up in Prussian stiffness on both sides of a pink parting line. I wondered to myself. Half of me was mixing colors, the other was so ashamed that I had a hard time keeping back my tears. "Today I let you Jew scum off for the last time," he flung the papers at me. "But beware if you don't move away! Once more, once more, you hear — come to this station once more and I will kick your dirty ass out of here!"

All the way back to the art school I ran so fast that I was still out of breath in the elevator. Trying to calm me, Mr. Hersch wiped my tears with his handkerchief. He took me into his arms, and suddenly we were kissing each other tenderly.

PART TWO

Brussels

JÜDISCHES UNTERNEHMEN
JOODSCHE ONDERNEMING
ENTREPRISE JUIVE

E i g h t

M R. HERSCH BECAME EUGENE. My demanding teacher changed into a gentle, understanding lover, and a day that had started on a very ugly note ended in the most beautiful evening. It was hard to believe — the mature man of my dreams was actually in love with me. That he was a little over-ripe did not matter. I would have loved nothing better than to crawl into the pocket of his smock for the duration of the Third Reich, a thousand years Hitler promised. For all I cared my teacher could go on painting instead of me — he was better anyway, and I would not have to continue searching for my own style. Having talent may be a good thing, but it leaves you with no peace. Like a slave driver it pushes you on. Woe to the artist who tries to take it easy. One look in the mirror drives the lazy genius to pick up his brushes and paint a self-portrait. Eugene often sighed that he would like to live his next life as a unionized janitor.

On a beautiful autumn day, we walked arm in arm through the rustling, dry leaves of the Tiergarten. By the Landwehr Canal, where as a child I had seen the liebe Gott, we stood waiting until a barge passed under the bridge. Torrents of water rushed and swirled out of the lock. My feet were icy, my head felt hot and strangely light, but still I was totally happy. As Eugene walked me home, we wondered why so many people were in the street reading the paper. We found out when we passed a kiosk. Huge headlines — a Jew had shot an attaché of the German Embassy in Paris. Then the news came that the attaché had died.

I was shivering less from fear than from the fever I was developing. Feeling better the next morning, I walked to the studio as usual. I stayed only long enough to listen to an announcement by a foreign radio station. In Paris a seventeen-year old Jewish refugee had committed a crazed act of desperation. His family, the same as my friend Ruth Klausner's, had been chased from Germany over the border into Poland without warning, without money, having had to leave everything behind. The teen-age son, studying in Paris, intended to take revenge on the German Ambassador there. By mistake he killed the third attaché.

For the rest of the day I lay dozing in bed at Miss Hopp's; she brought me aspirin and said that outside all was quiet. For once we seemed to be getting away with only the threats printed in the papers and flooding the airways. For the next 24 hours I felt terrible, though not even a temperature of 103°F could dampen my appetite. I gratefully accepted my landlady's offer to buy a pork chop and can of applesauce for me. When she returned, she was too upset to speak. The shop windows of the Jewish-owned pharmacy had been completely shattered — S.A. men were all over the place preventing people from entering. Many other Jewish shops had been ransacked. Everywhere she went she had to maneuver her way through broken glass.

"Wild horses cannot drag me out into the streets again. A pogrom, that's what is going on there," she said, repeating "pogrom" over and over. Miss Hopp then went into the kitchen to fry my chop.

My fever was gone on the following morning. Pogroms in the middle of the twentieth century, I thought on the way to Hardenberg Street. The word conveyed memories of the cruel stories in my Jewish history book, those pages with horrible old woodcuts of basins filled with the blood of Christian children illustrating medieval accusations of ritual murder. However, I used to turn the pages as fast as I could, as I always did with grim stories. Miss Hopp must have been exaggerating with her stories of "pogroms." Perhaps she wanted to dramatize the risk she took in shopping for me. However, I soon saw for myself the shattered shop windows and shuttered doors. In addition to the crudely brushed Stars of David, white letters dripping paint screamed "Jew!" "Germans, do not buy from Jews!"

Still, barely a trace remained of all those shattered and broken windows. People walked the streets as though nothing had happened. As usual when something of immense importance occurred, I came too late. Perhaps strangely, I felt a similar disappointment as a child when I believed that a building before me engulfed in flames turned out to be windows ablaze in the evening sun. I had yet to see a house on fire, though I once witnessed a terrible scene, a woman on fire running out from a building. An explosion had reverberated through the entire Eisvogelweg. We later learned she had been cleaning leather gloves with gasoline in her kitchen. Following the acrid scent as I was turning the corner of Fasanen Street, I saw that I had come too late. Only smoldering ruins were left of the beautiful synagogue where I had only a few weeks earlier been to Rosh Hashanah services with Karl and Suse, though that was enough to satisfy my curiosity for thrills.

In our old neighborhood, in Uncle Tom's Cabin where my father lived in a rented room, everything seemed calm. We were in urgent need of passports, he said, taking me to a photographer. Next we had to try to obtain visas. I asked, "What visas? Where will we go?"

"Anywhere." Many Jews had been arrested, he said; measures against us had been tightened and now, in a perverse irony, we would have to pay a heavy tax for the broken glass and burnt synagogues.

During this winter, I would either stand behind an easel in Eugene's studio or in front of consulate windows where the Jews of Berlin were converging, vainly trying to find a country to go to. After long weeks of queuing, we found out that the only visas still legally available were for either Shanghai or for Santo Domingo. My brother chose the latter and began his Odyssey-like travels to the Caribbean via Denmark, where Christian missionaries helped him. His non-Jewish wife with their small daughter wanted to remain behind until my brother could find a foothold. The outbreak of war separated them not only for the duration of the war — after seven years of separation, my brother asked for a divorce. The only relative I have left in Germany is his daughter.

Now, when it was too late, Uncle Max provided affidavits for Papa and me. But the American authorities informed us that the quota for German Jews was so low and our number so high that we would have to wait three or four years before we were eligible. Meanwhile, Eugene's ideas about the cosmopolitan nature of artists and its incompatibility with kibbutz life in Palestine had strongly influenced me. I had of late neglected my affiliation with the Zionist organization. Anyhow, lists for immigration to Palestine were no shorter than those for any other country. In vain we stood waiting until our legs gave out at the consulates of Central and South America with the names of exotic countries like Uruguay, Paraguay, Guatemala, San Salvador and Venezuela, far-away lands we had barely heard about in Miss Vogel's geography class. Standing in one line after another, we overheard all kinds of rumors, though they were seldom good ones. Still I learned via this grapevine that the England of my carefree, long-past summer vacation had opened its gates a crack, letting in young Jewish women who were willing to work as domestics, for example, as chambermaids or kitchen workers. However, to qualify for such a visa, you had to demonstrate experience.

I was eager to try my luck, even more so because Eugene had applied for an entry permit to Great Britain on the basis of his being a noted artist. One morning I went to a Jewish boarding house to take my chambermaid test. A severe looking lady (from all appearances she was the housekeeper) led me into a disorderly bedroom and left. Never in my life did I have to make a bed that large and that crumpled. Spending quite a while pulling and smoothing sheets and covers without much success, I turned to the washstand. Having rid the basin of soap scum, toothpaste and hair, I now puzzled over whether I should clean the floor with the same rag. There was more! If I was to pass the test I decided, I would do well to also wash the window sills and the radiators. After I had spent about two hours in the room the housekeeper came in. She assessed my progress and said goodbye. I would have to await the decision in the mail. I flunked.

Papa then received a letter from Uncle David and Aunt Johanna — with the help of a smuggler, both of them and two of their sons and daughters-in-law had fled on foot from Aachen into Belgium. At least one piece of good news had reached us on my 18th birthday. That same morning Hitler's yearly speech included the most vitriolic language ever against the Jews. For my eighteenth birthday, Eugene had made stuffed cabbage, one of my favorite dishes, which took so long to prepare that dusk was coming on as we sat by the window sipping coffee. Snowflakes were dancing in the halo of the lanterns below. On the opposite side of Hardenberg Street, the academy of my lost dreams all in white, looked more sugary than my birthday cake, and I wished the day would never end. A futile wish, of course, for even in this warm nest, we were but sitting in a trap.

While I had been laid up with the flu, many Jews during what came to be called Kristallnacht had been beaten, jeered at and some even killed. Jewish shops, whether destroyed or not, were taken over by new owners. Meanwhile, Aunt Hanna's apartment house was confiscated. How my father scratched together enough money for his portion of the one billion marks German Jews were forced to pay as restitution for their destroyed property and synagogues was a mystery to me. According to the Nazis, the Jews had provoked the German people into the "spontaneous" and justified retaliation of Kristallnacht. Before we could get exit visas stamped into our passports, we had to prove we owed no money to either the revenue service or the "winter-help" and that we had no police record. Having completed these formalities, the all-important exit visa stamp finally joined the large red "J" gracing our passports. At that point the merry-go-round came to a stop. Germany would permit us to leave, but no other country would let us enter.

The offices of the Jewish community were indescribably crowded during this January and February — they represented the last desperate hope of thousands of Berlin Jews for legal immigration. Had officials there known of ways to emigrate, they would have tried to save themselves. We were trapped. Shanghai and Santo Domingo were the only places still issuing visas, though we lacked the means to get there. That wasn't the case for illegal immigration — with a gold ring or two, we might have enough to pay a smuggler to get us to Belgium. Consequently my father and Gerda and Karl-Friedrich Schmidt decided that all of us should follow Uncle David's trail. First my Aryan brother-in-law with little Peter were to leave legally on a train; my sister and I were to follow, fleeing Germany at night with the help of a smuggler. If our escape went well, my father would follow the same way.

Papa's former driver had reached Brussels in the same manner and was to be our contact. In the middle of March, on the day the German army was marching into Czechoslovakia and all of Berlin was ablaze in swastikas, we received news a smuggler had been found for us. My brother-in-law and Peter should leave at once for Brussels by train, while the driver's sister, Gerda, another woman from Berlin and I were to stand ready at a designated hotel in Cologne. My brother-in-law agreed to pack some of my things in his luggage; having brought him some of my clothes, a few books, family photographs and my paint-box, all that was left for me to do was to say goodbye to Eugene. In the evening, for the last time, he and his old German shepherd accompanied me to the entrance of Miss Hopp's flat. A last promise, a last kiss, a last wave. With a heavy heart and my head brimming with wildly romantic thoughts, I finally entered my room. I had to hurry. Little time was left for feeling sorry for myself if I wanted to make the train that was to take my sister and me to Cologne.

Having shaken Miss Hopp's hand and put my gloves on, I suddenly missed the sapphire ring Aunt Johanna Spicker had given me for one of my birthdays. I had left it on Eugene's sink. Like someone possessed, I sprinted back to Hardenberg Street, rang the bell to the studio, found the ring in the bathroom and bolted out again, all the while aware of the ridiculousness of my sudden reappearance — what an epilogue to our long, dramatic adieus. The irony was that I could neither wear nor even take the ring with me — Jews caught on the way to the frontier with jewelry or more than three marks were sent to a concentration camp. Through the compartment window, I gave my father the ring and my golden, heart-shaped pendant with tiny photos of my parents inside. He said he would give them to Mr. König for safekeeping.

The cathedral of Cologne towered over our hotel — I had known of the cathedral in my childhood because it was the shape of my usually-empty coin bank. I could not leave my room for more than a short period, since we did not know when the smuggler would contact us. In the meantime, two Jews from Vienna joined our little group. We sat separately in small rooms pretending not to know each other, waiting for the call that did not come. Idleness and the ugliness of the hotel room was an ideal feeding ground for self-pity; to think I might never see Eugene again felt unbearable. Gerda huddled with the sister of my father's former driver; once more, perhaps out of habit, she treated me as the little Reni who had to be dragged along.

I felt lonely, abandoned by everyone. Trying to boost my morale I ate a sandwich, though it did not help — it was my first taste of margarine, which made me think of axle grease. Gerda cautioned me that from now on I had to get used to it. Through moist eyes and a grimy window, I contemplated the cathedral. Not that I was sorry to leave Germany. Why then did I have to feel sorry for myself? Because of Eugene? Because my sister preferred the company of silly Miss Frei to me? Fine, so much the better! From now on I had to get used to margarine, and I had to get used to relying on myself. I had been eighteen years old for more than a month and I was ready for adventure.

On the fifth day the call finally came. The six of us were to take the train to Aachen where we were to go to a pub; there we would meet the smuggler, described to us as a man who would have a Great Dane on a leash. We arrived at the pub and had just been served cups of coffee when indeed a man with a huge dog came in and introduced himself. Smiling, he sat down at our table; no sooner had he joined us than we heard a siren that was becoming louder and louder. The six of us were arrested — the smuggler was apparently a stool pigeon — and a "green Minna" transported us to the police lockup. (The Grüne Minna is German slang for a police van with siren.) The policemen there were surprisingly nice. We might be Jewish, but they saw we were not the criminals or customary prostitutes they were used to bringing in. They locked up Gerda, Miss Frei, the other woman from Berlin and me in a cell by ourselves. At least we were together — the two men from

Vienna were shut up separately. The farce began later that evening
when I found it impossible to sleep. A heavy woman with a reddish-
blond wig, a devout Jewess from Lodz, was shoved into our cell. At
once she poured out her troubles in Yiddish. Since we could not
understand her, she tried to ease her burden walking back and forth all
night in the small space between our bunks. Tap, tap, tap, tap, her bare
feet made a sucking noise on the linoleum floor.

"Woe is me, nebbish, bitter is my life," she bemoaned her fate —
this was the first Yiddish sentence I learned during the sleepless night.
The name of the unhappy woman happened to be Mrs. Honig
(Honey).

In the morning, one of us had to empty the latrine bucket, after
which we were locked up again so that our guards could pass us breakfast through a flap in the door. Whenever they had nothing better to
do, they would open the cell door to speak with us. One of them even
took orders to buy food for us in town. Having no idea how long our
few marks would last, we asked only for the cheapest items such as lard
and cheese. On the day Hitler marched into the Memel — a region
of Lithuania incorporated into north-east Germany in 1939 — the
patriotic cook treated the prisoners to marinated herring. Everyone fell
on this gift from heaven, except for me — I had an insurmountable
disgust for herring from my childhood experience with our grocer and
so I ate dry bread.

After a week in the police lockup, we were transferred to the
women's prison of Aachen to await our trial. I wore the chic, black
winter coat with the beaver collar that our tailor Herr Gesekus, nicknamed "Cheese kiss," had fashioned from Papa's old ulster. I also had
a modest felt hat with a round rim, then worn by "good" girls. At the
gate to the women's prison, a well-stacked Valkyrie in uniform looked
us over with contempt.

"So young and already so rotten," she spat the words in my direction, each one separately. "Get moving . . . get undressed . . . take off
everything . . . don't play shy, you slut. Here, all goes into this bag, you
won't need it anymore." Under her watchful eye, I now had to scrub
and shampoo myself with kitchen soap, then put on prison clothes that

I remember being striped blue and white. All week long the four of us had discussed what we were going to say at our interrogation and before the judge. Now we were shut up in isolation, each alone in a cell; during the daily round in the courtyard, we had to remain apart. My cell must have been occupied at one time by a seasoned criminal who had scratched an entire calendar into the otherwise bare, whitewashed walls: rows upon rows of days stretching into months and years. Each bundle of six vertical scratches crossed by a diagonal, evidently Sunday, represented one week. With hours passing into days in wearying dullness, with nothing to look at apart from those little bundles of time, I sat counting them over and over; to think how many months of loneliness and boredom were hidden in that calendar! I lost heart. And yet, there was something to be grateful for even in this place. Unlike the police lockup, I could use the bucket without spectators. My flight to Belgium was nothing like the adventure I had imagined. I have often thought since those days that death is preferable to a life in prison.

On day three of my stay I was promoted to sewing rows of buttons on cardboard; on the sixth morning I got my own clothes back. We were going to appear in court, a summary court it turned out. No prosecutor or defense council was present. A young man in a business suit, apparently the judge, posed a few questions, condemned us to two weeks in jail for "attempt at illegal border crossing," subtracted this fortnight from the time we had already spent in prison and set us free.

The background for our arrest had been a complaint, which the Belgian government had recently lodged with Berlin: the government claimed that the German border police were not making a strong effort to stem the flight of Jews across the border. We were neither the first nor the last refugees to walk directly into a police trap. In and around Aachen, Jews were being caught by the dozen. Since they rarely carried more than three marks in their pockets, it fell to Aachen's Jewish community to provide the fugitives with tickets to return to their homes. Watched by a policeman and accompanied by a functionary of the Jewish community who bought our tickets, Gerda, Miss Frei, the fourth woman in our group and I embarked on a train to Berlin. The constable waited on the platform to make sure we really left.

Although the train headed for Berlin, three of us bailed out as soon as the train reached Cologne. The other woman had had enough of this kind of travel and remained in her seat; the two Jews from Vienna were so discouraged they returned to Austria. I never learned what happened to them. While still in the police lockup with the friendly guards, Gerda and I had been allowed to write home. When we arrived in Cologne, we went to the same hotel we had stayed at before. An answer to our letter was awaiting us: an envelope with money. We settled down for a new waiting period, which turned out to be considerably shorter than the first one. Papa's former driver assured us of a more reliable smuggler — we were to avoid Aachen and meet our guide at a farmhouse on the outskirts of the city. When we arrived, our contacts took delivery of us as of any load of merchandise, whether it was cigarettes, razor blades or Jews that had to be lifted to the other side of the border. What mattered was that the transaction brought bread to the table. Their rough, professional bearing inspired trust.

The three of us sat waiting in the dark until about 4 a.m. when a delivery truck arrived. We were stowed behind a cargo of milk cans and potato bags, in addition to being hidden under layers of leeks and carrots. We were off. Unable to see anything, I had to crouch most uncomfortably, but was happy we were rolling toward the border. After a jolt that rained aromatic leeks on my hair, the driver came to rearrange our camouflage, commanding us to keep completely quiet. No coughing, no sneezing, he warned — we were approaching a checkpoint. Then there were voices, and the beam of a searchlight moved over the vegetables and milk cans. I could literally hear the pounding of my heart. We continued without incident, and after a while I concluded from the rattling that we were no longer on paved roads but on field-paths. I was right. Coming to a halt at dawn, finally able to stretch our legs, we were standing by a barn in an open field.

"No-man's land. . .terminus," yawned our driver laconically. "Now you wait here in this barn, and don't budge until my replacement comes. Good luck!" And he was gone. Hoping to get some sleep, we threw ourselves into the straw. We were well into March, the straw smelled of spring and I was dead tired. Dozing off, I abandoned myself to a dream alive with the sweet twittering of birds.

"Are you asleep, Irene? We have mice here," Gerda whispered. No birds. Instead the salami and rolls we had lived off since our departure from Cologne was making the little creatures squeak excitedly. Having to choose between sleep and salami, I, of course, opted for the food. I kept watch and since we had to wait a whole day in that barn, I heard a lot of squeaking. Only late in the afternoon, when we were almost sure we had been abandoned, someone came to tell us to stay ready during the night. Gerda's Karl-Friedrich and Miss Frei's brother would meet us in Brussels.

In fact, around midnight, a new face emerged from the dark stubble-fields, commanding us to follow him in silence and to step it up. The weather had turned to our advantage. Though it did not rain, the sky was cloudy, the moon illuminating for short stretches the meadows and fields we had to cross, the ditches we had to jump over and the fences we had to climb. Once we made it into the woods, progress became easier and faster. So much so that when our guide pointed to a large stone marker designating the point where Belgium, Holland and Germany met, it made me think of school excursions. Marching now on Belgian soil we nevertheless had to remain cautious. Since we had not yet registered with the committee for Jewish refugees in Brussels, we still ran the danger of being returned to Germany. There were some more meadows and fences; then we came to a road, which on one side was flanked by a lonely looking house.

"Heil Hitler!" a voice rang out of one of the black windows. "Heil Hitler!" responded our guide. For a second I stood transfixed to the cobblestones. Again we had been betrayed? Again we would go to prison? Giggling like a schoolgirl about the success of his joke, the smuggler explained that "Heil Hitler" was his password. He had inherited his sense of humor from his grandfather, he added proudly. Still laughing he brought us into the house, which was quite cozy. While we were warming ourselves by the stove, drinking coffee and eating Belgian bread with real Limburger cheese, an antiquated little vehicle had stopped out front. It would behave the way it looked. The motor failed every few kilometers, the battery balked and sometimes we had to push. Nevertheless, by early morning we arrived at the arranged meeting place in Brussels where my brother-in-law, little Peter and

Papa's driver were waiting for us and where, after a good breakfast, we went to register with the committee. We were in the Kingdom of Belgium, legally recognized refugees and free.

That is to say we were free, as long as we were not caught working without a permit. Flooded by immigrants, the small kingdom was suffering from unemployment. Refugees caught working illegally were jailed. Gerda went to live in her husband's furnished room and I went my own way. I could have squeezed into the narrow house Uncle David and Aunt Johanna lived in with their two sons and wives, and a woman from Breslau who had a large family. Each couple occupied one room. But ever since feeling blue in the hotel room in Cologne, I wanted to be independent.

The monthly allotment from the committee, which was sufficient enough not to die from hunger, was like being on welfare and, to me, only one step above begging. With the money I received on registering with the committee, I rented a tiny garret on Uncle David's street, gray, grimy Rue de la Chaumière. Situated behind the Gare du Nord, the quiet little street would come alive at night with a peculiar kind of traffic I had never before experienced.

The money that was left after I paid my rent was barely enough for margarine, certainly not butter. I often ate a warm meal at Aunt Johanna's, otherwise I consumed large quantities of bread with syrup and on Sundays allowed myself a cheap blood-sausage.

Brussels was a cozy old city, easy to explore on foot if one did not mind the constant rain. Public sculptures were everywhere, one for every two inhabitants! There was a surprise at almost every corner. A crusader on his steed, some king dripping with rain, a war memorial, a mother clasping a green child to her bronze bosom in the middle of a flower bed, and on the next bend in the street a sailor in black patina standing eternally against the wind. Suddenly I found myself in front of "Manneke Piss," whose small replica my father had for years kept hidden from me in the depths of his desk. He thought his souvenir from Brussels, complete with rubber syringe, was too indecent for my eyes. The narrow, twisted street paved with cobblestones where the naked little boy stood piddling through the centuries opens quite unexpectedly onto the Grand Place, an ancient stone-mason's setting for a grandiose fairy tale.

I had promised Eugene I would draw daily from nature for at least a quarter of an hour, a promise I tried to keep. Here and there I also earned a few francs with small pencil portraits. Some of the more affluent refugees would add those to letters to their families instead of photographs. Also my landlady, a Belgian widow, commissioned me to paint in oils the soulful little face of her lapdog. All this, however, did not butter parsnips and since I had resolved not to accept anymore public assistance, I had but one legal way left to make a living — the way through the kitchen door. As in England there was a shortage of maids, and so Belgium also allocated work permits for domestic help. Here I did not have to first pass a test. With the help of the committee I found a position with a young Jewish couple who had a baby. No longer having to worry about food and rent, I promised myself not to touch my salary until my father joined me, hoping I might then be able to continue my studies. On my wanderings through town, I made a wonderful discovery. Above the gate of a low, sooty building stretching over a whole block of the Rue du Midi was an inscription that caught my eye: Académie Royale des Beaux Arts. The name rang even more magnificently than the Akademie der Künste in Berlin. Still better, in this school nobody cared whether I was Jewish. White plaster casts of Michelangelo's marbles, "The Day," "The Night" and "The Captive Slave," were shimmering through the dim light of a lobby where students in lively discussion sat among the sculptures of the Medici Chapel. For a while I lingered at the door just looking. Though I had no money for tuition, things were to change.

My first day of domestic service was May 1st — I began by making my employer's family shake with laughter. I had mistaken the guttural Dutch they were speaking among themselves for Yiddish! While I was unfamiliar with Flemish, thanks to Miss Kleckel and Doctor Kadner I had no difficulty expressing myself in French, though the torrent of words bubbling up in the street and in shops was at first too rapid for my sober German ear.

The black dress with the white apron and tiny white cap suited me, though my employer's mother, a former opera singer, had overheard me singing at work and decided I should take it off. Someone humming Bach cantatas while doing dishes should not wear a maid's uniform, my patroness declared. That I had to continue eating my meals in the kitchen seemed to be a different matter.

With her imposing sounding board, her light pink powdered face and coifed hair in salmon-colored curls, the aging diva was retired from the stage. However, the newspapers furnished her with plenty of material for the melodrama of everyday life: earthquakes in South America, famine in China, leprosy in Africa, epidemics, sex and mass murders — the bare headlines alone were enough to dissolve the diva's delicately wrinkled cheeks in tears, compassion and cosmetics. Sentimentality kept neither her nor the rest of the family from exploiting me soundly.

"Mon enfant, dans la vie il faut toujours savoir sa place," she would say to me as I stood cleaning carrots. "Today you play the role of chambermaid, tomorrow it may be the baroness. What is important is to give each role all that you have . . . and you will see, everything will take care of itself." Madame Gomez was giving advice from experience, and for me her advice has withstood the test.

Whatever role I was playing, it seemed to be my fate to live in garrets. Again I was sleeping in a little mansard, this time under Madame Gomez's roof, her daughter having no room for me in her apartment. Even though her flat was small, there was plenty to do. Since flunking the exam in housecleaning, I had learned a great deal. Washed and combed, I had to show up at my employer's kitchen at 7:15 each morning to prepare Monsieur Rosiner's breakfast. Afterwards I would feed little Frédéric, change him, clean the rooms, do the wash or ironing, take Frédéric in his pram for walks, change him again and then cook and serve dinner. When the young couple went out for the evening, which they did most of the time, I would sit by the radio mending socks until Monsieur Rosiner returned around 11 p.m. to take me back to my quarters. Nevertheless, left alone for a while, I would still make time to read and produce my daily sketch after the baby fell asleep in his pram. Cooking presented no problems. Madame Rosiner's menu was restricted to six dishes: Monday, Flemish carbonade; Tuesday, steak with green salad; Wednesday, Belgian endive au gratin; Thursday, liver with carrots; Saturday, fish; Sunday, chicken. On Fridays, when I had half a day off, the Rosiners would dine at Madame Gomez's.

On those afternoons, I usually went to see Gerda or Aunt Johanna, or I went to a museum — and by "went" I mean walked. With the thought of the academy lending wings to my feet, I would walk from one end of the city to the other so as not to spend my precious francs for the tramway. To visit with Gerda was no great pleasure — she and Karl-Friedrich eked out a living altering and repairing the clothes of other immigrants. Their one room was always strewn with bits of fabric, strands of wool, irons and tape measures. In the midst of all this was little Peter crawling on the floor. Karl shortened or lengthened men's pants, Gerda knitted children's outfits. The sound of each step in the stairwell would frighten them. Were the police coming? Had a neighbor denounced them for working illegally?

In July, I accompanied my employers to La Hulpe, the countryside near Brussels where the Gomez-Rosiner clan had rented a villa. In addition to family members, friends also had been invited, which meant I had more work to do than in town. Standing for hours on end behind a washboard in the garden singing German folk songs and working in the open air did me good. I thrived. Perhaps it was my rosy cheeks that stimulated green shoots to grow in the sixty-years-old heart of Monsieur Gomez. In the morning, when the whole household was still fast asleep and I was serving him breakfast before he left for work in town, Madame Gomez's dignified husband would transform himself into a faun. The sudden metamorphosis always occurred while I was pouring coffee and stuffing his rolls with ham. Grinning from ear-to-ear like Rubens' satyrs that hung in large canvases in the Brussels museum, his dashing goatee reminiscent of a he-goat rather than of Velasquez, he would exploit my defenseless position to fondle me. I was not charmed, but apprehensive. I had to resist him and hold my tongue because I did not want to be fired.

After a week of this torment, Monsieur Gomez gave up on his own accord, deeply impressed that a female, a maid at that, had been able to resist him. Convinced that I must be as pure as the freshly fallen snow, he now proposed to help me find a husband. Several unmarried engineers belonged to his circle of friends, he said, engineers then being the most desirable catch on the Jewish marriage market. I was not looking forward to being tied down, least of all in an arranged marriage. The one man in the world I wanted was Eugene from whom I had until then only received a postcard. He was upset because I had left Berlin without paying my debt in an artist's shop that had given me credit on his recommendation. My father, whom I had asked to settle my account, had not kept his word.

All these concerns weighed heavily on me. The unpaid bill, Eugene's cold message, Monsieur Gomez's repulsive advances — to think that in a weak moment I would permit myself to marry an engineer and end up as a bored housewife seemed degrading. To make things worse, there were the tips. Every time a house guest said goodbye thrusting a few bills into my hand, I would have liked to disappear below the floorboards. Instead I said "thank you." I needed the money to bring my father out of Germany — he was still waiting in Berlin, and whether or not he paid my bill, we had to find a smuggler for him and find one fast.

Just a few days before the outbreak of the Second World War, my father arrived safely in Brussels by the same route my sister and I had taken. The German army attacked Poland and on September 1st, France and England declared war. Apart from Eugene, the only thing on my mind was the academy in the Rue du Midi. Having returned with my employers from La Hulpe to Brussels, I informed Madame Rosiner that in order to enroll in an evening course at the academy, I would have to leave my work three times a week at half past seven. To be sure she was furious, though apart from reducing my salary by fifty francs there was nothing she could do about it. Raising herself on the tips of her pumps, she was able to reach the upper side of the doorframe with her index finger. "Irene," she said bitingly, "this place is filthy!"

Nine

I REGISTERED AT THE ACADEMY as a German national, my profession a maid. While tuition for aliens was double that for Belgian citizens, I had passed the entrance exam with high marks and an exception was made for me, perhaps because I was the first domestic on the royal list of art students. One evening I entered Monsieur van Halen's fourth-year class of portraiture and life-size drawing from the nude. Unlike Germany, the students had no concept of either "Jewish refugees" or "dirty Jews." I was simply German, a "sale Boche" as Belgians used to sneer — Germany had conquered the country during the First World War. My new teacher addressed me solely in Flemish, though he spoke French as I did. He seemed unable to grasp the fact that I hardly spoke Flemish.

If I was resigned to the fact I would never really belong anywhere, by now I was toughened enough to not let such trivialities bother me. Most importantly, I had a new teacher, models and many classmates to compete with, though regretfully I could only participate in three of the five weekly classes. Madame Rosiner was reluctant to let me attend more often. Every maid's lot was to be exploited, or so I believed, and in my family those lowly creatures had not licked honey either. However, what really bothered me was something else, that for a few free hours in the evening Madame Rosiner reduced my pitiful monthly salary of three hundred francs by fifty. With my father's consent, I gave notice. How ungrateful, she said, squinting at me with the same beady eyes like her goateed father when he chased me around the kitchen table. Madame Gomez, however, was not too fond of her own daughter and gave me a twinkle of encouragement.

I would not be swayed from my intentions. At the beginning of December, I moved into still another attic room, a tiny one near my father's in the same row house of the Rue de la Chaumière where Uncle David lived.

It was the end of 1939, mid-winter of the "drôle de guerre" and the calm before the storm that followed the French and English declarations of war against Germany. France was entrenched behind the Maginot line; England believed herself safe on the other side of the Channel; Belgium and Holland lay cradled under the blanket of their neutrality. Germany was crouched, waiting for the signal to pounce on its prey. It was an eerie state of war — all seemed quiet, yet everyone was on edge. Life in that attic room with the small petrol stove discharging more reeking smoke than heat remains in memory as the winter of my cold feet. Of the half dozen or so destitute immigrant families, each dwelling in one room of the house in the Rue de la Chaumière, Papa and I, high up under the roof, were the poorest. Nevertheless we lived quite well, thanks to Aunt Johanna Spicker. She stretched the little money my father still received from the German Social Security into the hot meals she prepared each day. Before dawn, on icy winter mornings, Uncle David went to the market looking for bargains: fallen fruit, slightly rotten potatoes and soup bones, which Aunt Johanna orchestrated into a meal of broth with marrow dumplings followed by fried potatoes with jellied meat and fruit compote. Uncle David prayed three times a day and wore an old dressing gown and visor cap. Strangely perhaps, he seemed more at ease in his furnished room with its faded curtains and frayed bedside rug than in the magnificent villa in Friedenau, where as a child I had climbed on golden chairs.

Living once more in the midst of a much smaller and impoverished family, I was still with family; I now began to take courses at the academy as a regular daytime student. A Boche, one having registered as a house maid and who, believe it or not, could draw — what kind of a bizarre creature was this? The only one among my classmates who

approached me, though she was quite patronizing, was a Belgian officer's spinster daughter. Of enormous dimensions and nicknamed "The
Tank," she too was an outsider. She also had strong opinions, for example, anyone who would contrast green and red in a painting as I did
was necessarily without talent. Telling me so directly, she nevertheless
gave me a commission. She owned a portrait of her deceased grandmother, she said, which showed her without any jewelry and was
therefore not in accordance with her station. How much would I
charge to add a brooch to her dress? The "Tank" invited me to her
home and sat for me with the family heirloom pinned to her bosom.
What can I say? I needed the money so badly that I added a brooch on
the painting of another artist.

In my free time at the academy I also painted the busts of Racine
and Voltaire, staring so intently at the plaster the white seemed to turn
into all kinds of colors, pink, light green, gray, bluish and ivory. These
paintings aroused the admiration of my fellow students who now
began to ask me to go with them to a pub and discuss our work over
a glass of gueuze. We also went together to the medical school to study
the muscular system of cadavers. While one of the men fainted and
another felt nauseous, we girls sketched stoically. I only made a fool of
myself when I asked if the skinned torso of the dead was so dark
because it belonged to a black man.

With spring a nice letter arrived from Eugene who had finally made
it to England. On that morning, I studied each line word by word.
Wolfi, the old dog, had died while still in Berlin; Mrs. Lange had sent
money from Thuringia to pay my debt; Wolfgang was at school, and
Eugene himself had found a studio in a working neighborhood on the
outskirts of London.

Before getting up to eat breakfast at Aunt Johanna's and leaving for
the academy, I allowed myself to dream a little longer of Eugene and
his London studio. Sudden loud humming, dull thuds and crackling
sounds drove me out of bed, my astonished eyes following with each
thud the pink cotton wool cloudlets puffing up in the soft blue of the
skylight. It was a pretty spectacle. I did not know this beautiful spring
morning would become an important date in the history of World War

II — May 10th, 1940, the day when Hitler's armies against all pacts and promises invaded Belgium.

⟶

Since all German subjects in Belgium had become enemies, potential spies or saboteurs, my cousins Viktor and Herbert, and of course Gerda's husband, were arrested on the same day for transport to a camp. Neither their parents nor their wives would see Herbert and Viktor again. Uncle David and my father were apparently considered harmless because of their age, and now remained the only men in a house full of women and children. In the coming weeks of chaos I served as translator for all of them. Every evening the whole house would assemble in one room to hear me translate the news from the Brussels daily *Le Soir*.

Like Holland and Luxembourg, Belgium had been surprised by Germany, so France was not alone in trying to repel the sudden, massive onslaught. To judge from the Belgian newspapers those nations, together with their British ally, were resisting the aggressor heroically. Why then was one town after another falling into German hands? After only five days Holland was occupied and its queen fled to England; in France the "impregnable" Maginot line was either breached or simply bypassed. Each piece of news made it clearer that we were in danger of being trapped once more. Should we simply wait until the door snapped shut? Gerda, knowing only that her husband had been brought to some camp in France decided to flee with six-year-old Peter. I wanted to buy a bicycle to get away as well, but my father's refusal was categorical: he would not let me from his side. My sister's intention to flee under such uncertain circumstances he called pure madness, warning that bottled-up country roads were the best targets for air raids.

Instead of escaping by bicycle, I pushed a baby carriage full of bread through the streets. With bread rationing and so many to feed in our house, we needed a way, to transport loaves from the bakery to the Rue de la Chaumière — these were the only wheels we could get. Unlike

My class at the Académie Royale of Brussels. I am in the first row, third from left.

On the street in Brussels with my paintbox, c. 1941.

many Belgians who had been hoarding food since the beginning of
hostilities, people with our kind of income were dependent on rations.

The Belgian army defended itself better than the British, French
and Dutch combined and would have held out longer had King
Léopold not suddenly capitulated after two-and-a-half weeks of heavy
fighting. That surrender determined our fate.

All you heard now was, "Les Boches, les Boches!" People were leaving Brussels by train, by car, by horse-drawn cart, by bicycle and by
foot; just as my father had predicted, many of those fleeing were killed
by air raids on country roads. Helplessly in lifeless silence, Brussels
waited to be raped. Looters ran through the streets; if they did not
empty the storehouses, the German invaders would do it in two days
time. Under this rationale they broke down doors and carried away
what they could — sacks of flour, sugar, rice, sausages, and huge rounds
of cheese. An elderly man collapsed dead under the load of half a pig.
The looting was repulsive, though nothing in comparison with the
field-gray columns the next morning that called the city back to life
with thousands of stomping boots.

Nazi proclamations aimed at calming fear were soon posted at every
street corner and indeed, life seemed to return to a semblance of nor-
malcy: offices and schools reopened and buses were again running. The
shops, however, were empty. Our grocer's shelves, for example, held little more than jars of jam. Food was either rationed or hidden away
where only clients of long standing or those able to afford black-mar-
ket prices could buy anything at all. We belonged to neither category.

Those who had tried to escape the Nazis began trickling back into
the city. Emaciated, weather-beaten or wounded, they were the ones
fortune had favored over those cut down by the Stuka machine guns.
Amazingly, Gerda and Peter made it back to Brussels safely — getting
as far as the seashore near the French border, she was almost caught in
the same hellish gap that British and other remnants of the allied
armies were fleeing through in order to escape to England.

To translate for my neighbors newspapers censured by the Nazis and
edited by Belgian traitors no longer made sense. Like all of Belgium,
we now sat listening behind closed doors and windows to Radio
London, the one voice of truth that gave us some hope.

Though I had been able to escape Nazi power for only a short time and was trapped once more, I still breathed more freely than before my escape from Berlin. The fledgling artist became more independent, though the question still remained, where did I belong? Who was I? I was no longer a German, and I had lost contact with the Zionist movement. In my new Belgian surroundings there was little stigma to being Jewish. Was I nothing at all? A nobody in an attic room fancying herself a cosmopolitan?

I had lived the events of the last half-year as some kind of larva, a clumsy German caterpillar spun into threads of anonymity. With the start of the new school year at the academy, a butterfly tinged in Gallic colors broke the cocoon. When I learned to speak French fluently, to mock the enemy occupation and to read André Gide and cite Baudelaire, I was also invited to the homes of my fellow students and to participate in their excursions. I moved in a circle of bright, warm-hearted and liberal-thinking young people.

Even the Nazis understood that Belgians could not be transformed into Jew-haters overnight, so they went slowly at first with anti-Semitic measures. Most of the oppressed population often showed us their solidarity.

In summer we left the two tiny mansard rooms at Uncle David's, my father having discovered in a somewhat better neighborhood a nice room that was equipped with a stove. He slept there while I once again spent my nights in an attic room two flights up. One flight down we had the luxury of running water and a wooden toilet. Behind the wallpaper and its spring flowers we also had bedbugs — with the little rent we paid, what more could we ask for? I would live here with my father for two years, until the summer of 1942 and the onset of the great Jew hunt. Here I painted, cooked when there was food that lent itself to cooking, did our wash and received visitors. It should be understood that the army and the Gestapo were different entities and at the beginning of the Belgian occupation, army commander General von Falkenhausen seemed to have the upper hand.

Since Germany's surprise attack I had been unable to send letters to England; even so, when the Nazis began bombing London, I still took matters somewhat lightly. Why should Eugene of all people be in danger! Even as I assured myself, I wondered how good the British air defense really was? On my side of the war zone, I only had to fight bedbugs that could be expelled from our mattresses, temporarily at least, with the use of petrol (DDT was still unknown), though not from their hiding-places behind the wallpaper.

"The chin a bit higher, the left ear lower. No, you turn your head too much to the right," I directed the young man posing for me. On this afternoon of the second winter of the war, my greatest fears were neither air raids nor the notorious Brussels Gestapo. I trembled that Théophile Daumerie, a political science student, would notice the bed-bug crawling behind his head among the wallpaper flowerets. What would be more shameful in Aunt Hanna's eyes, a niece serving time in prison or living with bedbugs, I asked myself, trying at the same time to turn my model into a Greek god. Théo's appearance fit the elegance of his name, and I had asked him to pose for me only because of his classic profile. My new friends were not snobs — they even saw a kind of Bohemian charm in the shabbiness of my lodging. I did not have to ask him twice. Bedbugs, however, went too far. I was relieved when the wandering little spot disappeared through a tear in the paper and he was leaving.

The easel was a present from three academy friends, Renée, Françoise and Christiane, each of whom donated one leg. My paint-box, however, was still the one my brother-in-law had brought with his luggage from Berlin. Whenever I squeezed a tube, I thought of Eugene — "Irene Spicker, painting-pig," his son had etched into the lid to remember him by. How were he and his father really doing? During the last fortnight the London "Blitz" was massive so that even the thought of East Putnam being far from the center of London was still not very reassuring.

Rations had been tightened once more and I was often hungry and cold. In the folktale of a poor wood cutter, a good fairy grants his wish for a pot full of never-ending gruel. My miracle was a pot with pea soup. I discovered a soup that renews itself for seven days. Once a week I put dried peas in water so they would swell up overnight; I then cooked them with a carrot, a potato or whatever else was available, sometimes even meat from our small monthly ration. On cooling, the soup would thicken to such an extent I could dilute it with water day after day for a whole week. Pea soup was my specialty; my father's was rutabagas. I was sometimes invited to eat at the homes of students whose parents had secret pantries. At my friend Willie's, whose cache was powdered milk and Quaker oats, I would eat hot oatmeal. Françoise was the daughter of a physician whom a grateful patient kept supplied with eggs; she would treat me to omelets filled with jam. But the most hospitable home of all was Renée's where, to the sound of Bach's Brandenburg concertos, her sisters and other female relatives often baked English tea scones. Once her cousin Thérèse stopped short in stirring the dough to fly into my arms, crying, "It is so sad. After our death we will not see each other anymore. Jews do not go to Heaven, Irene, do you know that?" Half Chinese and a believing Catholic, Thérèse was too tactful to tell me I would go to hell. Tears were pearling over the ivory of her Mongol cheeks into the peaking egg-whites at the same time as the rueful "Agnus Dei" from the *Passion According to St. John* was sounding from the record player. Impossible to be so heartless as to answer that, believing in today rather than in tomorrow, I was more preoccupied with my empty stomach than with the next world.

On the other hand, every Thursday I looked forward all day to dinner at Miss Legrand's where I had lettuce salad and a sandwich with a hint of butter. Miss Legrand had been to school in England and exchanged lessons with me. Before dinner I taught her German — if she believed that Germany would win the war she did not tell me so; afterwards, over a cup of tea, I would get a first-class English lesson. My only paying student, a Belgian architect with a wife who often overdressed, apparently needed German to further his career and to obtain commissions from the victors. I could not abide him, but to make a living I accepted the most unusual jobs.

One of those was the restoration of an oil painting that had been damaged by bombing. Before the war it had been an old Flemish flower piece with fine detail, the owner explained, putting a square of torn canvas with jagged edges in front of me. My heart sank at the sight. However, needing work badly, I managed a confident smile and was entrusted with the artwork's miserable remains. The woman who owned it probably thought the delicacy of her laburnum, tiger lilies and larkspur were lost forever and so it might be wise not to throw away good money for a more experienced restorer. Applying the methods I had learned on Hardenberg Street, I ironed a new canvas on the back of the torn painting with the help of Venetian turpentine and wax, then filled in all the cracks with a mixture of plaster and glue and the patience of an ant. I finished with a good cleaning followed by retouching and varnishing — I could hardly believe the result. Though I went on to do other restorations, I never again experienced the degree of satisfaction I felt at resurrecting the tattered flowers.

For a time, things improved further when a middle-aged man came to me for drawing lessons, a job that included a weekly dinner of soup, entrée and dessert. It was too good to be true. All these years later, I still don't know why Monsieur Breskoff, the successful manufacturer of rubber articles and condoms, wanted to learn to draw. A Jew married to a cheerful Christian woman from the Rhineland, Monsieur Breskoff paid me well, though I would have done my best just for his wife's meals. She was a wonderful cook. Yet he never got further than working on the perspective of a bottle, matchbox and sugar bowl I arranged before him. Perhaps the couple had taken a fancy to me and the drawing lessons were only a pretext to help me? Or maybe they saw me as a girlfriend for their only son Serge. But caution, this is quicksand, Serge's beautiful face said to me. Shaded by long, silky lashes, his eyes were black pools swimming in milky blue — dangerous eyes. I imagined one could drown in them.

Still, as often as Serge and I were left alone, sometimes wandering among the beech tree woods surrounding Brussels, our friendship remained purely platonic. We intoxicated ourselves with voluptuous French poetry, mainly Verlaine and Rimbaud, and would sit together chastely side by side in his room until dusk when Charlotte, the family's household help, called us for dinner. Besides, my heart still belonged to Eugene and I was wary of a more intimate relationship, much as I suspected Serge himself was. After Monsieur Breskoff ended the drawing lessons, he and his wife continued to invite me to their home and also bought several of my paintings. When my father later developed coronary trouble, Monsieur Breskoff's nephew, a young physician, took care of him until his death. He would not take a fee from my father. I have often thought it was his uncle who paid for the treatment.

Bread was too expensive and difficult to find — so to celebrate my twentieth birthday, I bought a jar of jam on the black market. My father politely refused the jam. I ate it all myself, cleaning out the jar in one sitting until the glass shone like new. My sister surprised me with another sweet treat, an apple cake she baked in my honor. In the eyes of the Nazis, this third-rate wife of a second-rate German — a Jewess married to an Aryan — Gerda was nevertheless still a German citizen and was allowed to obtain regular work. She got a job as a saleslady in a delicatessen shop where the ingredients for my apple-cake came from. Gerda's job allowed her to round out her rations, even though the items she sold were mainly outrageously expensive fruit and bottles of questionable liquor and various ersatz goods. Her husband was liberated from the French internment camp by the German army. To be near the delicatessen shop, he, Gerda and Peter were now living in two basement rooms in the center of town. Aunt Johanna and Uncle David had been less lucky. Their sons Herbert and Viktor were still in the same camp in the south of France where my brother-in-law had been. Their wives Lina and Cilly were frantic, and Aunt Johanna, though not one to complain, was drawn, her skin like yellowed parchment. The news from her daughter Hilde in Berlin did nothing to improve the mood in the Rue de la Chaumière. Hilde had not fled to Belgium because she wanted to remain with her fiancée. They had indeed married, but now beautiful, blond Hilde, her complexion too delicate for anything but hand-hemmed muslin, was literally collecting trash — she and her husband had to work on a Berlin garbage truck. My cousin Karl the lawyer also remained in Berlin where he had a compulsory job as an electrician at Siemens. His and Aunt Hanna's trust in German law had cost them dearly. Tolerated as renters in their confiscated apartment house on Passauer Street, they, Suse and little Michael were still waiting in vain for legal emigration papers to America.

For a time, we were fortunate the Brussels Gestapo was too preoccupied with Belgian resistance to the occupation to deal with the Jews. Nevertheless, shortly after my birthday in January 1941, hundreds of Jews from Amsterdam were sent to Germany to serve as hostages. In March Bulgaria entered the war, then German tanks landed in North-Africa; in April it was Yugoslavia and Greece's turn to be attacked and to capitulate. Every evening I listened to Radio London, vainly hoping for better news. Every morning I returned to Monsieur van Halen's class at the academy to draw life-size nudes. All my renderings of men during that period turned out as muscular heroes, my females as powerful, defiant Sybils. My drawings did not reflect capitulation. It was strange to see how the same models in my work — they had seemingly escaped from the ceiling of the Sistine Chapel — compared with those of my friend Françoise whose drawings were like tortured symbols of suffering humanity. Françoise studied at a private painter's studio in the afternoons. She surprised me one day with the news that I had to accompany her there — you have been endowed with a stipend she said.

I had no idea how Françoise persuaded her teacher to accept me as a non-paying student. A wealthy physician's daughter, she had a marked sense for social justice. And so, accepting thankfully, I was delivered into the hands of Mademoiselle de Wappenaar. An aristocrat of bony elegant build and features that were a mix of noblesse and bitterness, she preferred a career of artist to wife and mother. Later, in order to provide her widowed mother with the amenities due her rank, she sacrificed her career as a painter for the position of teacher. She treated the young females entrusted to her as sternly as herself, a muse with a flaming sword pushing aspiring artists through a gate behind which there was no hope for a husband and children.

Mademoiselle Françoise, Mademoiselle Irene, and the rest of the exceedingly well brought up class did not dare contradict her, though we had not the slightest intention to consecrate ourselves to some kind of convent for female artists. After school, sitting in a café over vanilla ice cream that tasted of rutabagas, we juggled husbands, babies and canvasses, affirming our complicated future as painters and mothers. We would have it all, we would manage. Having long since come to realize that one could perfectly well live without starched tablecloths, ironed kitchen towels and waxed floor boards, I did not miss the fact I had remained "dirty vermin" to the Nazis, whether I rinsed my panties seven times or seven hundred. My eventual companion would have to wash and mend his socks himself; the cooking we could do in turn. This was how I visualized married life, worrying little about my future household. What preoccupied me was my style or, more accurately, its absence.

Mademoiselle de Wappenaar was in the habit of letting her students put their work side by side on the floor for comparison and criticism; even though my paintings would be regularly praised, I just as regularly found them to be the least interesting of the bunch. All the other girls had their own distinctive styles, I thought, all but me. What was the use of competent canvasses if they bore no individual stamp, in short, if they had no character? Could the Nazis be right in claiming we Jews were wanderers and condemned to be imitators. However sophisticated, a rootless Jew could never be a truly creative artist.

How striking my friend Christiane's still life was in comparison with mine, a few naively painted red apples in front of a blue tea kettle. Robust and Flemish, growing up in the countryside, she had never worried about style. She simply had it. And here I was, already twenty years old, producing paintings one after another with harmonious hues, a sensitive brush stroke, and without any kind of character. For years I would torment myself with the problem of soul and character and all that Nazi rubbish of blood and soil, until I finally saw the light. Unaware that you have to view your own work from a distance I had not seen the forest for the trees. Yes, even I had a style though I was as yet unaware of it.

With all the taking and giving of lessons, some small commissions, some restoration work, visits with friends, I still had free evenings. To spend that time in our one room in the company of my ever more taciturn father was depressing. Learning that I could take an evening course in clay modeling organized by the county, I naturally seized on the opportunity. Free of tuition, the course turned out to be just as morose as my evenings at home.

Tired after a day on the job, a few monosyllabic men were milling about a poorly lit room, each trying to copy the plaster of a death mask set up in the center. Copying what the others were doing, I began with the unpleasant task of making a wire contraption to cover with clay. Nothing disturbed the silence but the slapping of wet clay, until after a while a strange, hollow rattle punctuated the slapping. As it drew near, I understood that it came from our teacher. Deadly pale, his eyes devoid of expression and circled by black rings, he shuffled into the room. Before Parkinson's disease had reduced the poor man to a ruin, he had been a good sculptor, it was said. He shook and rattled so terribly that, although he gripped one hand with the other behind his back, I could not understand his instructions. To see him try to correct our work was almost unbearable; I later took up ceramics rather than continue sculpture with him.

⌒

The war news was increasingly depressing,. In February it was rumored that the situation of the Jews of Poland was worsening all the time, that all those living in Warsaw had been forced into one section of the city. Closer to us, hundreds of Jewish hostages from Amsterdam had diappeared, apparently shipped to a concentration camp in Germany. In late March bad news followed that was more concrete: Germay had invaded Africa, and shortly afterwards it was the turn of Yugoslavia and Greece. In May the B.B.C. reported that thousands of Jews had been arrested in Paris. When I finished the school year at the academy with a first prize and a diploma, Germany was once more baring its fangs. This time it would attack and swallow the Russian giant. While German panzers were racing eastward, I was running barefoot through a meadow in the foothills of the Ardennes, playing catch with Renée, Thérèse, Yvonne, Willie and Françoise. Théophile Daumerie and Jean Raemaker, a gluttonous student of philosophy, looked on.

We were spending our vacation in a stone farmhouse outside a small village surrounded by woods full of chanterelles and hazelnut bushes. To breathe the mountain air in freedom was invigorating. With no German soldiers in sight, we wandered arm-in-arm singing French folksongs. For Yvonne's best friend, Sara and her brother Simon, two fair-headed Jewish youths so innocent they did not even giggle at some of the more daring student songs we were singing, this would be their last summer.

But here, in the meantime at least, the war was far away. Jew hate had dissipated along with the morning mist. Running barefoot through the dewy grass I slipped on a heap of fresh cow manure — I stank to the high heavens while Françoise and Renée were in stitches.

That will bring you luck, Irene, luck and money!" Indeed, on my return to Brussels, I landed my best paid restoration job to date, not worried that I had to work hidden in an attic. I liked attics; nobody bothered me there. I never saw either my employer or her antique shop, only a mysterious contact who would climb the four flights puffing and panting every few days, look at my progress and bring me more merchandise.

"Here, this is an authentic Rubens, Mademoiselle Spicker, do what you can with the right eye and with the mother's hand," my contact would say, unpacking a painting with cracked color that had peeled in places. "I know you are good at doing hands — two, three fingers, for you they should be child's play." The painting was certainly damaged enough to be old, a nursing mother squeezing her breast with delicately pointed fingers — perhaps it really was a Rubens, perhaps it was a stolen one. What did I know about my contact? That he was a refugee like myself, a Viennese with sparse hair, long sideburns, eyes almost hidden by flabby bags, and that he hid his Adam's apple behind a smashing silk scarf. He was very polite. But someone who wrapped old masters in newspaper, paying me to "recreate" a Rubenesque eye and fingers could not have been the well-known Viennese art collector and restorer he claimed to be. That kind of story he could tell the lady from the antique shop. And who was I to patch up a possible

Rubens? Nevertheless I did, as carefully as I could. For the time being the scruples which my teacher from Hardenberg Street had instilled in me were holding me back from too much retouching. However, with each new painting I got to restore, the scruples that restrained me from meddling in someone else's painting grew weaker. One day near the end of this lucrative occupation, my mysterious patron climbed up to the attic carrying a pretty little genre painting. The problem was that only about half of the oil paint was still more or less intact — most of the other half was simply missing. Conjecturing that the painting had once portrayed a young woman delousing a child, I had to slip into the artist's mind and imagine what he was trying to do. With this long neglected little masterpiece, Monsieur Lindeman's source dried up. Politely taking his leave, he paid me and disappeared from the life of one who since has distrusted all antiquarians.

Driven out of my peaceful attic and having earned enough money to buy oils and canvasses, I now threw myself into painting. Mademoiselle de Wappenaar, possibly informed by Françoise about my restricted work space, had generously given me the use of her studio, which was empty during vacation time. I had only to take the key from the janitor to be able to paint all day until sundown without seeing anyone — or so I thought. As a task for the summer, Mademoiselle de Wappenaar had assigned her students to render a scene from one of Shakespeare's dramas. I had chosen the death of Ophelia. On the canvas in front of me the drowned young woman was staring at the sky, her long, red-blond hair floating among the leaves of a weeping willow. The composition worked, the lighting was dramatic — my teacher would not be disappointed. Hungry from the artistic exertion I sat down on a stool, reaching for the brown paper bag with my lunch. I had to fortify myself before going back to the wet, green color of the pond.

Satisfied I was, in turn, biting off pieces of onion and blood sausage consisting mainly of red cabbage, when the door opened and Mademoiselle de Wappenaar came in, looking from me to Ophelia and back at the purple sausage in my hand.

"This I did not expect from you, Mademoiselle Irene, that you would exploit my generosity in this fashion. Maybe it cannot be helped

— you are the same as the rest of your milieu. Given a little finger you take the whole hand. The nerve! To eat in my studio, and from a paper bag at that!"

Mademoiselle de Wappenaar was of course too refined to say the word "race." I was like the rest of my "milieu." But I understood. Only no bawling now. Forcing back the tears, I shouldered my paint box and, picking up the wet Ophelia and my lunch bag, said goodbye from the door. A "thank you" I could not bring to my lips. If I was really that tactless, then I might just as well be ungrateful. Blinded by tears after all, I stormed through the Rue de la Loi, la Chaussée de Wavre and past our ugly house, finally letting me, my painting and the rest of my things fall on a bench in front of the Gare du Luxembourg.

To be so bluntly put down as vulgar and tactless — in short, Jewish — by a teacher whom I admired hurt me more than the all the vilifications at the police station in Berlin and the poison spit out by the prison matron from Aachen. The most important thing in life was to know one's place, Madame Gomez had told me over and over. I should have heeded her advice. How could I have thought for a moment the little Spicker with a grandfather from Krojanke, who depended on good will and scholarships, belonged in Mademoiselle de Wappenaar's "milieu" like other students? Françoise, Renée and Christiane tried to smile away the insult. When I asked them to please tell me what unpardonable offense against the laws of etiquette I had committed, they only gently swayed their heads, Françoise making vague allusions to fine lines. Even though these lines were invisible one must not cross them, Renée added barely audibly. It was a problem of the geometry of good behavior that I have never been able to solve.

T e n

THOUGH WE HAD FINISHED OUR STUDIES at the academy, some of us returned to Monsieur Van Halen's class after the summer vacation. If not as good a teacher as Eugene or Mademoiselle de Wappenaar, M. Van Halen was nevertheless a good man — I am sorry to say that he was killed in the street soon afterwards by shrapnel from a bomb attack by the Allies. The third winter of the war was hardly a nurturing environment for art and young painters. Still, at the academy we at least had models, the rooms were heated, and we were in each other's company. Among the fresh faces in the class was a monk sent by his order — the study of nudes, I suppose, was to be at the base of his future church murals. I felt safer at the Rue du Midi among my classmates and plaster figures than I did at home where I would inevitably stare at the map that my father used to cover a tear in the wallpaper. In October 1941, the German divisions stood before Moscow, Kiev and Leningrad, and it looked as if the Third Reich would soon swallow up Europe in its entirety.

At this rather dismal time, Aunt Johanna died. She lay in her big double bed in the room where she cooked for us all and where we had so often gathered around her table. She died without having seen her children — her oldest son was in South America, the two others in a prison camp in the South of France, and her only daughter Hilde was still in Berlin doing forced labor on garbage disposal. Uncle David's daughters-in-law Lina and Cilly took care of him while my father visited almost daily. My little uncle turned more and more to his religion and worried over finding the money for a gravesite beside Aunt

Johanna's. He could have spared himself that worry — a year later Uncle David would go up in smoke in the Auschwitz crematorium. Nothing in the news, however, prepared us for what was already in progress in some places in the East.

Radio London reported serious German defeats for the first time in Russia and in North Africa. Meanwhile, America declared war on Japan after the surprise attack on Pearl Harbor on December 7th; a week later, Japan's ally Germany declared war against the United States. How could Hitler let the hated Roosevelt and his Jewish advisers declare war on the mighty Führer first? We breathed more easily. With an ally as powerful as the United States, things would go better, or so we thought.

New Year's 1942. While the B.B.C. was transmitting news about fleeing Germans, frostbitten limbs and frozen fuel, Renée gave a party at her home. She and her sisters fitted me with one of the evening dresses left hanging in the wardrobe from their more carefree times. It was a dreamlike creation of shimmering pink satin with lilac-colored ruffles; for the crowning glory, Thérèse curled my hair into corkscrews. That the rigged out Cinderella in the mirror seemed to have alighted from a somewhat common-looking coach did not detract from my enchantment. At last, my childhood dream of goyim naches had become reality. Needless to say I savored the evening to the last minute, to the last drop of sweet punch, to the last glimpse of the Christmas tree, candles and angel's hair. We danced to the rhythms of French music broadcast by Radio London: "Radio Paris ment [lies], Radio Paris ment, Radio Paris est allemand," kissing our partners as we passed under the mistletoe.

The next day was sobering. Our Belgian neighbor died of a heart ailment that morning. His wife was in tears and begged me to let her husband be laid out in my attic room bed until his burial the next day. She had no one left in this world, she cried, and in her one-room flat did not feel up to spending the night alone with her poor, dead husband. Having no choice, I at least wanted to use the opportunity to make a drawing of my deceased neighbor. Except for the skinless corpse at the Faculty of Medicine and plaster casts of famous people, I never before had a dead body for a model. Still imbued with my romantic notion that artistic maturity could only be achieved through suffering, I took up paper and pencil and forced myself to sit beside the dead man in my tiny room, alone with him for a whole afternoon. Afterwards, I was unable to sleep in my bed anymore and had to use a sofa in my father's room.

Although direct contact with the United States had become impossible after Hitler's declaration of war, we nevertheless received a letter from Aunt Hanna in California, which her niece Friedchen in Berlin had forwarded. It arrived via Switzerland. Aunt Hanna described in detail the exodus of the Meyer family. A miracle had happened, she wrote. Five minutes before closing time she, my cousin Karl, his wife Suse and little Michael were able to leave Germany for the United States — and all that legally, Aunt Hanna added proudly.

After years of waiting, the numbers on their affidavits had come up. Nevertheless, whenever they tried to get an American visa stamped into their passports, the cat had bitten its tail. The American consulate would not issue them visas without first seeing their tickets, while the travel agency would not sell them tickets without first seeing their visas. Since Karl was doing forced labor with Siemens from morning until night, it was Suse who had been running between offices and travel agents. Their bank accounts frozen, they had remained as renters in Aunt Hanna's confiscated house on Passauer Street, living off Karl's miserable salary. Although money was becoming tighter and tighter, Suse decided to try her luck with a bribe. Between the pages of one of the passports she handed to the employee of a travel agency, she had dared to slide a hundred-mark note. At first, the man who was surely accustomed to gratuities ending in more zeroes laughed. But looking at the pretty young woman with her bright three-year-old, his initial sneer softened into a smile.

"What do they call you, little boy? Michael Israel Meyer? My, my, what great names." He also had a little boy, the man told them, giving Michael a piece of candy. "What are we then going to do with you?" He wagged his head, addressing Suse, "Perhaps you have something at home I would be more interested in?" He returned the hundred-mark note. Indeed, during his noon break he came to have a look at Aunt Hanna's apartment. He seemed disappointed with the heavy, old furniture, worn-out carpets, the old-fashioned crystal and art deco vases, those vases I had dusted every second day. Not even the piano was to his liking. His eyes only lit up when he discovered Michael's rocking horse.

"That is more like it. Could you bring this to my place tonight?" he said to Suse. In his apartment, her feet had sunk into Persian rugs two or three layers deep, Suse later told Karl and Aunt Hanna, and she thought she had come to a museum. Still, no silver Sabbath candleholders or Venetian mirrors gleaned from other Jewish clients in peril could compare to Michael's rocking horse. In a category of its own, it had been sacrificed to obtain visas, flight tickets to Barcelona and ship passages from there to America. In order to avoid the lengthy train voyage to Barcelona, the agent had counseled them to go by plane. This way it would be easier to get the family with their J-marked passports through the frontier. Following this advice, they had another miraculous escape, Aunt Hanna wrote. The train they had originally wanted to take to Barcelona, which was full of Jewish emigrants, headed towards the east and Poland instead of towards the west and then Spain.

But they made it. Arriving in Barcelona, they celebrated by spending their German allowance of about six dollars on strawberries and cream, and then contacted the offices of the Jewish Community! Suse was able to get a job, which kept them afloat until they were able to leave for America.

At least some of our relatives had put distance enough between themselves and the still-expanding frontiers of the Third Reich to be out of danger. Two years earlier we had shouted joyously on reaching Brussels, confident we had shaken off our pursuers — we were now sewing yellow stars imprinted with "Jew" on all our clothes.

The Russian winter offensive was stagnating. Once more the German troops were progressing on all fronts, including North Africa as well. Not even the entry of America into the war seemed to help. At the very moment I was looking at the map on our wall, German

U-boats and planes were sinking allied ships in the Atlantic Ocean and the Mediterranean Sea. Even had I gone to Palestine like so many of my comrades, there was no guarantee of safety — nothing but a yellow stripe, Egypt, separated Rommel from the entire Middle-East.

On January 30th, 1942, my twenty-first birthday, I received an army bread from a German soldier. Stopping me in the street, he asked for directions. On such occasions I would have answered in the haughtiest French I could muster; however, this man's timid awkwardness moved me to reply in German. This occurred before the ordinance forcing us to wear the star. He wondered, naturally, why I was in Belgium. After I told him that I was a Jewish refugee, he began to speak, then said nothing, and continued on his way. Suddenly turning around, he ran back to press the bread upon me — even though this symbol of Prussian militarism should rather have stuck in my throat, the bread tasted better than birthday cake.

Rendered sentimental by his deteriorating health and moved by nostalgic memories, Papa would forget at times that Nazism and the Prussian army had become one and the same. Respectfully chewing, he recalled prouder times, though he was not allowed to forget for long who and where he now was. All German Jews residing outside of Germany proper were considered expatriates, meaning that monthly checks from social security were stopped. We now had to rely on my irregular small earnings.

Those earnings I put together in various ways. The Breskoffs commissioned a still life, the landlord asked me to paint a portrait of his young son and from time to time I had a painting to restore. Because I would also ask my friends, and friends of my friends, to pose for me, the portrait of a girl with dreamy gray eyes has remained in my possession. The young woman in the painting is Sara Yampolsky looking pensive and sad as though she knew the fate that awaited her and her brother Simon. She was wearing the yellow star, but it does not show in the portrait. Trying to make us laugh, our friends would joke about the star, while some strangers would make an effort to ignore it. Still, we felt branded. With Jews not allowed in the streets after eight o'clock, I circumvented the prohibition by ripping the star from my clothes at night on returning from the Breskoffs or Renée's house. Next morning I sewed it back on loosely.

"Before every fellow citizen with the Star of David I encounter in the street, I draw my hat," my friend Willie's father informed me solemnly. He was a Dutch Protestant in whose deep respect for the teachings of the Old Testament the people of the Bible were included.

For the first time in my life I was glad not to have the nose from the Zoegall's branch of the family; my short nose from the Spicker side was less conspicuous. Why would I of all people attract the attention of the Gestapo, I asked myself in my usual carelessness; and indeed I was never bothered in the street, with or without my yellow star. But on the day I was wearing the star and encountered a man with a bandaged nose, it became clear to me how degrading our situation really had become. In the Rue Neuve, one of Brussels' liveliest streets, he was walking casually in plain daylight without a star, but wearing his nose instead. Did he imagine that gauze patched criss-cross fashion over a big, unmistakably Jewish nose was camouflage? I am not even sure he was a Jew, but it was this grotesque image that etched itself into my memory as a symbol of Nazi derision.

The third year at the academy came to an end. With little food and less money, I was glad once more to be with my old group of friends who invited me to come with them into the countryside. We went to a farm not far from Brussels, located in the same broad, flat fields of Waterloo, which had seen the defeat of Napoleon in 1812. Taking up quarters in a barn, we made ourselves useful in the fields and were rewarded with fresh-baked bread, bacon and eggs.

The carefree atmosphere we had enjoyed on our vacation in the Ardennes mountains a year earlier was gone, yet without newspapers or Radio London we were able to keep the war at some distance. Since I did not want to think of what lay ahead once vacation was over, I ignored the fact that the Gestapo had ordered many Jews in Brussels and Antwerp to report to work camps. I did not know Uncle David was already on his way to Poland. Nor did I have any idea that Sara and Simon, in obeying German orders, were in a collection camp in Mechelen waiting to be shipped off somewhere else. Without mentioning they had gotten wind of this news, my friends decided to help me. I must not go back to Brussels, they said, but hide out in Waterloo. Monsieur Dessy, the owner of the farm, had agreed to keep me on the premises.

~~~

Though I had gone on vacation without my yellow star, Monsieur Dessy and his wife learned that they were sheltering a Jew and still were ready to accept the consequences — for him, it could mean the concentration camp if I was found out. Unbeknownst to me, he belonged to the Resistance, the secret Belgian opposition to the German invaders. Out of patriotism and his hatred for the occupiers, this father of three young children was already involved in illegal activities — I now became an additional peril. I was to play the part of a young artist earning my keep by helping in the house and kitchen.

My no less peculiar counterpart on the farm was Fernande, a girl my age. Each day I had to peel a bucketful of potatoes in her company. I should beware of her, my host warned me; she had been planted in our midst as a food spy, so to speak. Fernande was the daughter of a Belgian collaborator, a controller whose job was to make sure the farm produce was delivered in its entirety to the authorities, meaning that most of it went to the Germans. Had she not looked so pinched, she would have been pretty — sent to the farm on the pretext that she was anemic, Fernande needed country air and nourishing food. Everybody avoided her. I too should limit my chats with the poor girl, Monsieur Dessy warned me. On no account must she nose out the potatoes and sides of pork hidden below my quarters.

My quarters were behind the cowshed, far away from the others, in an uninhabited old house with a cellar that served the farmer as an illegal pantry. My job was to guard the forbidden provisions overnight. Thieves had lately raided similar hiding places in the region. In the event of suspicious noise, I was to alert Monsieur Dessy by an electric device that sent a signal from my house to his. During the five months I spent at Waterloo, the piping and squeaking of rats scurrying over the beams above me made such a racket that I would not even have heard potential thieves.

While I wanted to make myself useful, in the cowshed I really was only good at painting portraits of the animals. I tried to learn milking, which for the maid seemed child's play, but could only squeeze drops out of the udder. Under my groping fingers, the cow refused to spurt sonorously and rhythmically into the bucket. Once she kicked me in the shinbone and sent me flying into the dirty straw. After this experience, I gave up milking and decided instead to surprise Monsieur Dessy with a portrait of his prize-winning steer.

Having finished my potato peeling and helping Madame Dessy knead the weekly bread dough in a large wooden trough, I was free to work in the cow shed. The steer posed well. If he sometimes tired, trying to lie down in the straw, it was enough to buck him up with a little nudge of the pitchfork. Chained to the wall with a ring in his nose and giving me his profile, one blood-shot little eye would then stare at me so vengefully that after each session my painting developed more character. Still, he was in no position to retaliate, or so I thought, until one evening when I was walking to my quarters and passed through the cow shed warm with sleeping animals. This night I was greeted by snorting and stamping. Why are the animals so excited? Only when two malicious eyes blazed up in the dark did I understand who was coming after me. The steer had torn loose. I had never crossed the yard so fast! Monsieur Dessy arrived with the two farmhands, Vaclav and Pierre, bringing the situation under control. From that night on I respectfully kept my distance from the steer.

When winter arrived and I was no longer able to paint in the drafty stables, I was glad to help in the kitchen. Evenings before retiring, I would heat a brick on the stove, then wrap it in newspaper and take it back to my bed. But the hot brick could not resist the cold penetrating the straw mattress. Despite several blankets and woolen socks, I would become so chilled that I frequently had to run to the toilet. The more often this happened the colder my feet got and the more I had to run. The rats seemed to thrive in the cold, piping and chasing each other all night. They seemed to be living it up, though as soon as dawn broke they disappeared. Awaking at daybreak, once I had broken through the ice in my wash basin and brushed my teeth, things looked rosy for me as well.

The good white bread I had helped knead was served for breakfast. For lunch we ate fried potatoes with a thick slice of lard and more bread, better food than I had had in Brussels for quite some time. I sat at the table between the maid, who probably imagined Jews to be horned monsters (and so would never have suspected me), and the anemic, pinched Fernande, luckily too snooty to show interest in my origins. Then there was Vaclav, the Polish farmhand, knowing little French and too decent to betray me even if I looked suspicious in his eyes. Pierre, a Walloon, was another matter; almost too friendly, I sensed that I had better beware of him.

In Brussels where I ventured from time to time to bring my father food, Jews no longer had rationing cards. Nor did I see anymore yellow stars in the street — all Jews had gone into hiding. We had no sign of life from Uncle David or from his daughter-in-law Cilly, who the Gestapo had taken away; nor had anyone heard from Sara and Simon. The convocations by the Gestapo were not obeyed anymore, so Jews were now arrested wherever they could be found. All means of transportation as well as the streets now were subjected to Gestapo raids. Jews who dared to leave their hiding places did so at their own risk. Any Jews who remained in their apartment trembled in fear of their neighbors. One anti-Semite in a whole block was enough to uncover Jews in hiding and to betray them to the Gestapo.

At last, with the great turning point of fall and winter 1942, a slim hope appeared on the miserable horizon. Radio London announced immense German losses at Stalingrad and in North Africa — the Thousand Year Reich was seriously hemorrhaging everywhere and the liberation of the occupied territories seemed a mere question of time. But how much time, when with ever increasing speed we were being carried away toward some great rapids? I had been jumping from stone to stone without slipping — now I had to let myself drift along, carefully clasp at a branch here and there, and try to remain happy when over the torrential waters I might glimpse a dragonfly's wing flashing in the sun.

Shimmering in my imagination at that time was a Christmas crèche. On Sundays I accompanied the Dessy family and their hired hands to church, crossing myself and paying close attention to stand up, kneel and move my lips as if I were praying and singing with the others. I thought to make something nice for the children and let them have some fun at the same time by helping to shape clay figures and animals for the crèche. If I had to pass for a Catholic, why not also get some pleasure out of it?

In the early part of December, having spent half a day in Brussels, I made my way back to Waterloo with ten pounds of pottery clay. All went well. The day had been relatively calm with few raids by the Nazis and fewer attacks by the Resistance and arrests of Belgian hostages. It was late when I arrived at the Braine-L'Alleud station. Starting out on the five kilometer walk to Waterloo, I found myself in a thick fog, unable to see anything at all and with no one to give me directions. The string from the ten-pound package of clay was cutting into my hands; as I advanced blindly and seemingly at random through gray shrouds of mist, I felt cursed in having to wander like this all night. After a few hours, however, a compass in my head inexplicably brought me to the gate of Monsieur Dessy's farm.

As if there could be no Christmas without my crèche and as if my right to exist depended on finishing it in time, I now gave every free moment to working on the figures. I had plenty of models for the sheep and the ox, though they of course gave me the most trouble. The stable with the holy family and the three magi inside was the size of a big shoebox, watched over by two angel candleholders. Perhaps more piety was needed, for in the end the whole thing looked neither very Catholic nor even traditional. In any event, the children as well as the adults seemed to be more interested in watching a pig being slaughtered for the holiday. A little skeptically I scratched into the clay as a finishing touch, "Glory to God in the Highest, and Peace to His People on Earth," before going to help fill sausages. This in turn was an opportunity for Monsieur Dessy's nephews to heighten the general merriment by smearing my face with a handful of curdled pig's blood mixed with chunks of lard. I took this darker side of Christmas jollity in stride as simple goyim naches, though my next lesson on the subject of agriculture was considerably more unpleasant.

Monsieur Dessy loved pigeons. He talked to them, let them peck grain out of his hand and caressed their slick feathers — he also loved to eat them for his Sunday dinner. One day, pretending that he wanted to show me how beautiful and tame they were, he took me with him to the pigeon loft where a dozen cooing birds immediately descended on his arms and shoulders. Pointing out the delicate design on one pigeon's wings, he lovingly stroked its head; then, gently clasping the beauty in his hands, he suddenly wrung its neck with one quick gesture. The little head hung lifeless, blood seeping through the feathers he had caressed only a few seconds earlier. Monsieur Dessy gave me a strange look. What did he want to convey with this cruel scene? That townspeople are weaklings, easily forgetting how close life and death are to each other? That our necks too could be wrung at any moment? I was aware of that. Still I had felt the same cold pang long before in Uncle Tom's Cabin when the words, "Germany awake, Judah perish!" had stared back at me from the wall of the trash shed.

Silently going to peel potatoes, I wished Monsieur Dessy had not brought me to see the pigeons. Never again would I eat one. Roasted chicken, on the other hand, the taste of which I had almost forgotten, I would not refuse. And I did not mind filching those stupid bird's eggs out of their niches in the stables. Since I brought eggs that were still warm from the hen to the kitchen every morning, Madame Dessy became accustomed to passing an empty basket over my arm at bedtime. My ambition was aroused. Trying to find more of their hiding places, I sometimes would wait patiently until one of them, still proudly cackling for a while, finally got up from her egg. It was a game, like the Easter egg hunts of my childhood. The hens' sudden increase in egg production had not escaped Madame Dessy's notice, though I did not understand the underlying cause. Pierre, whose groveling friendliness I always had distrusted, was lately eyeing me sideways with the same kind of glance as the steer after I had nudged him with the pitchfork. I had committed an error, which would soon cost me dearly.

Monsieur Dessy and his wife spoke Walloon with each other, often looking at me while doing so. It was not a language I understand. "I am sorry, Mademoiselle Irene," Monsieur Dessy said, visibly embarrassed and scratching his head after one of these conversations, "but to keep you with us is becoming too dangerous for everyone. You have crossed Pierre's egg trade on the black market — that fellow is slick and tricky. It's possible that he has guessed for quite some time why you are here. He knows too much in general," the farmer went on in a low and angry voice. "I do not dare give a dressing down to my own farmhand, least of all for a few dozen eggs." Then he and his wife disclosed another reason why they had to let me go. The Resistance sought to hide a wanted terrorist with them and my presence attracted attention to the farm that it would not otherwise receive. I would not be sent away empty-handed, they said, as they tried to sweeten the bitter pill. Apart from being provided with an authentic Belgian identity card, I should make the trip to the farm once a week to receive some provisions.

One of the group of young people whom I had come to the farm with in the summer was a Jewish student from Antwerp — he had an older brother who had converted to Catholicism and was now a Franciscan monk. Through him, then Brother and later Father Stehman, I was now fitted out with a new identity as a Belgian baroness. (The real baroness, whom I of course did not know, was in a Swiss sanitarium with tuberculosis.)

The new role I was to play meant that in returning to my father's risky abode, I had to immediately take on the identity of the baroness, reverting from Irene Paula Dolorosa Sara Spicker to Marie-Antoinette Marguerite Ghislaine van Crombrugghe de Loringhe, née Verhaegen. I needed to leave my father's immediately since staying overnight in my old refuge with the flowered wallpaper had become too dangerous.

Although the baroness's card was authentic, the photograph was that of a married woman ten years older than I with two children and hair parted in the middle. Though there was no immediate resemblance, she did have dark hair and dark eyes like me, while the shape of her face, her mouth and nose were also like mine. To begin with, I studied my new name, and then parted my hair in the middle, pulling it back as severely as possible. I put on my coat with the stand-up collar that was ringed by ridiculous looking tails of unidentifiable animals — a whole fur collar had been too expensive. I now went to look for a cheap rental, another attic room, of course. In Brussels, attic rooms were never hard to find, though with my new identity I had a different problem: why would a baroness with four first and three last names and two children want to live all by herself in an attic room? Furthermore, how could I avoid the legally required registration at the police station? There they would compare me to the photograph on my card and begin to wonder.

In the hope my landlady might indeed be gullible, I had to show her my papers. (You can do the strangest and gamiest things when you have to.) Groping to bring to the surface the acting talent buried since my childhood, I took a deep breath, promising myself not to blush. Almost in tears, I begged the woman to make an exception, to accept me as a renter without registration. I was terribly afraid of my husband, a sadist who had beaten me and from whom I had run away; I appealed to her feminine solidarity. He was hunting for me, sure to find me at once if I went to the police. Their fate surpassing the limits of my fantasy, I left my children out of the story. Not yet twenty-two, I did not give the impression of a thirty-two year old mother of two even with my hair parted and pulled back into a severe bun. Whether the house owner believed my story or whether the rent money meant more to her than the law, she let me move into the attic.

"Today you are playing the part of the chambermaid, tomorrow you will be given that of the baroness," Madame Gomez had quite accurately predicted, surely not meaning her words quite that literally. The important thing was to know my place, she had always added. That place was once more a dusty little room under the rafters, where I could do little apart from reading, sleeping and dreaming. Since Uncle David's deportation, my father had been even more downcast. He had lost much weight and was in constant danger of being arrested.

"Can you tell me why a 72-year old man like my brother is sent to a work camp in Poland?" he would ask me. "That they took Cilly, I can still somehow understand — not yet forty and healthy — but they came for Madame Jonas too, 82 with a bad case of diabetes, and after her they took the Lichtmanns with their baby." Of all my relatives of the Rue de la Chaumière only Lina remained. She had not heard from her husband, my cousin Victor, since the German army entered southern France. My sister and her Karl-Friedrich, who in the meantime had learned enough French to work as a barman, were still living in the same cellar flat. Married to a Jewess, and therefore not a German of full value, he had escaped being sent to one of the fronts.

When my attic became too cold, I would visit those museums that were still heated or I would visit friends. Once a week I made the trip to Waterloo; Madame Dessy never let me leave empty-handed. By painting sprigs of flowers on silk scarves, I made enough money to pay the rent; my landlady, without asking questions, counted the Belgian Francs twice. The war went on and on.

January 30th, 1943, the tenth birthday of the Thousand Year Reich and my own 22nd birthday was not a day of celebration. My birthday present this year was a paroxysm of fury by the Führer, hoarse from shouting that the Jews were the culprits of everything. We had to be exterminated and destroyed ("ver-r-nichtet.")

They'll have to catch me first, I thought, closing the door to my room to walk down the creaking stairs, slowly as befitted the maltreated spouse of a baron. Wrinkling my forehead to appear older, I nodded in the direction of the landlady and left the house to go visit the Breskoffs. All day, from the moment I got out of bed, I worked as one possessed on a small self-portrait. Fascinated by my image in the mirror, the long, open hair falling over my face, the wine-red robe with a light blue nightgown, I started squeezing colors on my palette — as I was, unwashed, uncombed, the way I had crawled out of bed.

Whenever I was doing something worth the canvas and the paint, I sensed it, feeling at the end of my work tired and elated at the same time, almost cocky. Nothing could go wrong on such a day. Alone in the elevator up to the Breskoff's fifth floor apartment I did a few dance steps, playing with the idea of going back down and running home to take a second look at my painting. Instead I rang the bell. Charlotte opened the door with a smile, her gold tooth blinking.

"Come in, Mademoiselle Irene, the family is waiting for you. I have my evening off and am leaving soon, but you will still get a cup of tea." I did not intend to stay for dinner anyhow. Under cover of darkness I wanted to visit my father, to make an omelet and pancakes with the five eggs and the flour from Waterloo I was carrying in my bag.

Once more the Breskoffs had found a job for me, restoring their antique trunk. I was to exterminate the woodworms they suspected were boring away through the oak, nothing but tiny holes giving away their presence. Taking off my shoes, making myself comfortable on the carpet, I wished I could be as invisible anytime I wanted to. That is, I wished it up to the moment I prepared to attack the worms and their abode with the help of a medical syringe. Completely absorbed in this task, I did not notice the three men who had entered the hall without either ringing the bell or knocking. As if they grew out of the ground, they were suddenly standing over me. With the syringe in my raised hand and completely bewildered, I was unable to move. I remained seated on the carpet.

"Secret State Police! What are you doing here, what is your name?" I did not even attempt to play the card of the baroness. A Belgian aristocrat sitting in her stocking feet on the floor of a German Jew's apartment — it was hopeless. I would only get smacked in the face.

Monsieur Breskoff, not in immediate danger of deportation because of his mixed marriage, had been unjustly informed against, and the irony was I had been found instead, an unexpected catch. Only one of the men — he wore a raincoat and hat — looked the way I had visualized the Gestapo. His companion wore the uniform of the Wehrmacht. The third, in civilian clothes was a Jew, the notorious "Jacques" I later understood from the descriptions of his victims. With his natural instinct for spotting Jews and anything Jewish, he served the Gestapo of Brussels as their bloodhound.

He was the one who hit me in the face when I was asked about my family. My brother is in Santo Domingo, my sister is married to an Aryan, my mother died long ago in Berlin, I said truthfully and without endangering anyone. In my deeply rooted belief that the German police and Gestapo were omniscient, I was sure that each of my answers would be investigated. I was indeed questioned about my mother's date of death and place of burial. I was intimidated and did something unpardonably stupid.

"And where is your father?"

"I won't say." Smack, I was slapped in the face.

"Put on your shoes, you are coming with us. You'll tell us all right, you can be sure."

There in the same elevator, which half an hour earlier I rode up in such high spirits, I was now going down with a burning face. "You will tell us all right. You'll tell us," echoed my aching ear. With these miserable men I should have felt scruples if I declared my father dead? Had I lost my senses? Whatever mess I got myself into, I had it coming. Who knows where they were taking me? Perhaps to a torture chamber? And with all that, I was still thinking of my silly painting. Was I ever to see it again? A thousand thoughts were tumbling helter-skelter through my mind.

After a short drive the Volkswagen stopped at the gate to the elegant building on the Avenue Louise, which the Gestapo used as their headquarters — a place the population of Brussels would go a long way round to avoid. The outside of the building gave no hint of the spaciousness of the cellars beneath.

"Into solitary until she says where her father is," the Gestapo commanded an S.S. underling, shoving me through a door and turning the key. There were brown stains on the white walls, evidently blood smears, though for a torture chamber the room was too bare.

"Here," a uniformed man said, handing me a warm, brown drink and a piece of bread. "Come to the toilet now. Later you can catch some sleep — nobody will take you up for questioning before tomorrow morning." Sleep? Easy to say. How could I sleep with so much confusion racing through my mind? And where can I lie down? On a narrow wooden bench standing against one wall or on the concrete floor? In the course of the night I tried both, in turn, spreading my coat under me for softness or as a cover for warmth; but even on a bed less hard I could not have slept because of the cold. Next morning, something to eat and drink; the same at noon. No interrogation. No one came to see me apart from the warden and someone in uniform who held a whip and stood at the door looking me over:

"What a pity," he pointed with his whip first at me, then at the brown smears on the wall. "Better say from the start where your father is — we'll get it out of you anyhow," he shut the door again. Like a carousel gone haywire, my thoughts went round and round in circles. What to do to withstand the interrogation? I had to do something to stop the mad rush of fear, take myself in hand, and concentrate. A drawing. Yes. But what could I draw? At this instant anything from my imagination would come out a frightful mess. From my purse I pulled the sketchbook and pencil that were always with me and decided to draw my left hand — the only thing visible apart from the wooden bench, the walls and part of my feet. Not leaving out the smallest detail, I became so absorbed, so concentrated on my drawing I almost forgot where I was. Afterwards the hours passed faster, and I became so tired I dozed off sitting. The second night was better than the first.

Next morning, again no interrogation. Instead, I received company, a young man, disheveled, a greenish-white face, contusions and terribly red eyes, stumbled into my cell. His first words were to ask for something, anything, to eat. Here I was able to help, still carrying in my handbag Madame Dessy's flour and eggs that were meant to make pancakes for my father and me. The flour was useless to him, but he avidly drank the content of one egg after another, telling me he was being interrogated as a communist, the most wretched of situations in which any prisoner at Avenue Louise could find himself. Whether a terrorist or not, the Gestapo with or without success would use any means to get the names of his collaborators out of him. There was not much hope left for him. With the absent-minded, searching look of a man believing his days to be numbered, he spoke little during the short time he remained in my cell. The least punishment awaiting him was the notorious concentration camp of Breendonck. I don't know if he survived.

The presence of this unfortunate young man deflected me for a while from my own preoccupation. Soon after I was left alone again, a new visitor entered. A clean-shaven man with sallow skin stood in the door — from under the rim of his slouch hat, icily cold eyes glanced at me.

"You are Irene Spicker and will not say where your father is?" he closed his dossier with a clap. "And what have you got in there?" he came nearer, opening my handbag. Luckily the purse with the identity card of the baroness inside attracted his attention less than the brown paper bag with Madame Dessy's flour.

"Bakersman, bakersman, bake me a cake," he said bitingly, opening a meticulously folded handkerchief to wipe flour from his fingers. Getting next to my sketchbook, he glanced at my drawing and back to me. "Did you do that? Where did you study? With whom?" he sounded me out then, led me out of the cell and handed me over to a warden. "Shut her up here," he ordered, stopping in front of a door, "and nothing more to eat or to drink until she says where her father is. Understood?"

My new cell might have been a broom closet, perhaps even a toilet, during the more seigniorial times of the original landlords. By the dim light passing through a small glass pane in the door, I could see that from now on I would have to either remain standing or sit on the floor, as there was not enough room to lie down. Relieved that the man with the slouch hat had not taken me for interrogation as I had feared, I felt almost grateful for these few cubic feet of space. This hole, hunger, thirst, cold — all were better than an interrogation. Knees raised, I sat down on the floor, propped my head against the wall and tried to bring the events of the last few days into perspective. For sure Monsieur Breskoff had informed my father about my arrest, but what could Papa do except worry? Would I be strong enough to resist a series of steadily worsening interrogations, or would I eventually betray my own

The identity card of the Baroness van Crombrugghe de Loringhe (née Verhaegen) whom I tried to impersonate in Brussels.

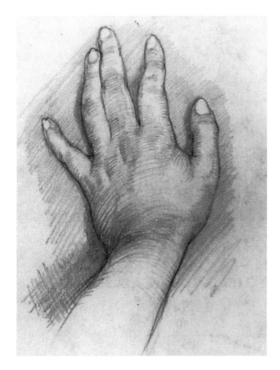

Drawing of my left hand that I did in the Gestapo prison cell in the building on Avenue Louise. (Ghetto Fighters' House Museum, Israel)

father? And where would they take me? To a concentration camp? Thousands of Jews that the Gestapo in Brussels and Antwerp arrested during the last seven months were transported in cattle trains to Poland. Behind them a heavy curtain had come down. Their voices had been smothered by the snows of Poland's gloomy forests, and no one had since heard from them. Soon I would see for myself what lay behind the mystery, I thought, letting my head sink forward. Maybe I could nap in this position? Judging by my stomach, it had to be afternoon by now. I had just dozed off when a key turning in the lock awakened me.

"Take your bag and come with me," the warden commanded. With eyes swollen from lack of sleep, I peered into a gray February rain. I was not the only one. Several dozen shivering men, women and children emerged from the depths of the cellars and were assembled in the yard around me.

"March, march, Jews, up with you — I do not have all day!" We were pushed and driven onto a truck.

No words can express the relief I felt. Nothing more about my father, no interrogation, no isolation cell — I would not have to prove to myself that I could withstand torture. I was simply brought to a camp like all the others, and if not for the sighing and moaning all around me I could have shouted for joy. Yet my sudden release was a riddle. To be let out of this den of sadists without a scratch after the stupidity I had committed, how was that possible?

The truck was rolling along the Avenue Louise, the open tarpaulin at its end dripping with rain. Naked trees racing by were uniting on the horizon, exactly in the middle between the mounted guns of the two S.S. (Schutzstaffel)* accompanying us. A perfect example of per-

---

*Hitler formed the Schutzstaffel in 1925 as his personal bodyguard, soon appointing Heinrich Himmler as its head. Himmler separated the S.S. from the Sturmabteilung (S.A.) and was among those responsible for the purge of its officers. During the war, the S.S. Death's Head Units were in charge of Germany's concentration camps. At the Nuremberg War Crimes Trial, the S.S. was declared a criminal organization and numbers of its leaders were executed.

spective, my eyes, independent bystanders as usual, were noting with satisfaction. A voice beside me brought me back to reality:

"Rabboinu shel Olom, why don't you help us?" whispered a mother with two small children, each jolt of the brakes throwing the three against me. I observed the woman's husband taking something out of his pocket and pushing it into one of his shoes. The last things I saw of the Avenue Louise were the art galleries. I had hoped that some day I would open my first exhibition in one of them, had dreamed of the foule des grands jours, of flowers and of astonished art critics. This kind of future lay now in the past. My one sketchbook would fast fill up — what I now had to hope for was toilet paper.

Mechelen

E l e v e n

AFTER WHAT SEEMED LIKE A LONG TRIP past bare, wet meadows we drove into a town shrouded in the darkness of a blackout.
One could only guess at names and signs, but then the somber silhou-
ette of a cathedral came into view.

"Mechelen," someone beside me whispered.

The truck passed a big gate, then stopped. Thin rays of flashlights
and a hell of a racket startled us.

"Off your ass. Out! Line up with your bags!" With my shopping
bag of worldly possessions, my purse, the flour and the sketchbook, I
jumped and landed in a puddle. I found myself in a square yard with
high walls, under an equally square, black rag of rainy sky. This patch
of sky with its procession of clouds, wind and stars connecting me to
the outside world was to become my imaginary escape hatch into freedom for the next year-and-a-half.

"Papers! Put all money and valuables on the tables. Woe to whoever tries to hide anything," a voice grated with a Saxony accent. Our
group of about forty men, women and children was shoved into a
room, rattling with typewriters, manned by a dozen young women in
aprons ready to "receive" us. S.S. guards continuously scrutinized them,
so I concluded they themselves must be prisoners.

Not much fell out as I emptied my bag on the table. I had left the
heart-shaped gold locket in Berlin, together with my parents' photographs and the ring, which I had so desperately run to retrieve from
Eugene's studio. My purse as usual contained nothing but small change.
A silver-plated compact, the only "valuable" in my pocket, was promptly

confiscated, while a used lipstick was thrown into a big basket. Would its contents be sent to bombed out Germany? Waste not, want not!

My keys were sorted out and classified, no doubt with the intention of clearing out my attic room. I would never know if my self-portrait was as good as it had seemed on the dark afternoon of my arrest. Let them search my place. There was nothing there but paintings and drawings. I never saw them again.

Many of the prisoners came with suitcases. All their clothes and canned goods, anything they did not wear on their bodies, had to be left here at the Reception desks. (Reception is for the German Auf-nahme, the office where the Gestapo processed new arrivals at the bar-racks.) Here they would be sorted and transferred into crates by other prisoners. When the Jews travelled east to Poland with the next trans-port, the wagons carrying the crates would be uncoupled in Germany.

Cries of pain, curses in German were followed by sobbing and moaning in Yiddish and French. With the back of his hand, an S.S. beat a woman, his blows landing indiscriminately — he had found a dia-mond in the lining of her coat. A few children were still whimpering, but soon everyone fell silent. Wordlessly, grim and despairing, some of the men pulled banknotes and gems out of secret pockets and the hems of their coats. The banknotes they turned over were their last reserves which they had hoped to buy freedom with for their families or, if it were to come to the worst, to ransom their own lives.

Until the day of my arrest, I had tried hard to resemble the baroness I was supposed to be. I was still wearing my hair parted in the middle, with a stylish bun at the nape of my neck. My coat with its fur collar of unidentifiable animal tails, and my silver-plated compact lent me an air of refinement — add to these my dazed aloofness, due to lack of sleep and the terrible stress of the last several days. When I handed over my so-called aristocratic papers to the apron-clad prisoner reception-ists, they were impressed. Minnie and Evi, whose job it had been to file my I.D. data and "receive" my "valuables," could laugh with me many years later over our first encounter. Not then. Evi sat at the table and was suddenly struck in the face by an open inkwell. One of the S.S. — he was scrawny with a face cut in two by a red scar — was furious because Evi had dared to speak with one of the arrivals. Having recognized a former schoolmate, she tried to allay the newcomer's fears with a friendly word. Spattered with ink for her audacity, Evi continued filing names, dates and places of birth. Nobody's address was asked for, and under the heading "nationality," she had to enter "stateless," whether the prisoner had a valid passport or not. The scar-faced sadist in a leather jacket did not take his eye off Evi for a second — he was one of the leaders. His name I learned was Krull.

By now I was too tired to react to anything at all. As though from a far away place, I was hearing a long litany of prohibitions. A gray blanket was thrust into my arms as I walked up worn-out stairs into a long narrow room with rows of roughly hewn, two-storied bunks. Passing through the aisle between them, I was greeted by a hundred pairs of eyes, the anxious eyes of trapped animals for whom the cage had been slammed shut. These prisoners feared that they would find relatives, friends or just a familiar face among the newcomers. The senior inmate gave me a piece of bread and a small slice of margarine and assigned me to my "accommodations," a straw mattress on the upper row of boards. I drank some warm, artificially sweetened liquid, coffee in color only, from a tin bowl, and ate part of my ration. Folding my coat into a pillow and crawling under the gray blanket, the thin mattress was a blessing after the narrow wooden bench in the Gestapo cellar.

"Lights out!" The darkness was alive with voices. Mothers tried to calm their little ones, shoes thumped on the concrete floor, a babbling noise came from the direction of two large latrine buckets. One hundred Jews, some loud and angry, some hushed and resigned, most of them without a word, were wondering why they suddenly had been discarded here. To my right, a prisoner who had been allowed to keep his guitar was strumming a melancholy melody. Beside my left shoulder, a young man said "good night." Then I was out, though not for long.

Loud enough to awaken the dead, two giants in the black uniforms of the Flemish S.S. bellowed, "Foot control!" I sat up, startled, blinded by a flashlight searching the rows of sleepers. Apparently I looked clean — finding favor in the eyes of the guards, I did not have to show my feet. They didn't know that I had not washed for five days. If the guards or S.S. didn't like you, they would find fault regardless. This searching for dirty feet was the nightly pastime of the guards and some of the S.S. They now inspected the prisoners' toes, taking three men with them. First they had to go to the washroom, and then they had to undergo drill and abuse in the yard. Through the window, I could hear sneering at slovenly push-ups, until at last two of the punished men returned. Before finally falling asleep I learned that the third had to be brought to sick bay. (One foot control victim whom the S.S. Kommandant's assistant Max Boden personally disliked died of a heart attack after such exercising.)

Much too soon, I was reawakened by shrill whistle-blows. A naked bulb was hanging on a wire above — was this a new day, was I still trapped in a bad dream, too tired to wake? My fingers touched the piece of cardboard on my breast — I was no longer me, no one, not Irene Spicker from Berlin with her string of names, not the Flemish baroness from Brussels born in Canada. Those two I had to leave at the Reception. I had become a number.

There was little time to think, and soon I was fully awakened by the stench of the toilets at the other end of the yard. How did one bear this? One inmate dealt out paper — in the women's washroom, mainly a long pipe with faucets, I was given a towel.

"Not before ending up here did it occur to me that toilet paper was one of the foremost attainments of civilization," a young woman smiled in my direction. "The Judenrat sends toilet paper." The Judenrat was the Association des Juifs en Belgique. Its members, chosen by the Nazis, were noted Jewish citizens who initially thought they would be able to help their co-religionists during the occupation. However, the Gestapo used them to facilitate the liquidations of Jewish citizens. "Unfortunately no one can get any soap," the young woman went on, opening one of the faucets. "Could be much worse, cold water is good for your health. I am Dina Hirsch, from Frankfurt am Main," she said, wholly naked. She was right. A rub with ice cold water drove the blood through my veins. I felt invigorated, almost like a human being, if only a numbered one. Fine, numbers did not need to be embarrassed. All around me, washing or drying themselves, were more nude models than I had ever seen at the academy, young slender ones, old wasted bodies — no fat ones. By 1943 fat had shriveled away. Looking at so many shapes, lines and shadings, l was no longer merely a number. The painter in me was struggling back to the surface. I observed my surroundings more intently.

"Hi, honey, don't stare so hard. You're eating me up with your eyes. I might need my boobs and butts for better times," one of the nudes teased in my home slang of Berlin. She was Tilly Sachs, saucy Tilly, later to become my next bed neighbor. Back in my dormitory there was still no sign of morning coffee. In its place one of last night's foot inspectors was waiting, the one called Ferdekopf behind his back. To see him now in daylight, the name horse face did not seem far-fetched, though for a beautiful animal like a horse Ferdekopf's nickname was an insult. With a small soldier's cap pulled over a low forehead, a short, broad nose saddling a massive jaw cut by a mouth bristling with mammoth teeth, in a crude way the man really reminded one of a horse (see page 301). So much for the head. For the rest, with his stooped posture and forward falling shoulders, he reminded me of a question mark. As he slouched through the aisle separating the rows of mattresses his mean Aryan blue eyes penetrated into each and every rabbit hutch.

"Out, out, lazy bunch of Jews. Exercise!"

Prisoners were running down the stairs from everywhere, pushing into the yard through eight narrow, doorless passages. The yard was as ugly during the day as it had been in the evening. Bare of trees or bushes, it was closed in by walls the color of soiled diapers, yellow ocher. A man with a black dog silhouetted on the wall was giving orders. He was our Kapo, Dago (for Dagobert) Meyer. (Kapos were Jewish foremen in concentration camps responsible to the Nazi officers for keeping order among the inmates.) Meyer's features were as brutal as the faces of the S.S. officers, but his gestures were more theatrical than Il Duce's. No wonder. In Antwerp he was known as an opera singer. Here, even though he was a Kapo, he was but another Jew.

"Attention. Get in line. March." His dog joining in the barking, Dago Meyer's voice carried for miles.

"Heads up, backs straight. Knee bend. Damn it! If you don't shape up you can stand here until tomorrow for all I care."

"That monkey with the bull neck wants to impress the Nazis — he sounds like a sergeant in the Prussian army," Tilly Sachs said in a low voice. "You know the old Berlin bicycling law — upward you stoop, downward you trample."

The knee bends, the jumping and stretching in the fresh morning air did me good (strange as that may seem) but less so for the older people. Barely able to stand on their feet any longer and completely bewildered, they could not grasp what was wanted of them. What else, bewildered eyes questioned. I have been wrested from my family, torn out of my life, everything taken from me, treated worse than an animal. "It's not enough. Now I have to play jumping jack," an elderly gentleman gasped in French. "Why? What for in God's name? Can someone explain it to me?"

"What for? It's great for our muscles," Tilly Sachs wisecracked. "We need big biceps to haul stones in those camps in Poland." No one but Tilly herself laughed; all the Jews around us, including me, took her sarcasm as a bad joke. Had it been revealed to us what lay in store beyond the barracks, at the end of the railroad tracks, how could we have believed it? We would have taken the truth for tasteless and fantastical rumors. Indeed, the absolute absence of news from the thousands of Jews deported earlier from Mechelen was difficult to comprehend. Had the earth swallowed them? Or what else? The "what else" was a thought too sinister to pursue. Any train of thought was throttled with Dago Meyer's order for a final sprint: "Everybody upstairs!"

Drinking the saccharine sweet ersatz coffee made me feel almost full, though only for a while. The piece of bread, which I had saved from my dinner, so gooey it should have been great for sculpting, I chewed as slowly as if it were a delicacy. My neighbors were very nice to me, newcomer that I was. Some had been in the camp for weeks and had received food packages. Rather they had what had not been confiscated. They gave me little gifts, a few rusks, a dollop of jam — the friendly young man from the mattress to my right gave me half an apple. Suddenly everybody pushed to look through the windows facing the yard. (All windows overlooking the street had been walled up.)

Another truckload, this one from Antwerp. Beside the gate stood a guard with a machine gun. Next to him was Kommandant Schmitt with a whip in hand. Behind him were his representatives, the scarred man in the leather jacket, and Schmitt's assistant Boden, the stocky S.S. with the Saxon accent. A doctor and two nurses in white helped some of the sixty newcomers get off the truck. If not for the machine gun and the whip, the scene could have deceived a viewer into thinking that this was some kind of a mental institution. Lulling myself for a second with this peaceful image, I could see that the inmates of my dormitory were more worried than before.

"We are more than a hundred people in our room. It's full. The new arrivals go to room nineteen, the last room that is still free. Once number twenty is full, we go on transport."

The logic of this simple addition was sinking in. For a while the room fell silent. Nothing but sighs and the babble of children were heard. Sitting or squatting on our mattresses, all of us were looking for a means of salvation, a way out of this nightmare, some solution that must be there if we thought hard enough, a life-line from the Almighty. Being helplessly packed into a cattle car, shipped to who knows where and what for? Those still disposing of assets outside weighed the best approach for bribing a Gestapo officer. "Good grease makes for good driving," a Yiddish expression teaches. Professor Edelmann was fed a few crumbs by his wife every three hours because of an ulcer — he hoped aloud that the Belgian secretary of education would intervene with the Wehrmacht to obtain his release. Tilly expressed everyone's sentiments, "I don't have much cash and a Nobel Prize they've forgotten to give me, but lowbrows don't want to go on transport any more than you do."

For my part, I was ready for the cattle car so long as no one forced me to tell where my father was. For quite some time in Brussels I had tried to resign myself to the realization that I might end up in a concentration camp. And even though I had neglected to prepare a valise or a backpack for this possibility, unlike any Jew with a sense of responsibility, my customary carelessness had not been misplaced. Whatever I might have brought with me would have been confiscated anyway. To this day I cannot understand how this news had not sunken in.

Were we simply ostriches burying our heads in the sand, not wanting to know? Did we willfully want to believe the German S.S. who reassured us about our fate and our luggage? In any event, the summons for deportation to work camps ordered the Jews to bring with them woolen blankets, solid shoes, warm clothes and canned food.

How pitiable and abandoned I felt on my escape from Berlin to Brussels! Now I was glad to be on my own — when I looked into the eyes of other inmates, especially those of young mothers, I sometimes sighed with relief. Apart from Papa nobody would mourn me for long.

"What will happen, will happen," my neighbor Egon cheered me up, giving me a tiny bit of chocolate. "We are both alone, strong and healthy, we will make it. The war cannot go on forever and in the worst case you can die only once. For the rest, I have an old friend here, Albert Clément, who has a job as a yard worker. He is trying to put a word in for me. Maybe they'll let me join his team or clean the men's washroom." I glanced at him, his face, as it was said in German, "like milk and blood." His fresh complexion, shiny black eyes and clean fingernails brightened the dark disorder of our rabbit hutches. He smelled of good soap. Where might he have gotten such a precious commodity?

"If someone is qualified for that job, it's you," I said with the last taste of the chocolate on my tongue and with conviction.

One of us always had to be on the lookout to warn the others if the guards were coming.

"Ferdekopf is on the second floor, be careful! They are on their way up from room fifteen. It's time for our promenade." The Germans called it a promenade when all transport numbers, by now more than a thousand, walked around the yard in a circle. Planted straddle-legged in the center stood our trainer with his whip, the same thick-skinned Boden who the evening before had stage directed the Reception.

"I know that fellow from Leipzig — he was a plainclothes man." Someone from the row behind me stole out of the ranks to approach Boden.

"Forgive me, sir commander, I am a master tailor with the highest recommendations. My wife sews children's wear." He did not get any further. As if all those Jews around him did not exist, Boden contemplated the partly cloudy square of sky above him. "In my opinion it's raining today," he proclaimed dourly, motioning the tailor back into the ranks. With courage born of desperation, other prisoners, fathers, mothers, now also tried to get within earshot of this Saxon who held their fate in his hands. They were ready to do anything to save their families from deportation.

"Excuse me, Sir Stormtroop commander, my cousin has been working in the leather workshop for over four weeks. I am a first-class craftsman of ladies purses."

"Sir Stormtroop commander. In Berlin I used to be a cook at the Adlon Hotel."

"Sir Stormtroop commander, please, I beg you, my sister is in room five and I am in room fifteen. May I move?" Fed up, Boden threatened with his whip:

"March, back with you. Today is Shabbes." It is Monday but Shabbes — Yiddish for the Sabbath — seemed to be his pet expression. He thought himself very witty, paying the Jews in their own coin, Yiddish. How fortunate I was to have no children, I thought, not to have to beg for anything from this petit-bourgeois scumbag, member of the master race.

And still, however distasteful a situation was, it never took away my appetite. I could barely wait for the midday soup to arrive. At last I saw inmates emerging from the kitchen by pairs, carrying steaming cauldrons through the courtyard and up the stairs. A whistle blew, and I returned to the third floor where for the moment an aroma of rutabagas replaced the stench.

"One ladle per person, you don't have to push." Under Ferdekopf's eye our room elder doled out the soup. What filled our bowls was mostly water with a few beet cubes, a hint of cabbage and onion, and the pièce de résistance, three small cubes of potato. Hungry as I was, it did not taste too bad. Once over the year-and-a-half, I fished a bone with a grizzle still attached to it out of my bowl. A unique event — never again did I find a pearl in my tin oyster.

How much can I say about my first afternoon in room number eighteen? Women brought armfuls of dripping wash to hang on a rope stretched in crisscross fashion near the iron stove. Socks, shirts and

underpants hung from rafters everywhere. Parents dabbed their children with the red liquid the infirmary distributed against impetigo
though since most of the little ones were disfigured by pocks from
head to toe, the remedy did not seem to be working. In one corner,
the young man with the guitar practiced soundlessly — he had been
asked to take pity on those trying to sleep. Was the air near the ceiling
really so sticky? Was it my surroundings, people packed like sardines,
children covered with red spots that depressed me? This misery would
not get the better of me. I would fight it, I decided. Taking up my
sketchbook I began drawing and listening to stories.

There was nothing to read, but there were stories. No writer could
invent what was unburdened here, the hundreds of desperate hide-and-
seek games, betrayals by neighbors, self-sacrifices of strangers. The end
of the stories was always the same. There was no escape.

During the afternoon exercise of walking around the courtyard,
rumors circulated in the ranks.

"Porter Wald, who packs crates in the warehouse, says he is sure the
next transport will leave in one week. He has it from Lieutenant
Noppenei."

"Nonsense. They don't have enough wagons to transport troops.
Why then would they use a whole train of them to cart Jews from here
to there?"

"You know that house painter Adolf Salomon from Aachen? As he
stood on a ladder painting the casino he overheard a conversation by
Wehrmacht officers. The Russians are near Kiev, and the Allies are. . . ."
The shrill sound of a whistle interrupted the speaker and our walk,
begun only minutes earlier.

"Everybody upstairs. Go. Go. Faster!" Again a transport had arrived
from Antwerp.

I did my wash and sat on the mattress with nothing but a skirt and
sweater. Legs dangling from a beam beside my wet stockings, I listened
to the story of the young woman to my right.

"I am Fanny, Fanny Kimmel from Antwerp," she began and sighed.
"Already in September the Gestapo came for my husband. In the
morning he went to work but never arrived there — they took him

from the street. All I could find out was that he had been brought to Mechelen," she said wiping away a tear. "With my yellow star I could not simply go to Mechelen, present myself at the Dossin Barracks and ask for my husband. You can just imagine what kind of a winter I went through. Waiting, waiting, while left and right my family and friends were disappearing, one after the other. You hear nothing more of them, you see nothing more of them." She was crying and I joined in, something I had not allowed myself to do since my arrest. Then she went on. "An old friend from school, a Christian woman, wanted to hide me, but I said no, when my husband comes back he will find me at home. And really, none of my neighbors informed against me. Maybe I would still be sitting in my flat if I had not gone for five minutes to Molly Schwartz just to see how she was doing. She had four children. Her husband got his orders for a labor camp in August and is God knows where. He was so afraid they would take the whole family if he did not go that he didn't even try to hide. He went voluntarily. The four children were just coming home from school, still standing in the doorway when we heard German voices, 'Your papers.' One swine in gray, the other in civilian clothes — they were already in the kitchen. I showed my identity card with my Belgian nationality. They took all of us anyhow. I said, 'Sir, I live just around the corner, may I get my backpack quickly?' While he went with me I asked him if he could please bring me to my husband.

"'That can be arranged,' he said, 'but first shut your door, otherwise the White Jews will come and carry away everything.'"

"'What White Jews?' I asked."

"'What White Jews could there be? The Flemings, of course,' he grinned, 'they are not much better than you Jews.'"

Here she shook her short brown hair, as if to say that the whole world had gone crazy. Then she continued, "On our arrival in Mechelen I went straight to the man with those things on his shoulder-straps. 'Herr Kommandant,' I said, 'my name is Fanny Kimmel, I want to find my husband. He has been here since September.' He looked at me in a funny way.

"'Kimmel, eh?' he said, laughing dryly. 'He's not here anymore, but

we can send you to him. It depends on you. With your Belgian nationality you can get a B-Number and remain here if you wish.' Nothing
doing. I'll get myself a transport number, I want to find my husband."
With sad eyes Fanny stared into the twilight that was beginning to
soften the harsh outlines of room eighteen, stroking the number hanging from her neck.

The lights went on, the bread ration was passed out. Combining
Fanny's leftover margarine, my spoonful of jam and Egon's half onion,
we crouched down on my mattress for dinner. After a few bites Fanny
again began fingering her number this way and that, fumbling the
piece of cardboard as if to ask it for forgiveness:

"Tomorrow morning I will go and ask Kommandant Schmitt for a
B-number," she sighed again. "You know Lévi, the young lawyer from
room fifteen? Yesterday he kept harping at me for an hour to do it. He
saw no way out for himself, he said, but if I went on transport voluntarily with my right to a B-Number, that would be criminal stupidity.
'Criminal stupidity,' he said. I would not get to see my husband anyway, he kept saying. Before they came to arrest him, Lévi had listened
to a Swiss radio station with stories from American newspapers. He
was beating about the bush on the news, said it was too incredible. But
one thing he assured me of, the moment a train arrives in Poland men
and women are separated."

Fanny would probably remain here in Mechelen and perhaps Egon
too, I thought, which meant that I would be shipped off without my
new friends. Feeling discouraged, I swept the crumbs from my mattress. The little girl in the bunk below held out her hands wound with
a thread of wool, her only toy; a few minutes of cat's cradle tired me
and I joined in the exodus to the washroom and toilets. Later, in the
dark, I could not fall asleep. I heard feet shuffling in the direction of
the buckets, whispered conversations, snoring, whimpering children.
Better warm air thick enough to cut with a knife, than a room full of
cold ozone, they used to joke in Berlin. But the air that the 120 Jews
penned up here breathed in and out was not only stale; it was charged
with deep anxiety, powerless fury. What had the young lawyer from
room fifteen hemmed and hawed about, I asked myself. What was the

big mystery? What in those camps in Poland could be worse than here? I was still brooding as the beams of the guard's flashlights pass over me.

"Show your feet, don't try to tell us you washed them, you skunk!" the two Flemings screamed at a shy little Jew, a mathematics teacher from Liège who rarely opened his mouth. "Now show your hands. Sure, soft and pink like a marzipan piglet. Yeah, we know, you were in business. We work and you make money. But you'll see, we'll make you calluses all-right."

How could I fall asleep like this? Furthermore I was hungry. Open-eyed I dreamed of brisket with horseradish gravy, real fruit raspberry Jell-O, a fresh roll with liverwurst. Perhaps there would be more to eat in the new camp. I speculated that undernourished slaves would not be worth much to the Germans, not for hard work. I had no doubt that hard, backbreaking work awaited me in Poland and worst of all, work to help the Nazis. Would I be in an ammunition factory? In the fields? I remembered from my school days that Poland was an agricultural country. But why did the Nazis send old, sickly people and mothers with little children there? To dig out potatoes? To milk cows? I turned and turned and could not fall asleep.

"Irene, can't you sleep either?" Egon whispered from somewhere near my ear.

"Yes, I am hungry."

"So am I."

"Tomorrow morning I will be sorry," I sighed, biting deep into the rest of my bread ration.

Four years had passed since I left Eugene. I was twenty-two-years old, Egon was a little older; and here we sat in the dark, slowly chewing on our piece of bread, holding hands like children who had lost their way in a forest bewitched by evil gnomes. The branches of this wood were so entangled, so grotesquely torn and knotted — only our kiss was true, warm and simple. Hotter kisses followed, until I came suddenly to my senses. The string around my neck, the cardboard number, my hot breath, brought me back to the night in Monsieur Dessy's stable, the cows stomping and snorting after the steer had torn loose. Had I gone crazy? What did I know about Egon? That I had enjoyed his company for twenty-four hours? That he seemed to be a nice fellow, was handsome and smelled of soap?

"Egon," I said softly, "I am sorry. Don't get me wrong, I like you, but there is someone in England whom I want to be true to," not mentioning that I had had no sign of life from Eugene for three years.

Understandably feeling hurt, Egon would give me the cold shoulder for the next year-and-a-half.

Twelve

TIME PASSED SLOWLY, hunger was my companion. Every few days the lucky prisoners chosen to be porters stacked packages of food under a roof in the yard. Would today at last be my lucky day, would my name be among those called up?

It was mail call time, and Dina, the nice girl from Frankfurt whom I had met in the washroom, accompanied me in the yard even though she had no one left outside who could send her a parcel. Her only hope was a small package from the Judenrat in Brussels. Several hundred prisoners were waiting, standing between yellow walls in the gray snow and puddles of black. Muddy gray, dirty yellow, murky brown black — the flag of people without a country, our flag.

A nostalgic melody rang in my head, the hymn of the German Social Democrats that as a child I had so often sung with fervor. "Black, red and gold, the banners unrolled," I hummed, disconcerting Dina who looked at me strangely.

"Well, what's so odd about a flag?" I asked with a straight face. "We are citizens all right — of an insect state. You are high above my caste, a slave worker. I am only one of those tiny ants running around, looking for something to eat, until some shiny black boot comes along."

Our anthill was functioning like a well-greased machine, geared to maximum productivity without costing the Nazis a pfennig. No German personnel were needed apart from a handful of officers, some policemen and the guards, all of them armed. Jewish prisoners did every kind of work and in this way paid for the expense of their captivity. The Nazis took care of punishment and beatings.

Veteran prisoners "received" the newly arrived Jews, helped relieve them of their possessions, searched them and later on opened the packages of food sent by their friends and families. Jews cooked for the military, served the officers and their "ladies," cleaned, washed and ironed. One inmate bred pigs for the officer's table, another trained the Kommandant's dog, a third was the court watchmaker. There were the female cooks and their helpers, a whole troop of porters, washroom, yard and latrine workers, electricians, plumbers, carpenters and house painters. A doctor with two nurses and precious little medication worked in the sick bay, while a pregnant dentist sat in a room one flight above. She and her dental technician husband brought their dentist's chair and drill with them. On the first floor of the old Belgian barracks was a repair shop for army uniforms, and work spaces for furriers, tailors, leather and paper craftsmen. All of the work they produced was sent eastward to Germany, along with trainloads of Jews shipped to Poland. Other areas in Mechelen were used for the Reception, Gestapo offices, sleeping quarters for the S.S. and Kapos, the casino, the punishment cells — the prisoners were cramped into rabbit hutches. However, the storehouse where prisoners registered and crated all that had been taken from the incoming Jews, occupied the largest area. So many scissors, so many watches, pocket knives, coats, baby carriages, so many pairs of shoes. The Judenrat in Brussels had to supply the raw material for the workshops, food, toilet paper, even screws for the carpenters — this meant that wealthy Jews who had not yet been arrested and sought to protect themselves from deportation had to pay until they were bled dry.

The Judenrat also provided some of the food for prisoners. Dina and I stood looking at the undistributed packages. Our safest bet was a small one from the Judenrat, for even if an inmate still had family members hidden on the outside, they were probably unable to help. We waited for Voss, one of our three Kapos, nicknamed the "postmaster," to finally distribute what the S.S. had not already taken.

"Sorry, Irene, but I have to go back to the washroom if I don't want to get in trouble with Ferdekopf. Listen to me, never attract attention here, not with your presence and even less with your absence. I have to go heat water — it's the turn of the lucky girls from the witches' den to take their monthly shower." (The witches' den is Hexenstall in German, the Nazi's name for the quarters of the Jewish girls working at the Reception.) Walking backwards while she was still talking, Dina landed smack in the arms of Voss. If my feet had not been so cold and I had been less hungry, I might have laughed at the blue-eyed giant with dark-haired little Dina. I disliked men like Voss, so terribly Teutonic, especially when they were Jews. Voss's Teutonic features were easily explained. He was from the Rhineland where during pogroms in the Middle-Ages, girls and women had been raped. When he was not cursing in Kölnish, he beamed such Rhinish radiance as if we all had come to Mechelen for the carnival. Sending Dina on her way with a good-natured little slap, he began to distribute the packages.

"Sarah Fishbein!" Happily smiling he threw a parcel into the arms of a young woman. "Herbert von Ledermann Wartberg [see page 238]! With such a name on it the package should not smell of Limburger. Eh, you, Moishe Schweinetod, what do you need food parcels for, each month slaughtering a pig," and so on. For me again nothing. I hated to be pitied — that included self-pity — but now I had to swallow hard anyway.

"Irene Spicker!" When had my name ever sounded so sweet? The package must be from my sister and Papa, who did not have enough to eat. I had to find out about the contents right there, carry it up to my dormitory to share the good news and some of the food with a friend. But Fanny was not there anymore. She had resigned herself to stay in the barracks, rather than to try and find her husband, God knows where in Poland. With her B-Number returned to her, she now worked in the tailor's workshop. Egon moved to a mattress far away from me. I decided to go to the washroom, to Dina, who had nobody anymore, neither inside the camp nor outside. We were of the same age and spoke German with each other, occasionally reciting poems we learned at school.

A low, wooden bench, customarily serving the women to dry their feet, was our banquet table. I have mentioned that my sister Gerda was very inventive, especially when it came to cooking. From fried onions, yeast and a whiff of powdered eggs, she conjured up a spread that she put on rusks — it reminded me of chopped liver. For dessert we had an apple and marzipan potatoes, which tasted of Quaker oats and almond essence, topped with a dusting of something resembling cocoa.

"Mmm. Ah," sighed Dina, "It has been a long time since I ate so well." Satisfied I leaned against the water pipes, stretching my legs.

"Isn't it quite cozy here, what do you say Irene?" Dina had been an inmate much longer than I and said this without any irony. "Private too. Ferdekopf does not nose around here so much." My new friend began to whisper, "Something fishy is going on in Major Schmitt's office. Klara and Edith are beside themselves," she said secretly. My blank expression apparently conveyed that I had no idea who Klara and Edith were. "You know, they are part of the witches' den. Tonight they'll all come for their shower," said Dina. "Edith Silberman is Kommandant Steckmann's secretary and Klara Sander works with Meinshausen at the Reception. May he rot in hell. I tell you, Irene, something is not kosher with our high and mighty. Some girls from personnel have overheard bits of a phone call. A Gestapo boss from Brussels was giving Steckmann hell. It smells of bribery," she said and even claimed that Jews in the camp were mixed up in the scandal. "In any event," said Dina, "after the call Klara and Edith ran at once to the infirmary, to Doctor Basch and Medic Wolf to warn them, I suppose. How do you like that, two married men with wives and children in Brussels. They are not young, not even good-looking, and Klara and Edith carry on with them openly. Perhaps they believe, poor fools, that a doctor and a medic can save them from transport?"

For the first time in two weeks I had enough to eat. I yawned. I was not yet well informed about the hierarchy in our insect colony, nor interested either. Dina's talk was after-dinner gossip and probably nonsense. Why would Gestapo officers who could easily pilfer whatever they wanted make common cause with Jews?

Dina, however, got so excited about her story that I tried a diversion — "How about another apple?" She did not even hear me. "Perhaps they'll send Major Schmitt and Kommandant Meinshausen to the Russian front. Remembering what they did to my brother, my ardent wish is that they both freeze to death there, miserably, member by member!" For a while Dina stared at the wall. "Don't be afraid Irene, I am not going to bawl, I'm done with crying," she said, and then as if in a trance she began to tell me the story of how she wound up in Mechelen. "We fled from Frankfurt to Antwerp in 1939, over the green border. The German occupation in Antwerp was gold compared to the hell Frankfurt had become for us under the Nazis. Even with the German Wehrmacht Antwerp was not too bad, not until the Gestapo took over. The yellow star, going into hiding, more and more arrests — left and right Jews were disappearing. Lightning struck us one morning in September — my brother and I had gone on the first train to the countryside, hoping that farmers would sell us some food. We had barely left home when the Gestapo arrived with police and pulled my parents out of bed. They brought my mother here in her nightgown, Papa in his pajamas." Dina stared at the black mold on the washroom wall. "That was a few days before Rosh Hashanah — in the beginning they caught Jews like flies, one transport after another rolling out of Mechelen. How long did my parents stay in the camp, two, three days, a week? We never heard from them again." We both fell silent. Two women entered with their wash. Dina gave them a handful of soap powder and moved closer.

"For two more months my brother Hermann and I struggled, but in November they caught us during a raid on the tramway. We were put in the same dormitory where you are now, on the street side by the third walled-up window. Hermann was not yet seventeen, still growing. You can imagine how hungry he was — there was no one to send us food. I helped him where I could, but I had nothing to eat either and only two eyes to watch him. With another boy he managed to filch food from the kitchen, some bread and potatoes. It got around. The two Flemings found half a loaf under his mattress, and after blows that sent his head spinning they led him away. His nose was bloodied but Ferdekopf in his black uniform and the other raven — it was Journée — did not stop.

"'I am going to give it back, tonight I am going to give it back!' my brother kept shouting. It didn't help. They pushed and poked him into the office of the Kommandant. Naturally I followed, I don't even know anymore what I was begging, promising and babbling — they did not let me enter."

An old woman came in, let down her gray hair and began to wash it. Two girls with armfuls of dirty clothes positioned themselves by our improvised table. Dina gave them soap powder and stared with dry eyes at the rusty faucet. "They pushed my brother and the other boy through the door — then Meinshausen and Schmitt and his dog came out. I watched from the window. There was no one else in the yard."

"'Off with your shoes, you scum!' Meinshausen shouted, 'socks too!' Now barefoot in the snow my brother hopped from one foot to the other. 'Are you cold? Why, you are shaking. Then run, man, run,' Schmitt laughed. A cold hand gripped my heart when I suddenly understood. It was the first of January, the New Year, the Kommandant and his deputy were drunk. 'Can you count to thirty? Then show me thirty knee-bends. One, two, three, up, down, up, down. Faster. Faster. Faster, I say. Here, Lumpi, you show them now!' Schmitt takes the leash off. 'Catch the Jews, Lumpi, catch the thief!' My brother runs, the dog sets at him, barking, and all the while Meinshausen was laughing. The dog snapped Hermann's leg, held on, he tried to shake him off. 'Ah, ah, now the thief is shaking. Don't shake, I tell you! Dance, you two, dance! Here, Lumpi, back. Let the Jew boys dance pretty in the snow, I say dance, don't you understand German?' Half jumping, half limping my brother staggered around, flapping his arms in desperation. When he finally fell to the ground the people in the dormitory had to hold me back. I only wanted to tear free, to get down to him." The brown velvet of Dina's brown eyes turned dull and black but soon her clenched fists opened up again to distribute one more handful of soap powder. Then she continued.

"Whether I was upstairs or down, it did not matter anymore, there was nothing I could do. While Schmitt and Meinshausen shouted at the inmates upstairs not to dare look through the windows, Ferdekopf and Journée were dragging Hermann and his partner to the cells. During the afternoon walk around dusk, I sneaked out of the ranks and made my way to the cells down in the cellar — the kitchen help pretended not to see me.

"You have been here such a short time Irene, be glad you don't know these cells. Each has a door with a small, barred window. That is how I saw him, in his bloodied, torn pants crouching in a dark corner. In the next few days he recovered a little. The moment I knocked softly, he limped to the door, pointing to his empty bowl, raising his shoulders and crossing his arms, to tell me how hungry and how cold he was. Risky as it was, the girls from the kitchen tried to get some food through to him — it could not be much. His partner was in the next cell. Unlike my brother who had a fever, he was all right. Only after Hermann ran a high temperature was Doctor Basch allowed in to examine him." Dina got up, stoking the fire in the furnace furiously.

"Cold fish that he is, Basch just said 'gangrene — his leg must be amputated at once.' But the infirmary did not have the equipment."

Dina got up again, this time to load coal into the furnace. With her back to me, she talked on and on, about how she went to visit her brother in the Mechelen hospital, finding him with one leg. How, barely out of his sick bed, he had been put on the next transport on crutches. Not allowed to go with him, Dina was "promoted" to washroom monitor.

"Can you find any reason in all this?" she asked. Still waving a poker, Dina turned back to face me. "A cripple is shipped off to work in Poland, and on my two healthy legs I am kept here in Mechelen in the washroom. Who said 'even if madness, it still has a method?' Was it Faust or Mephisto? Can you remember? It seems to me a good description of the Nazis. It doesn't make sense with the transports though, and doesn't fit drunken swine like Schmitt and Meinshausen at all. The day they're sent to the Russian front maybe I'll be able to sleep again. Irene, one day my parents will come back from the camps, they have to, and how can I justify myself, what am I going to tell them?" Leaning the poker against a pipe Dina rocked her head in both hands.

She had such a gentle face, a soft little snub nose and full, red lips. When Germany still was normal, girls like Dina were called Black Forest lasses. Maybe even a Meinshausen in sober moments had been moved by her sad eyes. Why had he tormented Dina's brother almost to death and then gotten him to the hospital to save his life, afterwards sending him on a transport? It was sadistic and cruel. What was there to understand? I tried to comfort Dina. "You did what you could. Is it your fault that you weren't sent on transport, that you're still allowed to crawl around in this hell hole?"

"Guilty or not, how does that help me when I cannot sleep? I should have taken better care of him, given him more of my bread." As the whistle sounded for our walk around the yard, I drew Dina outside, trying to stop her from further reproaching herself. "Explain to me why so many prisoners have a letter in front of their number," I pointed to some of the those in the yard, "What do those B's, W's and E's mean?" "Oh, Dina said, "B is for Belgische Nationalität, which means they usually remain here. W means Werkstätten, the workforce, and E is for Entscheidung [decision], which means each case is examined separately for transport or liberation."

⟶

Sometimes the young women working at the Reception joined us in the yard. I especially liked to walk with two of them in the same row, Minnie Feldman from Brussels and Evi Fastag from Antwerp. They were about my age, friendly and open-minded, and we got along well. Both had been in Mechelen since the Nazis opened the camp on July 28, 1942. Their knowledge of German, French and Flemish and their typing experience had so far saved them from the transports East.

It was now late March. Both said there had never been such a long interruption between transports. Toward the end of summer and in early fall, Jews were being hauled in twice a week — the barracks had been filling up — and Minnie and Evi were working day and night. From the first weeks of August until the end of October, they counted seventeen transports leaving with prisoners. A double transport was sent off in the middle of January. Since then, however, nothing. The camp was full once more and Minnie and Evi were working day and night. Still we had not yet heard the screeching brakes of the cattle train coming to a halt on the tracks outside the gate. After months of turmoil, the present lull seemed eerie, Minnie said, like the calm before the storm. Or maybe the optimists were right — they argued that after the defeat at Stalingrad the Germans needed their trains for more important cargo. Our barracks would have to burst before a transport could be economically justified.

I later discovered the real reason for the pause, which was simple enough. After six months the camp had swallowed more than eighteen thousand Jews living in Belgium — those who remained did not give themselves away so easily. They were no longer succumbing to threats nor were they taken in by promises. To fill the prescribed "Jew quota," the Gestapo now had to rely primarily on raids and informers.

"What do you do over there when no Jews come in?" I asked Minnie and Evi somewhat sarcastically as we passed the miserable geranium at the Reception window for the fourth time. What an ironic welcome, this lone representative here of the blossoming world. "Thank God, when no new prisoners arrive, then we open food parcels," Evi said bitterly, "so that Steckmann, the Major [Schmitt] and Meinshausen, Krull and company, and anyone else of the Herren who is passing by can take what they want. Boden sends packages home to Saxony. Just this morning he dictated a letter to me to his 'dear family' and signed it, 'Your loyal breadwinner, Max Boden.'"

"When no Jews come in, then they turn vicious," Minnie interrupted her, "then I have to scrub floors all day. Not long ago Boden caught me darning my stockings. The same evening, just when we were falling asleep, Boden, Schmitt, Steckmann and Meinshausen burst into the witches' den with their dogs and their flashlights. They do that often when they drink. They pass between the rows of beds, laughing when the dogs frighten us with their sniffing and snarling.

"'Ah, here they are, the two sisters, Minnie and Miriam Feldman go on transport! They have darned stockings at the Reception. The Anne Landes with the big ass too. She spelled Kontrolle with a C in my last report. Don't look so stupid you two, Fat Ass and Broad Ass, your turn will come too.' We could not sleep all night, but when we reported for work in the morning Boden only said 'Today's my Shabbes and took his greyhound out into the yard."

"With me he acts differently," Evi said. "When I have nothing else to do, he gives me lists to copy. What he needs them for is a mystery.

Long lists with very short entries. Name, number, place and date of birth. Nationality? Stateless. Address? None. Sometimes the list has the names of my parents and my three brothers among them." She looked with loathing at the pitiful geranium we were again passing. "Many here would like to have my job, but believe me, Irene, I am not to be envied. You were there when Krull threw the ink at me — only because I said a few words to an old school friend. Nobody should envy me." Hesitating for a moment, Evi fell into step with me. "It was the worst when I had to register my own family," she said quietly. "That was only three weeks after my own arrest. I was caught at the Antwerp railway station in July coming home from work with the yellow star on my blouse.

"When my family was brought here in August, the day was terribly hot. One after another the trucks came rolling through the gate. The yard was black with people. You cannot possibly imagine what it was like. We didn't even have time to cross the yard to eat our soup at the witches' den. Around three o'clock, Boden sent me over to the kitchen with a note for bread and cheese for those of us at the Reception." Evi stopped walking. Minnie and I had to pull her along when she continued. "All around me people are sitting on their bundles, red and sweating in the heat, dejected and dead-tired. Winding my way through to the kitchen I suddenly hear, 'Evi, Evi!' and find myself in my mother's arms, for one second safe and happy, until I grasp that my greatest fear has become reality. They are all here, my father, my mother and my three younger brothers, all five of them looking at me so expectantly as if I knew the answer, while I had to hurry to the kitchen and back to Boden. Believe it or not, I managed to mollify the monster. My family was left out of a half dozen transports. My mother was even allowed to sleep beside me, until the middle of September when none of my pleading helped anymore. Fewer Jews were being caught, so people with transport numbers were needed to fill the trains. I wanted to go with my parents, but they absolutely refused. 'Don't worry Evi,' my father tried to sound optimistic, 'We will soon be back. Even the Nazis must have noticed they have lost the war. Every night we listened to the French news from Radio London. In Russia they are running, in North Africa they are defeated. The British are bombing all of Germany. How will it help to ship Jews to Poland? Their generals are not stupid, they must understand that they're led by a madman. So don't worry. We will be back soon and we need you here to put the flat in shape for all of us!'" All seven, Evi explained, because she also had a younger sister, who would hurry home as soon as the war was over. Her sister had managed to escape to Switzerland just one day before her own arrest.

I can still assemble Evi's whole family in my imagination, seated around a white tablecloth on a Friday evening, her mother lighting the Sabbath candles, her father passing wine and challah to each; after the blessing, they laugh and chat. I knew that families meant everything to Polish Jews — but their flat? That sounded odd to my ear, rather a pre-text that Evi's father used to convince her to stay behind. Evi's eyes had long forgotten how to laugh. They told a different story. Making our eighth and last walk around the yard I glanced sideways at her. Maybe I'll have time to draw her portrait, I thought, before I am sent on a transport. A little chubby, she had small hands and feet. Her quick movements reminded me of a small animal, maybe a squirrel with big, brown, worried eyes that watered when she continued.

"In the middle of September the transports were still regular passenger trains — the Nazis did not want to alarm the population. Not only did Boden let me accompany my family through the gate up to the tracks, I was even allowed to keep some of my brothers' clothes — I have them in a box under my bed. Hundreds of young men and girls from Antwerp and Brussels left on that transport. Encouraging each other as they were walking up to the train, laughing even, they were too proud to let the Germans see their real feelings. With their numbers hanging from their necks, they began singing songs of the Zionist youth movements once inside the train, French patriotic marches, Flemish chants of defiance against the Walloons — my brothers' voices were the loudest of all. I could still hear them as the train was rolling away." Evi did not have to add that this was the last she had heard of them.

The barracks were now full. With every new load of prisoners our nerves became more tense. A warning sign, "Caution, high voltage!"

could have been hung at the entrance to each of our dormitories. Quarrels broke out about the last ladle of soup, about a few centimeters of space on a clothes line to dry one's wash, about a cigarette stub.

It was the beginning of April 1943. Evi and Minnie said that the previous transport, the nineteenth, had left in January in the snow. More than three months must have passed, and the stoves were not being heated anymore. Was it spring out there? Instead of looking for swallows in our square of sky, I rarely let the entrance gate out of my sight. Whenever the guard opened it, I expected an immense truck loaded with flour, which the girls from the Reception had described. If the guard then whistled for the porters, that was a sign the train coming to take us away would not be far off either. In each of the nineteen transports, Minnie told me, she had witnessed a cargo of flour for the Fatherland loaded together with a cargo of Jews.

We were grateful for each day the flour did not arrive. Though the wait was unnerving, I still had to pass the time. Blank sheets remained in my sketchbook and I drew what I saw around me, especially the children, young faces with sad, old eyes. I absorbed impressions like a sponge, rendering them with more sensitivity, though with little more self-awareness than a mollusk. Meeting with Dina, Minnie or Evi during our daily walks around the yard, I was reluctant to get too close — I was but a transport number, why come to regret the unavoidable separation?

The notorious flour shipment had still not been sighted when our three Kapos — Dago Meyer, Voss and Kraus — announced a festivity for the coming Sunday. An old trick to relax tensions in the camp, a maneuver to divert attention, said those with experience. I tried to believe that perhaps the S.S. had some vestige of a human side after all.

Having once been an opera singer, Meyer was ordered to prepare a program — he sought talent in every dormitory. We now let the young Dutch guitarist in our dormitory practice as much as he wished. For hours on end a melody he had composed rose slowly over shuffling shoes, clattering tin bowls and the commotion in our hutches. Now, more than half a century later, the gentle, melancholy surge still continues to renew itself in me. I cannot recall the young composer's name, though I remember the unforgettable name of his Dutch friend, Api Bueno de Mesquito. With such a name, temperament, striking features and pitch-black strands of hair, it was only natural that Api got the lead in the planned event. From the B-Numbers dormitory a professional stage designer emerged, Lon Landau of the Antwerp Royal Theater. From papier-mâché and old clothes from the storehouse, he created a female partner for Api. Some prisoners were opposed to Jews making a spectacle of themselves in front of the Nazis, and hoped the event would be cancelled by spring rains. Though they were probably right, they were also in the minority — after all, who didn't want to forget the present, or at least try to, if only for a few hours? Sunday came, and the weather was beautiful. This was the only day of the week when we were allowed to visit each other in the dormitories, people forming circles in the yard as soon as they had eaten their soup.

"Make room, you people, for our stride, we are the last of the Goths. Caution, here comes Thespis's cart," Landau exclaimed as the porters hauled tables, setting them up in a rectangle. He tried his best to create a receptive mood in the auditorium. "The walls encircling you are only an illusion." Lon rotated slowly on the heel of his cowboy boot, gesturing pathetically in the direction of the kitchen. "That's Venice for you, Ladies and Gentlemen, the palace of the Doges, San Marco, Cypresses and orange-trees." He pointed to the diaper-colored walls, "only the stage is reality!" His enthusiasm did not catch, the spectators stood in silence. Dago Meyer got up on the tabletop, pulling a little girl up with him.

"Ladies and Gentlemen, applause for our youngest diva, Jeannette Lévi. Number one, Olympia's dance, music by Jacques Offenbach." The ballet shoes and the accordion from the storeroom would surely be crated and sent on the next transport to Germany. Little Jeannette would be going even further, I thought to myself, clapping hard. The following number was a guitar duo by the two Dutchmen, then someone with a cardboard nose recited from Cyrano de Bergerac. After more ballet one of the yard workers told Viennese jokes. As a beauty in a cascade of black curls and pink bows now climbed onto the platform, the newest hit song rose from her lavish décolletage:

"Quand ca va boum, là, là, mon coeur," a song that had traveled from Paris to Brussels, penetrated our yellow walls. With her considerable charm, buoyant rhythm and all the passion she could muster, the young singer managed to carry away her public, hoping perhaps that not even the most hard-boiled of Nazis could send so much loveliness and talent on a transport East. While the guards could not help clapping, the officers leaning in the windows of the casino observed from afar how the Jews amused themselves. Schmitt, Meinshausen and the scarred face of Krull were missing among those looking on from the windows. They were replaced by a newcomer by the name of Frank.

Finally, after much applause we had the high point of the afternoon, Api Bueno de Mesquito dancing with a life-sized doll to the sounds of an accordion. Her head, formed and painted by Lon Landau, was a female caricature of Api. The lady's arms and legs were dangling from a dress of brightly flowered fabric, her hair was elegantly done. Was it a wig that had previously coifed the head of an Orthodox Jewish wife and mother? Most probably. But Api was too funny. Not even this sobering thought kept me from laughing. Dancing a passionate tango with his well-padded double, he tore her away from an imaginary rival, scolded her, slapped her and stroked her tenderly. The prisoners could not get enough of the two.

It was time for the next and last number — Dago Meyer in person. (His stage name was Dago Meybert, though his given name was Dagobert Meyer). Much as I later came to hate the man, I must admit that he had a beautiful voice. It boomed or quivered according to the score — his aria from the Gypsy Baron made the walls wobble. Then for an encore, melting away with longing and pushing the high notes through his nose, he sang "Kennst Du das Land wo die Zitronen blühen?" The prisoners were moved. For a brief time, too brief, they forgot where they were. Even before the applause had died down, a group of young people sang the "Song of Mechelen" (in French) to the tune of a fashionable hit song by the singer Ray Ventura. I do not know who composed the text in which, true to Jewish humor, a prisoner makes fun of his own misfortune.

We are all look-alikes,
A nose, two ears, two eyes,
Because of a small deviation,
Misfortune pursues our nation.

Refrain:
We all have a heart that beats, like everybody,
A stomach, brains and who knows what, like everybody.

The song was repeated, grew louder, more and more voices joined in the refrain — until the guards whistled, "Up, up, to your rooms!" Here is the French original, remembered years later by Evi Fastag-Dobruszkes:

On a les mêmes apparences,
Un nez, deux yeux et deux oreilles,
A cause d'une petite différence,
Un malheur nous est arrivés.

Refrain:
On a tous le coeur qui bat, comme tout le monde,
Un cerveau, un estomac, comme tout le monde.

Sara Yampolsky, sitting for me shortly before she and her brother Simon were deported in summer 1942. Oil. (Museum of Deportation and Resistance, Mechelen.)

PLATE 1

*The Two Seashells
(view of the courtyard
from the painters' work-
shop). My brushes and
two seashells on the
window sill. Oil. Irene
Awret. (Museum of
Deportation and
Resistance, Mechelen)*

PLATE 2

*Till Eulenspiegel, Marionette by Lon
Landau. (Museum of Deportation and
Resistance, Mechelen)*

PLATE 3

Redhaired Girl in a Green Coat. Oil. Irene Awret. (Museum of Deportation and Resistance, Mechelen)

PLATE 4

Playing Cards (the porters' dormitory). Watercolor. Azriel Awret. (Ghetto Fighters' Museum, Naharia, Israel)

PLATE 5

The painter Kopel Simelovitz by Azriel Awret. Watercolor. (Yad Vashem, Jerusalem, Israel)

PLATE 6

Distribution of packages in the snow by Lon Landau. Gouache. (Ghetto Fighters' House Museum, Israel)

PLATE 7

The Train Is Coming! Watercolor. Irene Awret. (Ghetto Fighters' House Museum, Israel)

PLATE 8

Arnold Dobruszkes, the Electrician. Oil. Irene Awret. (Courtesy Evi Fastag-Dobruszkes, Strasbourg, France)

PLATE 9

Napoléon. Watercolor. Irene Awret. (Ghetto Fighters' House Museum, Israel)

PLATE 10

*The youngest brother
Ehrentreu. Oil. Irene
Awret. (Museum of
Deportation and
Resistance, Mechelen)*

PLATE 11

*Pieteke Anger, born in the
camp. Oil. Irene Awret.
(Museum of Deportation and
Resistance, Mechelen)*

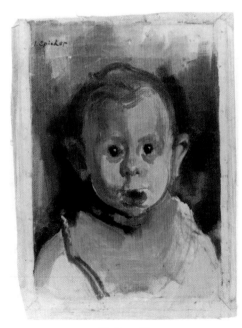

PLATE 12

Thirteen

T HE NEXT DAY WAS AN ORDINARY WEEKDAY. Dago Meyer was no longer singing but roaring through the usual morning exercise. After the breakfast of so-called coffee, I became wholly absorbed in a drawing when the flour-loaded truck rolled into the yard. Like brushfire the news raced from one dormitory to the next. Though tense and apprehensive, I was fixed to the portrait I was working on in order to finish it. My model was one of the Bachmann brothers, an important member of our hierarchy. He managed the store with provisions, under supervision of course. All that was sent by the Judenrat and much of what was taken from the arriving prisoners passed through his hands. He wanted to surprise his fiancée, one of the two nurses at the infirmary, with my drawing.

It's easy for him to sit still, I was thinking as I shaded his nose — he won't be going on a transport. When he later gave me a case with pen and pencil as a way of thanking me, and hinted that the pen was made of gold, I was at a loss for words. Gold is no more than a color, but this was metal, authentic, eighteen carats! Under the circumstances, gold and I seemed like a strange match. I had heard that a few weeks earlier a girl fished a gold watch out of her soup — who knows, perhaps she would have preferred a chunk of meat. Jews had to hide what was left of their valuables wherever they could — it could have been in a bag of semolina or inside a stick of margarine, a tube of toothpaste or a jar of jam. My elegant gift surely originated from a similar source. For Bachmann, coming across gold and gems might have been an everyday occurrence, so much so that it became humdrum.

Nobody had ever given me anything so precious, and yet what was I to do with it when the porters were out in the yard unloading the notorious bags of flour? It meant that I would leave on a cattle train in a day or two, allowed to take with me only the clothes I was wearing. After the first shock of the finality of our situation, the dormitory had fallen silent. Scared by the dejected mood of the grownups even the children made no noise. My neighbors were crouching over farewell letters with a faraway look, hoping they would be able to throw these last messages from the train while still on Belgian soil. Those in need of solid shoes, warm underwear or overalls for their journey into the unknown went to Cerberus, a bitter Jew who watched over a room full of clothes that were too shabby to be forwarded to Germany. Each pair of long johns or woolen socks was dear to him, and only with a coupon made out by Boden personally could one wrest them from him.

My problem was not too few but too much clothing, more than I could take with me. Inspecting the cardboard box with my belongings, all those things my sister sent, I had to decide what to wear and what to leave behind. Two sweaters, one on top of the other, would do fine, so what if my coat would not button up. My old ski pants from Bavaria and the ski boots Gerda put into one of her packages were just what was needed or so I thought. They would never wear out, and I could hide the case with the golden pen inside one trouser leg. If worse came to worse I would barter the pen for bread, for I well understood that it would not be needed to write picture postcards.

What was left was a crêpe-de-Chine dress, reminding me of the days when I was still a young lady of a more or less good family. Who would it fit best, Dina, Minnie or Evi? No answer. I jumped to the next question, namely where should I hide my sketchbook, when Ferdekopf's guttural bass battered my eardrums, then my consciousness. "Seven-hundred thirty-two, down into the yard!" he called. My number. There he stood in the door, waiting for me. No doubt about it, I was number seven hundred thirty-two, it said so on the piece of cardboard on my chest. Having been convinced of that fact, Ferdekopf to the astonishment of my neighbors led me downstairs into the yard. Would they have to pity or to envy me, I wondered fearfully.

A dozen flustered men and women already stood aligned in a row in front of the Reception, waiting for the new Kommandant, Johannes Frank, who now approached, visibly more sober than his predecessor and almost business-like. He held a list in one hand, explaining that those prisoners he was going to call had to hand in their numbers. They would get W-Numbers instead and be assigned to workshops. While I hung a new number around my neck, Frank seemed at a loss as to what workshop to assign me.

"Leather workshop," he said finally. I was perplexed at the whole proceedings and at being singled out. Having kept as far away as possible from our S.S. overlords, from the Kapos and from the guards, I had not asked anyone for the smallest favor; nor was I the kind of person considered worthwhile saving. Who had intervened? My family? Aunt Johanna was dead, Uncle David, my cousins and Cilly deported, Papa and Gerda were penniless immigrants. My friends? They were budding artists and students just beginning to wonder where I might be. That left the Breskoffs, whose flat I had been arrested in, the only ones in my circle with some means. However, they were having troubles of their own with the Gestapo. Who was it? Amazed at my good fortune and intrigued at the same time, I returned to my dormitory to pick up my things.

Farewell under this circumstance was not easy, especially saying goodbye to the children and looking them in the eyes. And what was I to say when my neighbors, the next day to be transported as so much cattle, warmly and in tears embraced and congratulated me? It was not my fault, I kept hammering into my head.

I had to move. Excited though with mixed feelings I reached for my cardboard box and tried to retrieve the golden set hidden under my blanket. The case felt strangely light. I opened it — only the pencil still lay in its velvet bed.

Of course I suspected those who slept next to me. On my left, on the mattress Egon once occupied, a very religious woman moved in, mumbling Hebrew prayers day and night. She never mentioned her family, a sure sign that her husband and children were in hiding, and that she was afraid for them. Nobody was as stupid as I had been, admitting to a father alive in Brussels, but refusing to give his address. No, this woman was not the kind of person to risk God's wrath for a fountain pen. Of that I was certain.

Of the neighbor who moved to my right after Fanny's departure I was not so sure. Like me, a Berliner but not resourceful, he was a gray-haired, mousy little man, unable to adapt. No one in the dormitory seemed to like him and neither did I. He received no parcels, and once I surprised him as he rummaged through my things. A shame about that pretty set, I thought, the golden pen and pencil should remain together. May the schlemiel keep both of them! If only he stopped giving me those scared sideway glances as if he believed I was going to denounce him. I pushed the case with the pencil into his hand, turning away so as not to see an old man blush to the roots of his gray hair.

No two-tiered rabbit hutches in this W-dormitory. I had a real iron bed with a straw mattress, and here, too, it seemed to be the guard's first duty to teach the Jews the rudiments of cleanliness and order. Our sheets had to be pulled as tight as in a school for nurses. My welcome to the world of W-Numbers was just as warm as the goodbye from the transport numbers, though as yet I had no idea how much I would have to rely on my new neighbors. For the next seventeen months I would sleep in this narrow bed between Tilly Sachs from Berlin and Monsieur and Madame Heiber from Brussels, with my feet pointing at Fritz and Trudi Handler from Vienna.

⌒

One day before the transport departed, the camp resembled a wasp's nest in disarray. Only one thing was sure about the approaching journey — it would be very long, and since nobody wanted to arrive in unknown territory with dirty clothes, there was hectic activity in the washroom. Prisoners stood in line in front of the infirmary to secure one last bandage, a small amount of ointment, a few pills or at least a piece of medical advice. The girls from the Reception hurried back and forth carrying lists. Meyer, Voss and Kraus, the Kapos, were running upstairs and downstairs to inform those leaving of all they were not allowed to take with them.

Meanwhile, dozens of crates were hammered shut in the storeroom. Two artists from the painter's workshop were detailing their contents in big black letters on the lids — 438 pocket knives, 223 pairs of scissors, 516 leather belts, 36 fur coats, 17 pairs of silver candlesticks, 862 wrist watches, 118 pocket watches, and no end of shoes and clothing. The most feverish activity, however, reigned in the kitchen, where Mama Goldberg, the dean of the witches' den, and her helpers, prepared travel provisions for the 1400 to be transported.

And where was my place among all those joints and screws that kept the German deportation machine of Belgium busy? It was in the leather workshop. I was good at crocheting and knitting, I sewed some, I could restore old paintings, paint walls and make plaster molds, though with leather I was at a loss. Kid or cowhide, to me it was all the same. The only thing resembling leather I had ever tinkered with was the scroll of imitation parchment paper, which years earlier I had inscribed in Hebrew letters with the Purim story as a wedding present for my cousin Karl.

Arriving at my new place of work, I found only men, hard-working family men, no-nonsense men. These serious faces bent over purses, briefcases and valises, assessed me with looks that said, what are we going to do with her? I was at a loss myself. But since not one of them wanted to have my deportation to Poland on his conscience, they told me to sweep up the scraps of leather and to clean the desks. Once the transport leaves, they may find something else for me to do, a bearded maroquinier (leather worker) said and shrugged his shoulders.

Later, after the workday ended, the mood in my new dormitory was just as gloomy as in the rest of the camp. In twenty-four hours, the barracks would be empty, apart from the workers, the personnel and a handful of B- and E-Numbers. Even Tilly Sachs who had seemed happy to have a neighbor to exchange barbs with, especially in Berlin slang, did not say a word. The Flemings were clumping up and down the stairs, shouting, "Lights out and shut up!" The camp lay black and silent, but who could sleep. Stretched out on my back I saw a few stars through the half-open window. They made me think of the tears that were choked under a thousand blankets.

Not even on holidays did prisoners get a taste of meat. However, before each transport the kitchen workers fried hamburgers into the early morning hours. Under the window of the second floor, I got a whiff of their tempting aroma. In the blacked out kitchen, onions were chopped, bread was soaked and meat was minced all through the night, so that everyone leaving the next day was handed a small package of food including a hamburger.

If I had known the whole story behind those hamburgers, I would have shut the window as fast as I could. I would have loathed the smell of fried onions. Mama Goldberg and her helpers also had no idea that the 1400 hamburgers they were frying would become a death meal. For whatever ominous presentiments we might have had, no one among us had yet heard about a place called Auschwitz. Nobody among us could as yet conceive that all women with children, all the elderly, anyone who did not look as if he could survive long arduous work on hunger rations would be gassed on arrival at the train's destination — the rest to be tormented to death more slowly. Of all those 1400 herded into cattle cars on the morning of the April 19th — the twentieth transport — only 150 would survive Auschwitz.

Though we did not really know what lay ahead, the East boded of disaster — experience had already taught me that it was best to expect the worst. But how did you simply snuff out human lives as though you were blowing out a candle? Years ago in Berlin I felt sickened at hearing the brown shirts singing, "When Jews' blood splashes from the knife, then things go twice as well!" When huge banners spanning the streets read "Judah perish!" When Hitler's hysterical voice screamed and cracked over the airwaves, "And I repeat, international Jewry has to be destroyed." Those words had been degrading enough but we could never have conceived that even a madman meant such outrageous sloganeering literally. That a government in Europe in the twentieth century would systematically organize the mass murder of millions had not yet sunk in. How could it? The idea itself, let alone its execution, still surpasses human powers of comprehension. Consequently it does not exist. To us, hamburgers were still just that. The Gestapo officers knew their significance — only the victims were oblivious to the fact that this would be their last meal, that at the other end of the railway tracks the gas chambers were awaiting them.

The sky was barely turning gray as I heard whispers, "The train, the train is here!" Since all windows faced the yard, the railway tracks were out of sight, though now the train was waiting just beyond the gate. Inside the yard some of the guards stood laughing and chatting with a group of schupos. Even in the semi-darkness of the early morning the schupos' silhouettes could not be mistaken. (Schupo is an abbreviation for Schutzpolizist, the German police.)

"What are they doing here?" I asked with astonishment. "You mean the schupos?" my new neighbor Monsieur Heiber said. "They have come with the train. They always accompany the transports," he explained, while he and his wife hastily got into their clothes. Both of them worked in the children's kitchen and wanted to prepare porridge for babies and toddlers in time for their departure. "On the roofs of each wagon sits a schupo. Anyone who tries to jump is machine-gunned," he added tying his shoelaces and hurrying off.

My childhood memories of schupos were rather pleasant. For a long period I venerated these wearers of green uniforms and their funny shakos (peaked military headdress) — they resembled upturned toilets — as some kind of guardian angels who helped blind people cross the street. True, they were known to sometimes overuse their rubber batons and their warnings to young trespassers in the Tiergarten were not always gentle. However, they never bothered "good children" and if ever I lost my way, the grown-ups had drummed into me, I should walk up to a schupo.

How ironic. Who were the schupos watching over here, who were they protecting the Fatherland from? The dangerous Jews? From all those squeezed into cattle cars behind lock and bolt, who would have to remain standing by stinking buckets, because in the straw covering the floor there was not enough room to sit? Or did they protect the passengers, taking care that all of them to the last baby reached their destination? What went on in the heads of these schupos who were pacing back and forth in front of the gate and cracking jokes?

It was light outside. The courtyard was swarming with porters carting crates and sacks from the storerooms destined for Germany. Throwing their weight about, the officers strutted out of Kommandant Frank's office, Boden and a Gestapo dignitary in front.

"Room number one!" The first group had to line up, all the prisoners with their tags well in evidence, so that names and numbers could be compared to those in the lists. This happened two, three times until our handlers got it right. One more body count and then forward march to the railway track. I recognized a little boy who showed me how to draw a tree with a bird on it — his mother was holding him by the hand. A schupo gave both of them their package of provisions, then they disappeared through the gate. Room number two, number three, number four. The children who just two days earlier had danced ballet in the same yard, the raven-haired beauty who rendered her hit song with so much vivacity and abandon, the dreamy Dutchman composer now without his guitar — neither talent nor charm helped them. They all received their parcel, they all went the same way. On and on the embarkation continued, incessantly and smoothly, groups of one hundred and twenty people disappearing one after another — for good, though we did not yet know that.

In the afternoon, when upwards of eight hundred numbers had been called, the traffic suddenly stopped. The lists had become mixed up — names did not correspond with numbers anymore, numbers not with names. Standing rigid with crossed arms like a tin soldier, the Gestapo boss from Brussels seemed to fix Boden with his icy glance, the latter bearing responsibility for the correctness of the lists. On those days when Max Boden must have imagined himself living in a dream world with a private secretary, he addressed Evi patronizingly in Saxon as "Miss Efa." But now Evi and two other girls working on Boden's lists, running up and down the yard like three shooed hens, were "stupid assholes" and "useless Jew-rabble."

Years later Evi told me what really happened. Though nobody could prove it, she was the one who caused the confusion, interchanging numbers and names. The majority of the mix-ups related to young people who had known each other, having once belonged to Jewish resistance groups. My new neighbor Monsieur Heiber, also Albert Clément the yard worker, Egon, Arnold Dobruszkes the electrician, a young couple from Holland who served the officers in the casino — all were members of underground organizations — were trying to help their comrades break out of the cattle cars once the train was underway. They furnished them with knives, files, small saws and screwdrivers stolen from the workshops and the storehouse, even giving them money so they could make do once they got to a town. In order to place those with the necessary skills to help the others break out of the cars, a trustworthy person was needed in Boden's office. That person was Evi. Her job was to combine names and numbers in such a manner that small groups of potential escapees met in certain cars.

Breaking out was hardly easy. For each wagon, the Nazis appointed one Jew who had to answer for the others and was under the threat of dire consequences if anyone was missing on arrival, dead or alive. This meant that whoever wanted to try to escape first had to persuade the wagon foreman to flee as well. If the foreman refused, a fight would likely follow. Only after the foreman was overpowered would it be possible to file through the iron bars of the tiny window and then bend them open. The opening had to be sufficiently enlarged for a body to get through. Often those about to escape preferred sawing through the floorboards and slipping out between train and track through the bottom of the car. You needed great courage for that kind of escape, for even though the distant end of the tracks loomed dark and sinister, no one knew the whole truth of what was awaiting them there. Few of the prisoners were let into the secrets of the escape network before their actual departure. Trying to live in a world of my own, amidst the gray reality, I had no inkling of organized resistance inside the camp until the day of liberation.

Having typed the lists, Evi needed no end of explanations to convince Boden of her innocence — the plan of the changed numbers proved to be successful. How successful is a story that I will return to.

With the train sitting on the tracks until dark, Boden must finally have resigned himself to faulty lists, the final count being exact despite the deliberately confused numbers. The remaining Jews were hastily loaded, and when the last two dormitories filed into the yard it was night.

"Lights out!" the guards shouted to us. In the morning the compound was completely still, resembling an ugly schoolyard during vacation time. The many doorways, which at regular intervals had spit out long lines of people who were then drawn back as though by magnets at the next whistle blow, had turned into black, empty holes. The children's kitchen had been closed until further notice. Walking to the leather workshop, I racked my brains on what to do there. Were leather leftovers and cardboard available? Could glue and safety pins be found? For the rest I would ask for tubes of oil color from the Judenrat in Brussels. My forced contribution to the German war effort would consist of hand-painted leather brooches, I decided. If I let the maroquiniers work in peace, they would leave me alone, I conjectured, especially since this work required little space at the work tables. A scrap of leather in front, another in the back, a piece of cardboard in between, and the brooch was ready for painting. Nobody but Journée and Ferdekopf, who would peek at my lizards and birds of paradise, took notice of my creations. With the exception of Meyer, that is, who regularly picked the most beautiful among the brooches as a matter of course. But even I grasped that those who wanted to hold on to their W-Numbers had to keep quiet.

Some of the married maroquiniers slept with their wives in the same dormitory as me. Though friendly enough, their permanently troubled looks were caused by worries over their children who they had not seen and of course had no word from — all married couples naturally declared they had no offspring and could not risk speaking about them. One thing was clear to all — though they might craft the most beautiful, elegant pocketbooks and their wives worked hard in the laundry or the tailor shop, nobody was indispensable. The officers, the guards, even Dago Meyer, all loved nothing better than to rub this warning in whenever they could. The need for a few more dozen Jews to fill a train, and one was gone.

Wagschal was the only person in the leather workshop seemingly at ease. Singing and cracking jokes, a bachelor who allowed himself to be carefree, Wagschal was a name that went well with the bald little moon-face and the puppy eyes. Monsieur Wagschal spoke in French, but sang in German the one song he knew, and sang it over and over: "Tell me that you love me, say it's only me, though it is a falsehood, say you adore me. Pain and heartache are the price, to look into your lying eyes, Oh you! the fulfillment of all my desires." Arriving at this point and not knowing how to continue, he would begin again. Was the serenade for me? So inspired, I began to decorate my brooches with sirens and fauns. One morning, as I was trying to reproduce Botticelli's Venus in a shell on a brooch, Journée and Ferdekopf suddenly pushed open the door to the workshop:

"Everybody out, step on it. The Kommandant is waiting." They shoved the last ones out into the yard. Since the departure of the twentieth transport, all officers and guards had been in an even worse mood than usual. You tried to keep clear of them. They did not speak anymore, they barked, and we were about to learn the cause of their temper.

All workers and personnel, about 500 prisoners, we were assembled in the courtyard, motionlessly looking at a wall by the kitchen where a row of large-sized photographs seemed to gaze back at us. Some of them were portraits, the others showed people lying or sitting in oddly contorted poses. Mrs. Fischbein who had slept opposite my bunk stared at me as if I did not exist — she had a black spot on her forehead.

"Have a good look," Boden growled. "That can happen to you too. It happens to all runaways — a hole in the head." I began to understand that all these photographs were of dead bodies, people whom I chatted with only a short time ago in this same place I was standing now.

Had the Nazis shot all of those trying to jump from the train? Not even Evi or Minnie had been able to overhear snatches of conversations on the subject, though to judge from the biting mood of their masters, something with the twentieth transport had gone wrong. Not until those who at first succeeded in escaping from the train but were then caught one by one and brought back to the camp could we patch together what had happened.

On its way to the frontier, the transport was held up by three armed men, all of them young — they had one pistol among them and waved a red-shrouded lantern. The schupos fired from the car roofs, but it was a moonless night and the three managed to break open several of the cattle doors. At first the schupos were shooting in the dark, but soon floodlights lit up the grounds, and a number of the fleeing prisoners were killed or wounded. The wounded were later rearrested in the hospitals — those whom the machine guns had finished off we had seen ad nauseam. Many others dared the jump to freedom after the train was rolling once more toward the frontier. Unfortunately, most would be recaptured over the next sixteen months, up to the liberation of Belgium, and would be brought back to Mechelen. Called "Flitzers" they had to wear a red ribbon at all times around their upper arm and were put on the next transport in a separate car. On arrival in Auschwitz they were driven directly into the gas chambers. We know now that 17 prisoners fled when the three young men opened the cattle train doors, 225 more while it continued rolling toward the German border. Two of those three, though later arrested and tortured, survived the war; the third, a young Jewish physician, was caught for a different exploit and executed.

May 1943. Rain had bleached the photographs on the yellow wall, winds had torn them apart. Almost every day trucks drove into the courtyard, unloading new prisoners — the dormitories were filling up again.

I got used to my routine — exercise, gluing brooches, standing in line for the midday soup, decorating the brooches. After hours, I joined the daily round in the yard. I often spoke with Fanny Kimmel, who worked in the tailor shop and continued to brood over her husband. For Egon, I was like a vapor — I didn't exist — while Dina lately seemed to prefer the company of Sam Levi, a yard worker. Since the episode of the lists, Evi and Minnie went back to the strict regimen and seldom had time to walk in the yard.

The people in my dormitory treated me nicely, especially Madame Rosenberg who with her son glued envelopes in the paper workshop.

From our conversations, she knew that I grew up without a mother and sometimes gave me small gifts of fruit and biscuits from the packages she received. With much tact, she also gave me the advice of an experienced woman and let me know I could confide in her. Having little to confide, I felt no need to let Madame Rosenberg into my intimate world and to a past where Eugene, my friends and even my family were slowly receding into dreams. Surely her interest in me, for which I was grateful, was motivated by the goodness of her heart, but perhaps she would also have liked to awaken in her son some more curiosity about women. However, I was as indifferent to him as he was to me. If he dreamed of anything at all it certainly was not girls. I could imagine his very Jewish looking curly head swaying in his sleep through India on the broad back of a war elephant, or see him absent-mindedly riding a charge against the Tuareg in the Sahara. Madame Rosenberg's son had read so much Karl May in his childhood that life in the barracks did not seem to repulse him. In any event, shortly after our liberation from Mechelen he was recruited by the French Foreign Legion.

What dreams haunted my other neighbors, whom fate and the Nazis had thrown together in this dormitory? Tilly Sachs by day with her dry sense of humor and standing on her sturdy legs was common sense itself — what about at night? Did she dream about her secure job as an accountant in Charlottenburg, about Sunday excursions to Potsdam, eel green with cucumber salad and a large beer with raspberry juice, or did she yearn for the man who never came, the children she would never have?

In the two beds pushed together to the left of mine, whispering often went on until late at night. Monsieur and Madame Heiber had no time for dreams. Before the whistle woke us in the early morning, they were already in the children's kitchen, pouring milk rations to young mothers. Children again gathered in the dormitories of the transport numbers and parents once more dabbed a red liquid on little legs and arms disfigured by impetigo. Except for their nightly whispers, the Heibers were silent people — he was tall and serious with fine, narrow features, she was seemingly more worldly. In Brussels they had neither been so reserved nor so serious. Minnie told me that the Heibers moved in the best society. Monsieur Heiber, a member of the Judenrat until his arrest, had been co-owner of an important cosmetics company, and was reputed to be a patron of the arts and a philanthropist. I later learned that he also belonged to the resistance movement, that in a smaller measure he was continuing this activity inside the camp, that he and his wife had played an important part in hiding Belgium's Jewish children — about all of this Minnie and I were in the dark. We just wondered how he had been able to talk the Nazis into opening a special kitchen for children.

At the time, I simply took the Heibers for a romantically inclined couple. Later I came to understand the meaning of their nightly whispers. In contact with personalities in key positions, they knew more about the destination of the cattle trains than we did. Their information about the "work camps" in the East was perhaps a fraction of the truth; still they knew more than the bits of rumor that passed for real knowledge. What could they do? Disseminating their information among the inmates of the camp would have caused general panic. To be whipped, thrown into punishment cells and sent to Auschwitz to be gassed? Try and organize a rebellion? In a revolt without arms, the first to be killed would have been those young men who maybe had a chance to survive. Inform the transport numbers who were on their way to the tracks about their real destination? Would the most endangered among the prisoners, women, children and the aged be able to survive jumping from a rolling train that was guarded by schupos and machine guns? Only a miracle could have saved them. And yet, the condemned also have a right to the truth.

My neighbors might have gone on non-stop weighing pros and cons, muffling their voices behind their blanket. They could not find a way out because there was none. Apart from a handful of courageous partisans there was no prospect of help from the outside either. The Allies? Sleepy little Mechelen had not yet experienced a single air raid. The only way out was self-help. The Heibers and their confidants decided to let small groups of reliable young people know that they should try and escape from the train at any cost. Provided with primitive tools to break out, they were encouraged to assist others to flee with them. To this end every worker in the camp who knew about these efforts stole tools wherever possible

While the Heibers on my left whispered in the night and Tilly Sachs on my right snored softly, Fritz Handler across from me told jokes every evening after "lights out." Nicknamed "Negus" by inmates and soldiers because of his black, woolly curls, he looked permanently sunburnt even in winter. His wife Trudi in the bed next to his was as delicate and reserved as he was loud and boisterous — she may simply have been weary from working in the laundry all day long. On the other hand, the Negus was one of the most prominent personalities in Mechelen — good-natured, broad-shouldered, he was foreman of the yard workers and the dormitory elder as well who meted out our soup. Taken together, however, all these attributes were eclipsed by his phenomenal memory for dirty jokes. Tilly Sachs with her Berliner's sassiness, even sarcasm, was an innocent compared to him. If my memory does not deceive me, every evening at bedtime he told at least half a dozen inane, smutty stories — more than two thousand jokes that came to an end on our liberation. Perhaps I exaggerate, since on some nights he was in no mood for fun or was tired. That still leaves at least a thousand jokes. Where are the inventors of a thousand such stories? In which of its nooks and crannies did a human brain store a thousand bad jokes? And yet, of all those jokes, I cannot recall a single one. For me, and maybe for most of us who listened, the Negus' jokes became a cycle of lullabies, the "Viennese Cradle-songs from the Semmering."

F o u r t e e n

I WAS NOW MAKING BROOCHES EVERYDAY. Perhaps it was during the fourth week that Kommandant Frank appeared in the doorway, followed by Boden and a man in civilian clothes, someone from the Gestapo to judge by his raincoat and slouch hat.

"An inspection from Brussels," one of the workers whispered. Everyone stiffened, suddenly and wholly absorbed in work — I too was bent low, gluing pins to the backs of leather brooches.

"How many attaché cases a week can you produce?" the visitor asked both Mr. Karwasser and Mr. Wagschal in an ordinary, businesslike manner, as he passed behind the rows of tables to better examine the work. I knew this voice, I had heard it before, hollow and without timbre. Casting a sidelong glance, I recognized Erdmann, the Gestapo officer who had asked me all those questions in the Gestapo cave of the Avenue Louise. The same one who then had given orders to keep me shut up in a janitor's closet until I would tell him where my father was. I never understood why, after a few hours of confinement, I had been loaded on the truck to Mechelen with all the others. No interrogation, no torture. That I arrived at the camp uninjured and in one piece had seemed like some kind of an oversight. But oversight or guardian angel, if that man recognized me I was lost. Miracles do not happen twice in one month and even though I was wearing a gray smock and turned my back to him, I was not invisible. Paralyzed by fear, I remained bent over my work, feeling like a mouse that found itself beside a cobra.

"If I had wanted to, I could have found out where your father is," said the hollow voice directly behind me. And though my heart was racing I had to turn and look up. Suddenly all became clear to me. It was as if scales had fallen from my eyes. It was he, this stranger with the sallow face under the slouch hat, the Angel of Death from the Avenue Louise and Chief of Security of the Gestapo for all of Belgium, who had saved me from the transport to Poland. Without another word, Erdmann passed on. I shuddered, yet I felt relief. When I summoned enough energy to continue gluing my pins, the three men closed the door behind them.

"If I had wanted to, I could have found where your father is." For the remainder of the day and most of the night Erdmann's words were ringing in my mind. Maybe he was right, maybe he could have gotten it out of me.

"I will not tell you," I had answered in the Gestapo cellar when he asked me for my father's address. Though not intended that way my words must have sounded like a provocation. They had simply slipped off my tongue. What I had really meant was, "How can I betray my own father?" So that Papa would disappear without a trace like Uncle David? At this point Erdmann should have delivered me into the hands of his specialists. If a good beating was not enough to make me speak, then they had other means. Would I still have refused to give that address? I will never know. Instead Erdmann, Himmler's zealous lackey, whose job as Chief of the Jewish section of the Gestapo was to "clean" Belgium of all its Jews, had treated me like a rebellious child, shutting me into a broom closet only to let me go a while later. Letting me go meant imprisonment in Mechelen but protection from deportation. Where was the key to this puzzling cat and mouse game? Probably in my sketchbook. Leafing through it, coming upon the drawing of my left hand, Erdmann had suddenly stopped to question me about my father.

"Did you do that? Let's see, show me your hand. Where are you from? Where did you study?" Harmless questions I could answer in a straightforward manner. Did the linear shading of my drawing remind him of old German masters? Did he wonder if Dürer had been resurrected in a girl, let alone one of the despised Jewish race? Or did he think that only great and irrepressible talent could have driven someone in my condition in a naked cell with bloodstains on the walls to draw her hand. In truth it was fear that drove my concentration, something, anything to deflect my thoughts from the impending interrogation. "Ars nemo odit nisi ignarus" reads the inscription above the entrance to the Kaiser Friedrich Museum in Berlin, and in Dr. Bart's class I had learned enough Latin to understand its meaning — "Only the ignorant hate the arts." It must be an ironic fact that this brutish Nazi saved my life because of a small drawing.

Erdmann's own hand reached still further. After the encounter in the leather workshop, I spent an uneasy night. Not even the Negus's bad jokes could lull me to sleep. The morning was foggy, raindrops drizzled on the few rows of inmates forming ranks for exercise — even Dago Meyer bellowed his commands half-heartedly. Bound in a ponytail, my hair swung more limp than usual as I yawned through the movements. Damp with rain and perspiration, I returned to my brooches, having no idea the gray frame of my days had somewhat brightened. Once more my life was to take a new turn. Once more Erdmann stood in the wings as though waving from afar. I was ordered to Frank's office. Dina's rumors about changes at the top had proven correct and her most ardent wish fulfilled — Major Schmitt, Meinshausen and their cohorts had been sacked. Though I will write more about this story later, for the moment I was being questioned by the new Kommandant.

" W-526?"
"Yes, Sir Storm-troop leader."
"Do you know how to decorate walls?"
"Yes, Sir Storm-troop leader."
"All right, come along."

Looking me over without much conviction, Frank got up from his desk to lead the way to the casino. It had little in common with the plush and luxurious gambling dens that Dostoevsky and other Russian writers evoked in their novels. In the center of a room smelling of stale cigarette smoke and beer stood a conference table. The only other furnishings apart from some armchairs were gold-framed photographs of Hitler and Himmler who were staring into dirty coffee cups. The aroma of melted butter seemed to confirm the stories Minnie and Evi had told me.

Among the things taken from new arrivals were their rationing cards that included monthly stamps for butter. Supposing each Belgian citizen was allowed a half-pound monthly — based on the number of prisoners brought in, that might have added up to fifty pounds for the camp's S.S. officers. So their meals abounded in French fries prepared in a huge pot of melted butter. After Boden's greyhound had run away and then returned in a pitifully emaciated condition, Boden nursed him with steaks broiled in butter. It is such details of memory that still astonish me — we were overjoyed with a small pat of margarine that we sometimes received with our bread rations.

<hr />

"Look, here you have walls." Frank's square index finger pointed in four directions. Indeed, but what was I going to do with Hitler and Himmler hanging on one of them, I asked myself.

"Make some nice sketches, something that is suitable for our casino. I will give you some time," he added in an almost friendly manner. "Take your stuff and report to the painter's workshop (Malerstube in German). That's your place of work from now on, and don't let me hear any complaints. Understood?"

"Yes, Sir Storm-troop commander." Deprived of my freedom, degraded and in constant danger of transport to some ominous place in the East — at this instant I felt as Michelangelo might have when the Pope commissioned him to do the frescoes for the Sistine Chapel. Thinking about the theme for my wall paintings, I went to say farewell to the leather workshop. I did not think that anybody apart from Mr. Wagschal with the faithful pooch eyes regretted my departure. So carrying the oil colors and brushes sent me by the Judenrat, I set off for unknown territory on the second floor left of the gate, the painter's workshop. I found a small room with one window, gray-green oil color peeling from the walls, the furniture consisting of a rickety office cabinet, a desk, a bench, a stool and an electric bulb. Though a far cry from the studio in the Latin Quarter I had been dreaming of, the little room promised the privacy, the refuge I was yearning for after months in a ward of concentrated humanity.

The two men staring at me from the bench behind the desk looked familiar. I had noticed them in the yard, but as they always wore the overalls of heavy laborers, the thought that they might be artists never crossed my mind. They were both sculptors. Baron Herbert von Ledermann Wartberg, the taller one with the nonchalantly sagging shoulders, introduced himself. The other was simply Awret. Having until a short time ago passed for a baroness myself, nobility conferred by a false identity card did not impress me. Here, however, I was confronted with a real baron with long teeth yellowed by tobacco and the airs of a true blasé. With a sniff of his aristocratic nose he pointed to the stool.

"There is not enough work here for three," he grumbled, walking out of the room as if in that instant my specific weight had displaced his lebensraum. Was he so petty or simply superstitious? Maybe he imagined himself in a boat on the high seas, and here I came, a female, a bad omen. More probably he just feared for his place of work and for his W-Number. As if that kind of reasoning mattered in a place where the only thing you could count on was chance. The Gestapo made its decisions at random — one Jew more or less in the painter's workshop was of no consequence. To be or not to be, or at least to be for the time being, was in the last resort a question of pure luck. Awret was the younger of my two new colleagues and seemed to look at life the way I did, preferably at the lighter side. On the contrary, he did not give the impression of feeling threatened by my presence. Pulling a funny face as if to say, "don't take that fellow seriously," he made room for me on the bench beside him.

"Irene, I understand you are a painter. It would be a great help if you could lend me a hand," Awret said. "We have to deliver fifty-eight new numbers tomorrow morning. I'll make the outlines and you fill them in with Indian ink," he added, pointing to the sheet of cardboard that he was cutting into rectangles. "Numbers three-hundred ninety-two to four hundred fifty. All transport numbers. More arrests." He drew me to the window to look down on a truckload of prisoners coming to a halt in front of the Reception. "Not the most pleasant occupation in the world making these dog-tags," he sat down again. "Would you rather draw or paint? I will give you paper. I can do these numbers by myself if necessary."

How could I not want to help someone who was so nice to me? As I cut cardboard, perforated and drew strings through the holes, Awret explained my new job. It consisted of making numbers for the prisoners, painting signs and labeling linen bands the various workers had to wear around their upper arms.

The guards did not often come to our wing and from now on working in the painter's workshop, I had more time to myself. Remembering *Candide*, the book Serge Breskoff had given me in Brussels, I mocked myself, "Eh bien, Doctor Pangloss, Est-ce que tout n'est pas pour le mieux dans le meilleur des mondes possibles?" (Isn't everything for the best in this best of all possible worlds?) More seriously I asked myself how much longer my luck would hold. Without even raising a finger, I had landed one of the best jobs in the camp.

All day Awret and I painted numbers. As neat as print, I commended myself and admired my teacher. The baron, who from time to time opened the door a crack to show his aristocratic nose, condescended at last to watch us work. He went still farther. When we had an evening snack together he raised his mug of ersatz coffee to drink Brüderschaft, brotherly friendship, with me. Never before had I smoked but here tobacco was a treasure that passed for currency, and so I felt duty bound to share a fag end with the men for dessert. We discussed my idea for the casino walls, which I believed to be very original — to decorate them with allegories of the four seasons. Later the baron, whom we sometimes referred to as Herbertchen, pulled an envelope with photos and newspaper reviews of his work out of the wobbling cabinet. Apart from a few "ahs" and "ohs," I could not bring a word to my lips — on the one hand because I did not like the sculptures, on

Prisoners taken from a truck are shoved into the Reception by a guard. Left foreground, Boden and Frank; right, Dr. Gleis, Parnes and a medic. (Muséee Juif de Belgique, Brussels)

Supplies are unloaded in the courtyard. Pencil drawing. Irene Awret. (Ghetto Fighters' House Museum, Israel)

In the Dormi-
tory. Pencil draw-
ing from my
sketchbook.
(Ghetto Fighters'
House Museum,
Israel)

In the Dormitory. Pen and ink from my sketchbook. (Ghetto Fighters' House
Museum, Israel)

Prisoners wore numbers around their necks; it is such numbers that Awret and I painted. The transport fate of prisoners wearing an E (Entscheidung, decision) was yet to be decided because Jewish identity had not been established. (Jewish Museum of Deportation and Resistance, Mechelen, Belgium)

Z stood for Zigeuner, Gypsy. (Jewish Museum of Deportation and Resistance, Mechelen, Belgium)

the other because my astonishment over the celebrity of his models left me speechless. All the royal houses of Europe were represented by their busts: a son and daughter-in-law of the Kaiser (God rest his soul), the Prince of Monaco's wife, King Carol of Rumania and family and even the Pope. According to the reviews, I was in the presence of genius. Herbert von Ledermann Wartberg, it was written, is the greatest European sculptor of the first half of our century. Never having seen any of the people he had sculpted, it could well be that his sculptures resembled their subjects. The Pope, for instance, stared at me out of pupils bored into his bronze eyes and through a pair of funny wire glasses. Then as now, he did so coldly, as in reality, with the indifference he showed toward our people and their fate. That was not an easy achievement, I thought of Herbert with some cynicism, to make such mawkish portraits out of bronze. The Holy Father and all the majesties in the baron's folder left me with the same kind of saccharine aftertaste, as did our coffee. Awret, who knew the photographs, smiled at me, looked deep into the Pope's bored out eyes, then gave me a little wink. We were on the same wavelength.

Two minutes before the guards shouted "lights out!" I arrived breathlessly in my quarters. When I told my neighbors about my initiation into the Mechelen bohême, Mrs. Rosenberg smiled indulgently. From the other side, Tilly wagged a finger. "I can see it coming Irene. Don't let them soft-soap you. If you get in the family way, you go on transport faster than you can count to three." Meanwhile the Heibers were whispering, and the Negus was telling his dirty jokes.

It was a warm June night. Lying on my straw mattress below the window I tried to visualize the plaster casts that I remembered from the lobby of the academy, Michelangelo's marble statues from the Medici Chapel in Florence. The Morning, the Day, the Evening and the Night, divine and timelessly leaning on their white arms, appeared before my closed eyes, bringing some calm and quiet to my mixed-up mind. And then I saw the casino. On the left wall Spring lay behind a flower garland; on the right Autumn leaned on a basket with grapes, apples and pears; between them Summer ate cherries, strawberries and peaches. How was I going to paint all those fruits from memory when

I could not even recall what they tasted like? On the wall with Hitler and Himmler I would paint Winter. And what was Winter holding in his hands, and what in God's name was I to do with the framed Führer? I fell asleep without having resolved the problem.

On normal days you would find time for painting, Awret had said, but normal days were rare. Constant change was seemingly the law in our restricted little world of the subhumans, the Untermenschen, which I now found myself in. The painters' workshop, this salon des artistes, was a molehill. I had plenty of new friends — my circle once more had been turned inside out and here among all the excommunicated, I felt at last that I belonged.

Dina might as well have been engaged to Sam Levi, the courtyard worker, and moved in a more bourgeois environment than I did lately. Fanny Kimmel was unexpectedly set free as a Belgian citizen. Since the sinister disappearance of Klara Sander and Edith Silberman — they had worked hand-in-hand with Evi at the Reception — Evi seemed troubled, worked for three people, and only rarely found a moment to take a breath of air in the afternoon. Nobody noticed when Klara and Edith had been taken away — one morning they were simply gone and with them Doctor Basch, the camp physician, together with Wolf the medic. It turned out that all four had been thrown separately into confinement, and weeks later they were still imprisoned. I had taken Dina's stories about Klara and Edith for gossip — I now knew she had been right.

It was hard to believe but true that the former leaders of the camp, Major Otto Schmitt the butcher, Kommandant Steckmann, Meinshausen and Krull had vanished even earlier. The reason, we later learned, was they had made common cause with Jewish prisoners. It was rumored that the four Gestapo officers used Jews from Brussels to sell a good part of the wares produced in the camp, and destined for the Fatherland, for their own profit. Basch and Wolf had been implicated as middlemen. On the other hand, while Edith and Klara were so efficient that they seemed indispensable, they had the misfortune of having affairs with the doctor and his medic. No matter how and where people live together, a class system forms itself and gossip becomes its currency. Even in our oppressed little society without newspapers or radio, the camp doctor, the medic and the secretaries of the Gestapo officers belonged to the aristocracy. Until they were caught, the families of Basch and Wolf had been protected from arrest and deportation. They were now hauled into the barracks to be sent on the next transport. Together with their wives and children, the two men and their mistresses would all be "reunited" in the same cattle car marked "for special treatment" on their arrival in Auschwitz.

Shortly before the twentieth transport, when Schmitt, Meinshausen, Steckmann and Krull suddenly disappeared, the prisoners felt some relief. Just some. If Kommandant Frank was less of a drunkard and not as sadistic as the Major, he did not rule with velvet gloves either. One had to be careful. While I could temporarily escape the reality of the yard in the painter's workshop, life between the yellow walls was mirrored in the window. How absurd that I sat here painting numbers for the prisoners, taking pride in the fact that they looked like print. Was I still right in the head? Here I was drawing a seventeen-year-old with beautiful blonde locks for my "Spring" — down in the courtyard two Gestapo were leading a pretty red-haired girl away for interrogation. I had long since finished my drawing when the two men dragged her back to the cell. She could not stand upright anymore, and if not for the red hair, I wouldn't have recognized her. A cold chill crept up my back. The same thing could have happened to me. Similar interrogations of Jews suspected of belonging to a resistance movement or believed to have information were conducted regularly. Cruelly as these young people were tortured they rarely talked.

The painter's workshop had many visitors. Meyer came in and out, curious children opened the door. We told them stories and while I sketched, Awret amused them with little conjuring tricks. I could even paint them in oils since the Judenrat had sent me colors and canvas.

One of our more frequent visitors was Lon Landau, the stage designer who drew and painted at least as well as I did. Before the last transport in May, he and Meyer made it possible to put on a variety program in the yard. We placed our sparse material at his disposal, but then at certain times he suddenly disappeared. Where did he go? What was so urgent for a B-Number? I asked him outright. At first he did not want to come out with it, he did not want to say that part of the day he took care of the old and the very young in his dormitory. I was unaware of his affiliation with the Communist party, and that he and his comrades were members of various resistance groups who were secretly working together and trying to help wherever possible. A wiry, short man, he had a powerful nose, a meager mane of brown hair and was always wearing top boots and an old corduroy jacket — he was the only one among us who looked like an artist. Landau brought life into the place. Evenings in our workshop sizzled with heated discussions about art, history and the history of art. For hours on end, we argued over a name, a date, a concept, until the guards whistled "lights out!" Did Leonardo paint his "Last Supper" on a Milano church wall in oils or was it a fresco? Who invented cubism, Braque? Picasso? Or perhaps the Russian modernists? And since we could not find either an encyclopedia or a dictionary in all of the barracks, we finally returned to our bunks in agitated states of mind, each of us convinced we were right. With the pride of ownership, Landau liked to make fun of his nose: "When I shall die one day, they will write on my gravestone, Ci gît le nez de Lon Landau, un mètre plus bas son propriétaire." (Here rests Lon Landau's nose, one meter below its owner.) Fifteen months later he would be buried in a mass grave at Bergen-Belsen without a marker.

Landau, like Awret, was in his early thirties. An older artist also joined sometimes, shyly sitting on the edge of our bench. He talked little and painted delicate, small watercolors, dreamlike memories of Palestine — blooming meadows where almond-eyed children played with young horses and cypresses swayed over flooded fields. I had imagined Palestine differently, rather like in the ballad I learned long ago in Miss Vogel's class of Kaiser Barbarossa arriving in the Holy Land on horseback. "The Knights from hunger were half-dead, stones there were but little bread." However, Kopel Simelovitz certainly did not just dream up his landscapes. He and Landau had lived in Palestine for a long time. They returned to Europe because they had come down with malaria.

Like all painters I knew, Kopel loved to cook. Since there was no way to prepare tasty dishes with the little that we had, he conjured them up. Having led the modest existence of a member of the artist's colony of Lathem Saint Martin, his recipes were so original and so within everybody's means that I still remember some.

"The best soup in the world is made with the lower part of chicken legs, twelve to fifteen — they're free, the butcher is glad to get rid of them. Naturally one has to first scald them, peal the skin and chop off the claws, then add herbs, salt and pepper. Once cooled, the broth is so strong you can tip the pot over and use it as a mold. That soup you have to cut with a knife." Punished by Frank with a parcel embargo, we were listening hungrily to Kopel's description of his soup. Reverently thinking of chicken broth, we were spooning up our mid-day slush when the baron, who was sagged over his tin bowl in elegant indolence, suddenly sat up.

"Damn!" he cursed, in an uncustomary language for one so well brought up, and removed a razor blade from his spoon. One of the compensations of embargoes — contents of confiscated packages were thrown indiscriminately into our soup. It could become a little tastier, even richer. I mean this literally. Together with a chunk of rutabagas you could have spooned up a soft-boiled banknote, or broken a tooth on a diamond or found a rasp at the bottom of the bowl. Someone not so lucky would have seen the limp legs of a cockroach dangling from his spoon.

~

The baron had barely recovered from his shock, when Meyer arrived with a commission. Frank had ordered him to make a bust of Dago Meyer's head. Why? Maybe the Kommandant wanted to see if it was worthwhile for a pure German like himself to be immortalized by the hands of a Jew.

That our workshop was too small for such an undertaking did not hold back Dago Meyer. He had the door to the next room broken down, so that we now had a real studio. The Judenrat furnished the clay, and with leftover wood from the carpentry workshop, Awret cobbled together a modeling table. Now finally the baron could show his talent. We never complained when he looksed on while we were working, giving paternal advice, only busying himself when the guards made their rounds. Painting numbers and signs was not for the likes of an artist who had made portraits of the Pope and royal heads of state.

The great day arrived. Imagining himself on stage no doubt, Meyer planted himself straddle-legged and took a deep breath to expand his chest. The baron slapped clay on the table: bang, bang, bang. Not to interfere with Herbert's inspiration, Awret and I retreated discreetly into the old part of the workshop where all we heard from the adjoining room for the next hour or so was the slapping of wet clay. When Meyer was called away to do some shouting in the yard, we went to have a look at Herbert's work. What had emerged from under the baron's slender fingers was a big pile of clay with a nose and two ears.

"It does not yet resemble Meyer," Herbert said to Awret, extending his clay-soiled hands. Tactfully silent, Awret first of all gave the mass the shape of a head.

"Look here, Herbert," he stuck a bit of clay below the nose, "Meyer's upper jaw protrudes, his nose is fleshy, and so are the lips." Awret padded the brows into a bulge, and added two furrows above the root of the nose that gave the hint of a threat. The opera singing Kapo began to emerge from the wet clay and was ready to be swathed in wet rags until the next sitting.

From that day on, the three of us never mentioned Herbert's manila envelope or his artistic past. One thing had become clear — the work in the photographs was not the baron's. He could not even have made those melted looking bronze highnesses.

The next morning was a repetition of the previous day. Awret and I painted numbers, the baron toiled at his creation — at the end of two hours Meyer called us to compare the sculpture's likeness to him. But there was none. Earth to earth, dust to dust, Meyer had reverted to clay.

Saying little, Awret waited for him to leave, then once more brought his head into being. After the third session, Awret's patience was gone. "Herbert, if you destroy what I have done once more, you will have to finish Meyer by yourself." He spit on a bit of clay, softening it to form an eyelid. Next he wet a bigger lump, padding the mandibles to get at Meyer's resemblance to a well-fed tomcat. "Do me a favor," he said to the baron, "when Meyer poses tomorrow, make believe that you are working. And if you absolutely have to do something, then do the hair." In this way Meyer's bust was completed, and Awret cast it in plaster.

Even though I had finished the designs for my wall paintings, all but the problematic "Winter," the Kommandant seemed to have lost interest. "Spring," "Summer" and "Autumn" were resting in grandiose poses on sheets of paper the Judenrat provided. Lon Landau, who as a stage designer was experienced in drapery, used a red pencil to correct the faults in my folds. Frank's decision to leave the casino walls bare may have stemmed from the Nazi's recent defeats on all fronts.

We had heard of the German defeat at Kursk from Arnold. As an electrician, he was charged with maintaining the garrison's radio sets and was often able to keep us informed about the war situation. First North Africa, then Stalingrad, now Kursk. (More than a year was to pass before Begium would be liberated.) With two souls warring in his breast — patriotism and opportunism — Frank may have convinced himself that in case of emergency wall paintings did not lend themselves to being carried back to the Fatherland. So in place of murals or busts he now wanted portrait paintings. If need be, they could be packed in a suitcase.

The Kommandant would never model for a Jew, so Awret was to do his portrait from a photograph. I was to paint his mistress from nature. Awret had little difficulty in rendering Frank's coarse features, his pug nose, his sly little red-rimmed eyes, though he had to be careful not to render them too realistically. My assignment was easier. While Frank's lover Lillian was not a beauty, she was not ugly. Half-British, she knew how to conduct herself. Dressed in the colorful summer dress that Mrs. Hamburger made for her in the tailor's workshop, she sat stiff as

Azriel Awret at work. Pencil drawing I did in the painters' workshop. (Ghetto Fighters' House Museum, Israel)

Artist Lon Landau. Charcoal drawing. Irene Awret. (Ghetto Fighters' House Museum, Israel)

Baron Herbert von Ledermann Wartberg. Pencil drawing. Irene Awret. (Ghetto Fighters' House Museum, Israel)

Painter Klaus Grunewald. Pencil drawing. Irene Awret. (Ghetto Fighters' House Museum, Israel)

Drawing of an inmate by Lon Landau. Pencil. (Ghetto Fighters' House Museum, Israel)

Drawing of an inmate by Lon Landau. Pencil. (Ghetto Fighters' House Museum, Israel)

a poker, obediently smiling whenever I asked her to do so. Our sovereigns were so well satisfied with their portraits they rewarded each of us with a pack of cigarettes.

Followed by a group of visiting S.S. officers, Frank opened the door to our workshop, a circus owner showing off his wise monkeys: "And here are our artists!" Embarrassed, with patronizing smiles on their faces our sworn enemies treaded lightly in their polished boots — I didn't know if they had to remember not to click their heels or greet us with "Heil Hitler!"

The days passed, some grotesque and repulsive, others warm with friendship. Among the new arrivals one morning was my cousin's wife, Lina Spicker, the only one of Uncle David's shattered family who had still held out in Brussels. With one of my numbers around her neck, she now walked every afternoon by my side in the yard, resigned to following her husband, her father, brother and sister-in-law to where people disappeared and were not heard from again. She did not even ask me to find a job that could prevent her deportation. Not because she hoped to find her husband at the other end of the railway tracks — she was not as naive as Fanny Kimmel. Rather because she felt that as the youngest in the family it fell on her to draw the final line. It seems ironic that her husband, by then a broken man, would survive the war, the only one of this branch of the family. He survived half a dozen concentration camps, a serious injury working as a lumberjack, and pulled through typhus and many other sicknesses and hardships. His wife Lina did not come back.

Toward the end of July the barracks were almost more crammed, if possible, than before the twentieth transport. Lina would stay only a few weeks before departing on transport, though she was there long enough to witness a particularly ugly day. It happened shortly before the great truck with its load of flour drove through the gate.

A young prisoner had tried to escape over the rooftops. He did not get far and when they brought him back he was limping and in bad shape. Of course the Gestapo announced a parcel embargo, after which more than a thousand transport numbers were ordered to assemble in the yard, forming ranks in a half circle. Unlike the former

Kommandant, Major Schmitt, Frank preferred leaving physical punishment to Boden. A designer with the most sinister imagination could not have produced a more ominous setting than the weather on that afternoon.

The darkness of the thunderclouds was so pervasive that in the workshop I had to stand by the window to see what I was drawing. I had been imprisoned seven months and there had been almost unremitting dreariness — the sky now, rather the patch of firmament that the yellow walls allowed, was a spectacular canvas. Above sheets of rain hanging over the barracks, thunder clouds reared their indigo, lilac and sulfur yellow crowns zigzagging as high as our narrow skyline allowed. The harsh glare of a shaft of light seared through the clouds and illuminated the corner of the building from where Boden now entered. The rest of the courtyard with its thousand Jews lay in deep, brown shadows.

Sometimes on warm summer days when all the windows were open, we could hear the voices of Hitler or Goebbels blaring from the radio in the casino. The word "Jew" figured prominently in every second sentence or so it seemed. What if we were as powerful and evil as we were made out to be, would we be imprisoned here! On this summer afternoon I was concentrating on the sky and my drawing, listening not to Hitler or Goebbels but to an orchestra playing the "Song of the Monastery." I knew the music well because my piano teacher Miss Becker used to play it for me as a reward on the rare occasions when I had practiced to her satisfaction.

"Ah, the Tango of the Ministry. That's beautiful, isn't it?" The guard who we referred to as "Moishe Baby" because of his youth wanted to impress me with his artistic taste and the fact that he had finished high school. That he had joined the Belgian S.S. and worked in a concentration camp he justified with his idealism.

"Here he is now, that flitzer, the guy who tried to get away — it's going to be interesting," he said, looking through the window, probably wondering what I found to draw in a black sky. Then he left.

Down in the yard Journée and Ferdekopf were coming from the lockup, leading the unfortunate fugitive between them. Though limping, he kept himself proudly erect as he was brought face-to-face with Boden. The radio, meanwhile, had changed to the first measured beats of Liszt's "Hungarian Symphony," a last sunbeam trembled on the roof that the prisoner had attempted his escape over. Guarded by machine-guns the Jews stood in silence. The music swelled and seemed to grow more agitated, its rhythm becoming so furious that only snippets of Boden's sneers and threats were carried to the window where I stood drawing. But when I heard the whip, it became impossible to ignore. I could draw no longer. At first the whip twitched over the poor fellow's legs, soon it aimed at his torso, and when the Jew still uttered no sound, smacked his neck. The crowd stood mute, only wild czardas rhythms and clapping filled my ears. When Boden at last released his victim, I did not understand how he could still set one foot in front of the other. From my window I was fortunately unable to see him clearly. The forced witnesses in the courtyard tried to avert their faces as they silently disappeared into the stairwells. Someone closed the windows of the casino, cutting short the rest of the "Hungarian Symphony," and I wished the storm would finally break. But amid thunder brewing in the distance only a few thick raindrops fell from all that splendor. The sun set, and a gray curtain rolled down over this day.

Fifteen

———

"ON TOP OF EVERYTHING you are now talking in your sleep, Irene," I heard Tilly's voice as if through a filter of cotton wool. "Nice and airy here under the window, you know, but you'll be moon-struck and start walking in your sleep. I rubbed my eyes. I had slept through the wake-up whistle. Tilly was combing her hair. Madame Rosenberg was already dressed and bending down whispering into my ear, "Do you know, child, what you just said? 'I love you terribly.' " Smiling, she wagged her finger at me. "Must have been a real fancy dream," Tilly said dryly, pulling the comb through gray-flecked hair. "And who's the fellow you love so terribly? I've warned you once, Irene — all artists are Don Juans. Don't come to me mooning and moaning."

"Dreams are nonsense," I cut Tilly off in German, shrugging my shoulders in the direction of Madame Rosenberg, who knew only French. I put my shoes on to go down to the washroom. "I love you terribly." How embarrassing. Why did my subconscious say something I would never have said awake, and in such a lousy French?

Who was the dream about? Not Eugene I hoped. Sitting in a London suburb, he probably no longer asked himself where I might be. After five years of one-sided faithfulness my fervent longing had by now cooled down. Still I often thought of him at work, having given him my word to draw from nature for at least a quarter of an hour every day, no matter what.

Whom did I moon over in such silly French I asked myself splashing water on my face to cool off. Already this early there was a foreshadowing of how this August heat would make the barracks stifling hot by this afternoon. The washroom door opened a crack and Ferdekopf's broad nose and black kepi became visible. While Dina shielded me with her floor rag, she went on raving, as she did every morning, about her wonderful boyfriend Sam Levi, the yard worker. Rubbing myself down without soap, I could not get Lon Landau's words out of my mind. "I am like a predator," he said proudly in the course of one of our conversations. "I will not mate in a cage."

Much as I was impressed by his comparing himself to a predator, I concluded nevertheless that I belonged to a different genus, of domestic animals perhaps. I was indeed in love, but I didn't know it yet. I was so busy in the painters' workshop I barely had time to breathe. Not that we had so many "numbers" to produce — Jews were no longer caught so easily — but because Meyer had developed an insatiable appetite for my paintings. He proposed to send my father, who was still in hiding and probably hungrier than I was, a food package in return for each of my paintings. My friends said that the parcels would never materialize, but warned me to do as I was told. Meyer apparently had no scruples and was thought to volunteer information about the inmates to the Gestapo officers. He would maneuver to have me put on the next transport if I crossed him.

And so I kept working. I painted carrots, onions and my tin bowl, all before a background of empty bottles; also more elegant still lifes: a jar of jam and a stoneware pot with and without my brushes in it, the grouping flanked by two sea shells and mirrored in the window. Minnie saved the two shells from a basket with goods the Nazis saw as too worthless to be shipped to Germany. The two shells and I have not been separated since then — once the inhabitants of foamy waves breaking on clean bright sand, they now sat on the smeared windowsill of our workshop, radiant and unearthly. To this day I can only wonder who brought them into captivity.

Meyer actually sent my father a parcel for the first of my paintings, apparently believing that in this way he kept up his side of the bargain for all those to follow. (My father was still living in the tiny room where I stayed before I went into hiding on the farm on Rue du Luxembourg.

I either gave Meyer his address without fear that he would squeal, or else I gave him my sister's address, which was legal.) For my part, I had to shut up and just continue painting — a little girl holding a shell against her ear, a blond curly-head in wooden clogs. I then painted a red-haired girl with pale skin and impetigo in a green coat. I was allowed to keep the redhead, which looked too sad for Meyer's taste. How could I suspect these good-natured children who posed so nicely for me would choke to death in the gas chambers of Auschwitz? Despite our foreboding, such a concept had not yet entered anyone's mind.

Hélène Koen worked in our studio temporarily and spoke of her husband who had implored her to be careful. "Even if they command you to scour the floor with your toothbrush you must obey without a peep!" Although her hands were red and rough from scouring, she sat skillfully cutting out a tiny costume for a marionette that was to be part of the puppet theater the Kommandant had authorized Landau to build for the children in the camp. Holding pins between her lips, Hélène mumbled, "Everyone envies my husband and me our jobs in the tailor shop. You ought to see his back — just before Meinhausen was sent to the Russian front, he still had time to dog-whip him for not saluting. The leather thong cut so deeply into his back that he was spitting blood and it's still not healing." Hélène pulled a few pins from between her lips and fastened a collar on the marionette, which represented Till Eulenspiegel, a mischievous figure of Flemish folklore. Her clear face never wore a smile, not at the grinning puppet in her arms or at my painting. "A nursing mother? Is such a sight in these surroundings not sad enough, why do you have to paint it?" she asked, "What for, for whom?"

More than for Meyer's sake, soft gray eyes, sandy hair, a rosy baby and the young mother's protective warmth attracted me — the painting became a composition of Madame Gutterman and her child in gray and pink. I remember it as the best I did in the camp. The Guttermans disappeared with the next transport, and the painting disappeared with Meyer.

How lucky I was not to be married and not to have a child, I thought again and again. Hélène told us something more. Before the last transport, she had to scour the schupo's quarters, and remained there alone with one of them, a tipsy Rumanian who had so cursed the Nazis and his work with the trains that she dared to ask him some questions.

"I knew what I was risking, but I simply had to," Hélène said, adding that she and her husband had had a large family in Antwerp, and that thirty-six already were gone without a trace. I understood why she never smiled.

"What is there to see in that camp where the train stops? What do the Jews do there?" Hélène needed all her courage to ask those questions. The Rumanian schupo was leaving the room when he turned in the doorway and said, "Whoever gets there, you won't see anymore and those you do see walk around in pajamas." Incomprehensible. Still, hearing Hélène's report, I shuddered.

With remnants from the tailors' and leather workshops, and despite her dejected mood, Hélène made beautiful, funny costumes for Landau's marionettes — Till Eulenspiegel, Lamme Godsack, farmers, soldiers, a princess, a king and a queen. With papier-mâché heads, wooden limbs and joints held together by leather strips, all kinds of figures from Flemish folklore joined us.

With the increasing population of the painters' workshop, we were lucky that since Meyer's bust was finished, we now had two rooms for our work. We needed them — there were the three official painters, then Landau, Héléne, the puppets, and a newly arrested young artist, Klaus Grünewald, who would become a life-long friend. After many months of hiding, running and zigzagging from place to place, Klaus and his sisters were caught in Brussels. It was rumored in the camp that their father, the former owner of a tool-making factory in Düsseldorf, had tried to buy his own and his wife's freedom with a huge sum of money; this occurred before the Gestapo arrested the three children. However, something had gone wrong. Perhaps the ransom money landed in Gestapo hands after the parents had already been shipped East — nobody ever heard from them again. And yet, oddly enough, these S.S. may have had their own perverse sense of fairness — the

Olga Puhlman, one of the B-numbers. Pen and wash. Irene Awret. (Ghetto Fighters' House Museum, Israel)

Little girl. Pencil drawing. Irene Awret. (Ghetto Fighters' House Museum, Israel)

Portrait of a boy. Pencil drawing. Irene Awret. All the children I drew and painted were transported to Auschwitz. (Ghetto Fighters' House Museum, Israel)

Young man in golf trousers, seated. Pencil. Irene Awret. (Ghetto Fighters' House Museum, Israel)

belated payment now seemed to cover Klaus and his sisters. Though held as prisoners inside the camp, they were not sent on a transport. In this way all three survived the war.

Things were lively in our place. In one corner, Landau was bent over a bucket stirring glue for the papier-mâché. Hélène squatted on the floor fixing a tiny purse on Till Eulenspiegel's belt. Awret was painting CAUTION, DANGER OF EPIDEMICS! on a sheet of cardboard that covered half the table. Kopel Simelovitz and I shared the remaining space. I produced numbers, while he used our finest brush and greenest green of hope to hide an imperfect world behind a row of watercolor cypresses and nesting songbirds. Klaus looked on — the baron sighing deeply stared holes into the air.

"A—ttention!" All jumped up as one, standing straight when Frank entered the workshop without any warning. Once more a number of prisoners had escaped from a transport, the twenty-first. The Gestapo bosses were more than just angry.

"You bastards, what are you doing here?" Frank snapped at Klaus and Simelovitz. "Out! Get where you belong! And you," his voice cutting the words he now turned to Awret, "Who the hell do you think you are to paint portraits without my permission? Did you think I wouldn't find out?" Klaus and Simelovitz bolted. The rest of us continued standing at attention. I could hear my fast-beating heart — out of fear for Awret and because I too had painted portraits without authorization.

"That's Jews for you, give them your little finger, they grab the whole hand." Frank thundered on, "You have painted Léon, you have painted van Rees — you like to paint porters? All right. From now on you are a porter and a painter — when the whistle blows you run, understood? Dare paint one more portrait behind my back Awret and you go where they don't serve you hot chocolate for breakfast." With this unmistakable threat Frank slammed the door shut.

Lodging in the same room with the porters, Awret had done the portraits to thank his neighbors van Rees and Léon for sharing their packages with him. Van Rees, co-owner of an important business, and Léon, according to his own account a burglar from the region of Lille, were both generous people. Their non-Jewish girl friends supplied them with delicacies too exotic for the taste of the S.S., so these packages were rarely confiscated. In this way, Awret had profited from snails in garlic sauce, from breaded frogs legs, from stuffed mussels and goat cheese in olive oil, a long way from rutabaga soup.

Only men were quartered in the porters' dormitory — they shared their food, living in a sort of commune. Not so in the witches' den, where the well-brought-up girls from the Reception seemed to think that if selfishness did not fill your belly it at least made you feel less hungry. There everyone feared a woman who was nicknamed The Spider (see page 302). She stowed packages under her bed until the food began to stink. Ugly, gaunt and sloppy, it was said that she was Boden's pet because of the reports she gave him about the other girls.

Evi was the Cinderella of the witches' den. She subsisted almost entirely on beet soup, potatoes and our sticky bread, that is, until the day Frank sent for her. A miracle had occurred. Though Evi's parents had been deported, her sister not only managed to reach Switzerland, but she sent Evi a package via the Turkish Red Cross. A Middle Eastern Fata Morgana unfolded before Evi's slightly bulging eyes — she thought she was seeing things.

"Fräulein Efa, I hope you don't object to my sampling some of these small things," Frank asked in the polite tone of a gentleman. "Pistachio nuts — I haven't seen them since before the war." One, two, they were gone. "Dates and figs, I've forgotten what they taste like" — the small bag landed in a drawer. "My God, what huge almonds." They disappeared into his pocket. "Ach, and dried apricots — can you spare some?" With a nod Evi mumbled, "You are welcome, Herr Kommandant," and returned to the witches' den with what remained of the package, mostly rice and beans.

Since the day of his punishment, Awret wore an armband that he himself had inscribed with the word "porter." Each time we had a few minutes to ourselves our romantic tête-à-tête was interrupted by the whistle that ordered him to get down into the yard. As each truck

arrived with prisoners the porters had to be ready to bring the newcomers' suitcases and bundles into the Reception. But Awret's main
job was to carry crates. Crates with bottles for the casino that had to
be unloaded, crates with provisions to be transferred from the storeroom to the kitchen, raw materials and finished products that had to
be pushed and shoved to and from the workshops; meanwhile Awret
had to do his painter's work as well. I have asked myself over these
years how in this situation, under constant watch, our friendship could
develop into a close relationship. All the while there was the running,
dragging, the interrupting whistle, the sign painting and Meyer's gluttonous appetite for oils and sculptures. But that was what happened.
The greater the pressure, the better we worked as a team, and it has
remained so to this day.

Besides, Awret was much tougher and stronger than his narrow, sensitive face led one to believe. For hours he carried hundred-pound
sacks of potatoes up to a third floor room and still had enough energy
for flirting, and not only with me. Lon Landau compared the camp to
a cage for wild animals but where the libidos go on strike — men like
Awret, however, were constantly bumping into the bars, unable to
ignore the many women fluttering about. Who knew if this might be
the last opportunity? Like an innate talent, Awret's ability to handle
women was as natural as the gracefulness of a young cat playing with
wool. Balls of all colors came tumbling and rolling, black ones, brown
ones, red ones, including Raymonde the blonde, a good-natured young
woman with broad jawbones, broad hips, a broad Flemish brogue and
easy morals.

To my eyes, all of them were prettier than me — with the exception of my friend Minnie Feldman who I was slowly becoming jeal-
ous of, they all had transport numbers. Jealousy blinded me to the fact
that the poor girls were not attracted solely by Awret's charm. In their
helplessness they probably hoped a gallant contact of this kind could
land them a job in the painters' workshop that would protect them
from deportation, at least temporarily.

With all that, the painters and all other W-Numbers, including the
"personnel," were in constant danger of being called up to fill the

quota for cattle cars. Despite the Nazi pressure on the Belgians to turn in their Jewish neighbors and as tirelessly as they tried to sniff out Jews with the help of Jacques the informer, the numbers in the barracks were not sufficient for a full cargo. The great Moloch somewhere in the East demanded his offerings, though we had not yet looked into his bloody eye nor breathed the poison he exhaled. We simply speculated that if the camp had insufficient numbers of prisoners, it would be liquidated as would we. We had no illusions on that account. Surely Kommandant Frank, Boden and their followers never had it so good. To make sure they didn't have to give up their honey pot of Mechelen for the Russian front, they would not have hesitated filling the trains with whoever fell into their hands. W-Numbers, B-Numbers, Gypsies, X-, Y- and Z-Numbers. Sentiments had no part in this equation. For someone like me who on principle always expected the worst, only a sudden windfall would be a surprise.

The optimists among us, however, those who still had not learned that reason amounts to wishful thinking, fooled themselves with logic. They said, or wanted to believe, the Nazis needed their railway cars for more important freight than Jews. Toward the end of summer 1943 the question was no longer if the Allies were planning an invasion of the continent, but when and where. We had also heard that in May the town of Cologne, almost in our neighborhood, was bombarded by more than a thousand British planes, and that in the East, the German front was in retreat. So what? As long as the Nazis wanted to boast of the Third Reich's invincibility, they needed us as vermin to squash under their shiny boots. Now, as the Reich began to disintegrate, they needed us as scapegoats. I was certain that even if Himmler had to find trains from under the earth, the Gestapo chiefs in Berlin would still have found the means to deport us to that place where "those Jews you can still see are walking about in pajamas."

Awret and I never talked about the future. That theme was taboo here. Happiness in the present was enough for me. My jealousy troubled me more than my captivity. "Don't take things so seriously, Irene," Awret said trying to cheer me up. "Declarations of love are not my cup of tea, but you know quite well how I feel," he assured me between painting signs and carrying potatoes. Though quite stoic when I had to be, and unconcerned to the point of recklessness in everyday matters, when it came to jealousy I was helpless. Through the window I saw Raymonde coquettishly toying with Awret's suspenders, and worse. For his thirty-third birthday, Minnie had dedicated a long poem in French to him about a genial sculptor kissed by the Muses — I feared not only the Muses.

Why did I take art and myself and romance with such unbearable seriousness? Sunk in a German fervor that is both deep and sentimental, I was envious of the Gallic esprit. Hitler had thoroughly torn modern art from its questing in Germany, and replaced it with the icily colossal and the idealized creations of the Third Reich. So it was that my world came to a standstill with the nineteenth century Romantics — the Nazi Weltanschauung was not a propitious time for a teen-age Jewess. Like a snail, my soulful German self had to retire into its shell — only under the cover of sarcasm did that self put out its head.

Nothing could lure me from my shell, not even the refreshing acquaintance with the Impressionists and the Fauves, with Aldous Huxley or with Rimbaud, Verlaine and Baudelaire. Four years of furnished attic rooms with bedbugs, half a year of a ramshackle old farm building with rats, the slaps in the face of my arrest and the shouts and curses of the S.S., nothing had succeeded in waking me from my very private, very romantic sleeping beauty dreams. Only now, after six months of captivity and over my head in love, I was finally ready to crawl out of my protective shell of cynicism, finding to my astonishment that I did not need it anymore. Strange as it may seem, in the ugliness and degradation of captivity, I found once more the faith in humanity that I thought I had completely lost during my Nazi years in Germany.

All of us who passed through the Reception had to abandon our belongings and also the masks that concealed our true natures. But "caught together, hanged together," a German proverb says. Here between prison walls, suddenly seeing the true nature of my fellow Jews, their inner selves as naked as their bodies in the washroom, my pride returned.

Our God allowed little children to be herded into cattle cars, but we Jews, the so-called chosen and cast-off people who prayed to Him for thousands of years, were more humane than He and the rest of the world that looked on, setting their immigration quotas and preventing refugees from disembarking from rotting ships. Thinking of the wonderful people I met in Mechelen, I came to realize that being Jewish was a privilege. There were the childless Heibers who slept next to me. Day and night they racked their brains on how to save other people's children — only much later would I learn how successful and how dangerous to themselves their activities had been. There was Lon Landau running from one dormitory to the next assisting the elderly and the young mothers without ever mentioning why he disappeared for hours from the painters' workshop. Still alive at the time of our liberation, he died shortly afterwards of typhus that he contracted as a volunteer aide in Bergen-Belsen. There was Evi changing entries in Boden's lists under his nose, Arnold the electrician, and a whole band of workers like Awret swiping tools for flitzers, prisoners who would try and break out from the cattle cars.

—

"We have to help ourselves," shouted Albert Clément, laughing as always, jumping high above the beds in our dormitory to accomplish a somersault. On this Sunday, the day we were allowed to visit, Albert was improvising a cabaret performance on a stage of six beds pushed together. Until his arrest in Brussels, he had been a market crier. Behind the Gare de Midi, he had promoted ladies' stockings, bananas, razor blades and yo-yos. No doubt a born comic, he exploited his talent to sell anything at all, making more money than he could have on the stage. A ray of light, he and his friend Wolf Epstein, another yard worker, could make us laugh on dark days.

The performance began. Wolf as a foppish Wallis Simpson lay flat on his back, pushing off the amorous Prince of Wales, piping, "Wait, darling, not so hasty! How can you do this in a castle as dirty as this one? Look up, two dead flies on the chandelier." The prince, alias Albert, kicked Wallis away and furiously jumped on the mattresses, stuffed a potato into his mouth the better to speak like a Brit. He cursed flies, domestics, Jews, Communists and, of course, his darling Wallis, in a princely manner.

Second skit. Wolf and Albert, transformed into an elderly couple, sat arm in arm on the side of a bed speaking Yiddish.

"Yankel," she sighed, "we've lived together for thirty years, don't you think it's time to get married?"

"You are quite right," he said, "but who will take us?" We may have laughed but applause would have been too noisy. One of us always had to watch by the stairs.

Laughing ourselves into tears at Albert and Wolf's comedy, as on many preceding Sundays, I was completely unaware of the part they had played during the week. Prisoners like Arnold Dobruszkes, the carpenters, the yard workers and others, used to stop what they were doing under the pretext that without a certain kind of material or tool, without more plaster, concrete, wire or screws they could not finish their jobs. Generally, they were then permitted to leave the camp accompanied by a guard to go shopping. This enabled those who had contacts with the resistance movements to secretly exchange messages.

I could not stand Albert van Koovorden who with his wife Milly served the officers in the casino. Repulsive lackeys, I thought to myself, seeing him bowing, her curtsying, both of them servile and smiling at the Germans — how much I didn't know. I never guessed that they were listening to the table talk in order to inform the Resistance about the composition and date of departure of the next transport. While I took him for a sneak, actually the information he and Milly were gathering was passed on as messages inside crates of empty bottles, which a knowing coachman came regularly to cart away.

Arnold had established his liaison with the underground in the back room of a Mechelen hardware store. While the owner's young wife entertained the guard in the shop, Arnold pretended to look for copper wire and radio tubes back there but was really transmitting letters. He was also able to smuggle food that he hid in his socks and pants and shared with those who received no packages. Like most of the workers in the camp, Arnold had come to his job by pure chance.

One November night in 1943, when Major Schmitt the drunken sadist was still Kommander of the camp, he wanted to shampoo his hair. (Because of his former trade, Schmitt was called "the butcher of Breedonck" and was executed after the war.) Fate, however, willed that his hair dryer, no doubt taken from a Jew, did not work. Since the Kommandant could not be expected to go to bed with a damp head, Journée and Ferdekopf were sent running through the dormitories to find someone among the transport numbers who could repair the dryer. "I can," Arnold answered sleepily — having fixed the hair dryer and overhauling the major's radio, Arnold was installed as camp electrician and thus saved from deportation.

Arnold Dobruszkes, Albert Clément, Wolf Epstein, van Koovorden and Milly, Maurice Heiber, his wife Esta and others were all in contact with underground organizations. I don't know whose idea it was to introduce arms into the camp, but an urgent appeal was secretly communicated to the Resistance.

"Shall we let ourselves be slaughtered when the Allies land to drive the Nazis out of here? Give us something, anything, to defend ourselves, guns, hand grenades." Indeed, arrangements were made, though I knew nothing about them at the time.

I laughed on Sundays about Albert and Wolf's antics, without suspecting that on weekdays they were risking their lives for us. I produced numbers in the workshop, painted sad children and suffered the pangs of jealousy, only vaguely aware that like a fly entwined in threads of danger I was swaying in a net of deadly secrets. Years later I was told the following story.

Albert and Wolf executed a plan to obtain weapons from the Resistance. Working on repairs to the punishment cells and the pigsty, they helped make a damaged wall cave in so that sand, cement and lime were urgently needed for its rebuilding. Permission given, they both left the camp with a cart and an armed S.S. guard, walking along a nearby canal to get to a hangar with building materials. They joined the guard in making fun of a pair of lovers in a meadow by the hangar. So absorbed in their kissing, the couple did not seem to notice the three men at all. The uncommonly pretty young woman was Rachel

Koperbac, an exceptionally courageous member of the Resistance. While Albert and Wolf were loading sand and cement, she observed the movements of the guard. Looking bored, the guard walked back and forth by the side of the hangar — as he was turning for the third time Rachel jumped up and ran into the hangar letting a package glide into the sand on the cart. When the guard was facing her once more, she was back on the grass, kissing her lover as before. Albert layered the sand with straw, and so the officer's pigs got fresh bedding and the Jews got a pistol or two. I never found out what exactly was in the package. In any event, these arms — their hiding place was known to very few — were never used. A year later, the end came so fast that our jailers only thought about saving themselves and did not even manage that.

⸺

At that time, the underground was active in many ways. It was rumored among the prisoners that the Flemish S.S. whom we had sneeringly called "Moishe Pisser" had been in the way of a bullet aimed at him near the entrance to the barracks. How well it had been aimed I came to know through Evi. Frank had taken Albert Clément and Evi along to the funeral. Albert helped with the shoveling, while Evi translated the Kommandant's condolences into Flemish for the traitor's widow.

"Imagine this comedy, Irene, me translating Frank's eulogy for that filthy traitor word-for-word to his sobbing widow, what a hero he had been, how much he will be missed, and with all that I had to keep a straight face and seem serious. I did not dare look at Albert or I would have burst out laughing."

One morning shortly after Moishe Pisser's funeral, Frank so scared me I almost fell over. "You could do something more useful than dawdling in the yard and painting empty bottles," he barked at me. He then took a photo from his breast-pocket and said, "Look here. This soldier fell on the Eastern front, and I want to surprise his widow with his portrait. Start immediately, in oil, life-size. On with it!"

Although I had seen Moishe Pisser only from afar, I instantly recognized his lightly grinning face in the passport photo. I knew that he had not been killed in Russia but here in Mechelen in front of the barracks gate. Now I had to explore his physiognomy in a tiny photograph and try to look deeply into the eyes of this anti-Semitic, Belgian traitor. Lacking direct contact with my model, I was like a damp match, unable to light up inspiration. Still, maybe out of pure hatred I painted such a lifelike portrait that Frank later told me, to my great satisfaction, that the widow fainted at the sight of my picture. This surprise so disposed Frank in favoring our workshop that he released Awret from his punishment — no longer did he have to carry heavy sacks but even better, he now had more time for me.

A few days earlier, however, while I was highlighting Moishe Pisser's glasses to give them the finishing touches, I encountered Frank's more brutal side in his treatment of Max Bauer, a wealthy pensioner who had fled Germany for Brussels, but then landed in Mechelen. Shortly before he was to be deported, the elderly Bauer managed to buy his freedom from the Nazis of the Avenue Louise for the astronomical sum of a million-and-a-half Belgian francs. In his elation after being freed, he committed an indiscretion that would become fatal to him. He boasted about what he had paid to be free, suggesting that a percentage had stuck to Frank's fingers. News of this sort spread quickly and Bauer was rearrested, jailed in Brussels, and then brought back to Mechelen.

"Get down, form ranks!" The guards chased all the prisoners into the yard, where the three Kapos, Meyer, Kraus and Voss, made us form a half circle. When Frank and Boden arrived they were in a foul mood — Boden exhibited his customary mulish demeanor, while Frank was in a rage, his eyes squeezed almost shut, his jaws tense like a bulldog baring its teeth. Bauer was dragged before the Kommandant. On similar occasions Boden had taken charge of the beatings — today Frank did. Only later did I learn about the background of his rage. A noncommissioned officer, Frank had been the one to expose the corruption of his bosses, Major Schmitt, Meinshausen and Krull. They had not been removed because of their cruelty, but for stealing valuables produced by Jews or taken from them — they then sold the goods, lining their own pockets. Apparently, for his honesty, Frank was appointed Kommandant of the camp.

Whether or not Bauer's allegation was true, Frank was going to publicly remove the stain from his S.S. honor. That was what he now did in the yard in the presence of all officers, soldiers and prisoners, pitilessly whipping the seventy-three year old man, mainly aiming at his head, his neck and his face. I could try to close my eyes, but not my ears. After Frank had beaten the unfortunate Bauer half dead, he had him dragged to a cell to await the next transport.

That happened toward the end of August 1943. Looking through the window of our workshop some days later, I witnessed a sight so ghastly that nothing will erase it from my memory. In the morning a big truck from Antwerp packed with people had already rolled through the gate. The yard was feverish with the kind of activity prior to a big shipment. "Paint only new B-Numbers!" Meyer called from the door. What did that signify, only B-Numbers, we asked among ourselves? And in such haste and so many that even the baron had to help us. Had the hunt for foreign Jews become so difficult that Jews of Belgian nationality, until then relatively safe, were now also being arrested? That is exactly what was happening. The S.S. headquarters in Berlin were demanding fuller trains, more Jews, no matter what nationality.

Moreover, they were demanding more money, more jewelry, more furniture, carpets and silver. Towards this end, all Belgian Jews, naively believing that they were protected by their country and its royal house, were lured into a trap by Erdmann. He invited them to appear on the same day and hour with promises of new identification papers. Everything went flawlessly. First, those summoned were relieved of their keys. Moving vans hired in advance were ready to empty their dwellings on the same day.

So many Belgian Jews had fallen into the trap that there were not enough trucks available to transport all of them to Mechelen, half an hour away. Shortly after this morning's arrival of the first truck with about eighty prisoners, a van drove into the courtyard.

The whistle blew. Two S.S. and a driver jumped from the cabin.

Frank and Boden, Parnes, the new camp doctor, Gertie and Rena, the nurses as well as a row of porters stood waiting for the double door at the rear to swing open. But nobody got off. There were no people, only a thick, white cloud pierced by cries and groans. Then like a wall, the prisoners were falling out. More and more like so many unwieldy packages. As Doctor Parnes and the two nurses tried to catch those who were falling, the porters were carrying lifeless bodies into the infirmary. Boden stood speechless, Frank cursed incessantly, the square patch of sky shone in radiant blue, and the walls glared with sunshine. All that yellow made me nauseous. How could one truck hold that many tottering figures? As in a bad dream there seemed to be no end to the unloading.

Among those straightening up and staggering towards the Reception, I recognized the face of Fanny Kimmel, my former neighbor from the transport dormitory. In June she had been freed as a Belgian national. Frank, too, noticed her. I saw how he stopped cursing for a moment to address her. I was too far away to understand their exchange, but Fanny later repeated it to me.

"Again? What are you doing here, how stupid can a person be?" he shouted at her.

"Yes, I was stupid, Herr Sturmscharführer," she said. "I believed in a German officer's word of honor." Either Frank did not understand or he pretended not to. Inexplicably it paid off and nothing happened to her. She and her husband had the luck of born survivors. She survived the war in Mechelen, while he emerged from camps in the East. They had children, and fifty years later I visited the two in their flat in Antwerp in the company of Evi and Awret.

One hundred forty-five Jews had been loaded into that furniture truck, women in the rear, men in front. The vehicle was so crammed that the last ones were squeezed in only under threat of being shot. The door had to be jammed shut by those pushing on the outside. It was impossible to move an arm or a leg. The heat soon became so unbearable many could not breathe and fainted. The driver and the two S.S. in the cabin couldn't care less. Halfway to Mechelen they had stopped — probably to pour down a few beers — thereby prolonging the agony of those trapped inside.

For nine among them it was too late. They could not be revived. Fourteen others hovered between life and death and were transferred to a hospital. For the rest, the doctor and his two nurses worked a whole day and night to get them back on their feet.

That happened on a Saturday, the Sabbath. It was the first time Boden did not strut in the courtyard, dismissing the Jews with a scornful, "Today is Shabbes." It was a dark Sabbath, one truck after another bringing in Belgian Jews. For two days Awret and I painted numbers until dawn.

Sixteen

THE GESTAPO HAD NAMED THE RUSE that enabled them to net more than a thousand Belgian Jews "Action Iltis." The most prominent and wealthiest among them were soon released to return to their empty houses and apartments. Even with those let go, the barracks remained full of B-Numbers and foreboding. On the daily walk in rows of five, I was now swarmed by protests and rumors in impeccable French."

"King Léopold has always been spineless, we have nothing to hope for from those quarters," someone beside me said scornfully. "He is licking the Germans' boots, thinking Hitler may still win the war. But his mother has her heart in the right place. Élisabeth will never allow Belgian subjects to be carted off to Poland!" another voice rose with indignation. "General von Falkenhausen has assured the government that not a hair will be hurt on the head of a Belgian Jew." The truth was that under German occupation the Belgian government had faded into a shadow of itself, powerless to do more than protest. Later I would learn that those government officials who openly vented their indignation over the arrest of Belgian Jews were simply replaced by willing collaborators. The Justice Department's unsuccessful attempts to prevent deportation to Auschwitz led to its acceleration — as I have already written, we knew only later what was happening in the East. Nobody had yet heard the name Auschwitz.

The request by the Belgian authorities reached Chief of the General Staff Eggert Reeder too late — the arrested Jews were already in Germany, he wrote, on September 17th. Reeder evaded responsibility with a lie. On September 20, 1943 (the 22nd transport), a train with the Belgian Jews first left Mechelen for Poland. Our colleague Kopel Simelovitz was to be on that transport. We who remained behind were the privileged — we felt guilty about our fellow prisoners and tried to help them. How could we say goodbye to Kopel and suffer his trusting, childlike face if Awret and I had not tried to do something. Never before had we asked to speak with the Kommandant — taking this step was fearful but one we had to do.

Awret and I crossed the yard to Frank's office. Awret brought his offering, a sculpture of a monkey with its young that he had carved out of linden wood and lovingly polished. Accepting the carving with thanks, Frank's face darkened when we pleaded with him to let Kopel stay as a helper in the painters' workshop. His crude, ruddy face turned redder, his pinched eyes almost disappeared and he bared his teeth, "Children," he growled in that seemingly friendly address with the repressed threat used to put the upstart young in their place, "be glad you are staying — but that can change if you once more have such nerve. Get out and back to your work!"

He did not have to repeat himself — the danger was palpable. Had Frank like many Germans not looked upon artists as children, possibly magicians but otherwise irresponsible, our meeting could have had a worse ending.

The day before the transport was to leave, Awret's luck and a portrait saved him from another serious mess. When the train arrived at the gate, a German S.S. by the name of Stark was charged by the Kommandant to ready the cattle cars for loading the next morning. Stark included Awret in the team of yard workers for this job, as a way of thanking him for the portrait he had ordered and which was almost finished. To move outside the gate, replace dirty straw in the wagons with fresh straw, secure the hatches with barbed wire to prevent breakouts, such a job for Jews was considered a special treat by the S.S. — strange as it may seem, it was like a summer outing for the prisoners.

Only years later did Awret describe the interior of the cattle cars to me, the darkness, the filth, the overpowering stink. He would say nothing in the camp.

While sweeping straw that was soiled with dried vomit and excrement out of the cattle cars, Awret had an idea that he gave voice to.

"Sweeping will not help much. Maybe we should paint the inside white — white and blue." He regretted those words even as they were slipping out of his mouth. Fritz Handler, the Negus and chief of the yard workers, Albert Clément and Wolf Epstein stood there grinning.

"What did he say?" Stark asked suspiciously.

"The wagons ought to be painted white and blue," Moishe Baby, the youngest and most literate of the guards, proudly translated from French into German. The colors were an allusion to Zionism. A Jew permitting himself such insolence? What probably saved Awret from a beating, denouncement and deportation in one of those very wagons was Stark's worry about his unfinished portrait. When he at last got his voice back, the knuckles in his clenched fists were white.

"Impudent Jew sow, march, back to the barracks! Don't show your ass here again," and he showed Awret the direction of the gate.

That night, as the aroma of hamburgers again pervaded the air, a poem by Möricke would not leave me. "Once more spring lets its blue ribbon flutter through the air, sweet scents full of promise touch upon the land." Before sunrise, shouts and whistles signaled the transport. Dogs barked, Frank gave orders, Meyer's rolling stage voice ordered everyone to stand in line. First to be called were ordinary transport numbers, followed by B-Numbers, and in the end, for the last wagon, a row of Flitzers with shaved heads and red armbands. Kopel Simelovitz was one of the first to line up. It was strictly forbidden to look through the window while a transport was leaving, but in the half dark I saw him waving goodbye with his free hand before disappearing through the gate. We never saw him again, nor the carving of the monkey mother and child, which Frank kept.

The morning bell that meant it was time for warm mash for the little ones did not ring anymore. Only a handful of children were left. Empty cardboard cartons thrown from the windows of the transport dormitories filled the vacuum. Frank surveyed the scene from a window above the gate with the air of a man content to take an hour's leisure from a job well done.

The straw on the plank beds barely had time to cool and the schupos only just bolted the locks of the wagons over the sobs and cries inside, when a team marched off to clean the vacated dormitories. An

S.S. we called Moishe Ear Boxer chose the cleaners from among those saved from the transport at the last moment — they were B-Numbers, wealthy people, noted scientists and artists. Others, with E-Numbers around their neck were able to prove that the substandard Semitic mix in their veins was sufficiently diluted with high grade Aryan blood. In some cases, being married to an Aryan partner was enough to save one from deportation.

A journalist, a professor of philology and the owner of a department store were among those Moishe Ear Boxer chose for cleaning up. From third floor windows, they flung empty cartons to the yard below. These were collected, stacked and bound together by a pianist, an expert of the art of Oceania, and a pharmacist. Letting nothing go to waste had always been a sound German principle. That it applied to gold teeth, body fat and human skin would not have registered with us.

Readying the dormitories for new occupants fell to the women. A muscular ballerina with a Slavic pug nose, a lanky high school teacher of ancient Greek and a very pretty young actress dealt with bibs sticky with jam, broken yogurt bottles, torn socks, used hygienic pads, shredded prayer books and abandoned clothing that littered the two-storied wooden hutches and concrete floors.

In the painters' workshop I had already met the young woman who gathered straw fallen out of torn mattresses, stuffing it back with bandaged hands. This was Dunia Sadow, a rising star on the Brussels stage. Only vaguely aware of her Jewish origins, she could not comprehend why she had been arrested, let alone in the middle of a play. Brought to the cellars of the Avenue Louise, she cut her arteries and was rushed to the hospital. Having arrived in Mechelen, she came to the painters' workshop frequently, hoping to find congenial company that would cheer her up.

Considering the conditions under which we lived, things in Dunia's own dormitory of B-Numbers were quite lively. Nadia Bolotine, the robust ballerina in her early forties, gave young girls dancing lessons in the passage between the hutches. At the same time from the upper row of mattresses an art historian lectured a more serious audience on

Tolstoy. Teens of high school age were invited to participate in algebra lessons, and the rest passed their time as best they could. The art historian, an anthropologist and an archaeologist, for example, knew some twenty living and dead languages — they trisected an imaginary globe to write a history of the world from memory. Each had a third of the known landmass to write about in the tiniest handwriting, so as to use as little paper as possible. But among the Belgian Jews there were also more colorful figures like Napoléon, a giant in a striking blue shirt and a red scarf who had worked as a helper in a Brussels slaughterhouse. As if to remind the others where they really were, he came along the aisle swearing through his long, yellow teeth. Loudly thumping his wooden leg and cane, he tore straight through all that bel esprit.

⟶

The brutal "collection" actions, the suffocated, the half-dead — none of those heart-rending scenes managed to dampen my passion. After the twenty-second transport in 1943, more than the nights cooled off. No doubt the leaves outside were turning and chestnuts were raining down on Brussels' avenues — closing my eyes I imagined I could hear them bursting. No fall colors here, where the geranium on the window sill of the Reception was disturbed by frequent digging and looked more pitiful than ever. My friend and rival Minnie confided in me that sometimes amid the cries and confusion of arrival, she had observed new prisoners hiding a ring or a diamond in the plant's roots. Later the owner would beg her or one of her colleagues to dig up the gem and return it.

There were other changes as well. The Wehrmacht's broken promise not to deport Belgian Jews, the treachery of Action Iltis and the speed with which those arrested were deported provoked indignation in the former governing circles. What was really happening behind the dense forests in the East and at the end of the railway tracks had begun to trickle out, news much too unbelievable to be taken seriously by ordinary Europeans in the west. So why startle the horses, the Nazis may have speculated, when so many transports had rolled smoothly and in orderly fashion toward the so-called Final Solution? When here and there someone sat up and took notice, it was possible to allay suspicions with fairy tales about tolerable conditions in the work camps. The Brussels S.S. therefore permitted three Jewish old age homes, three homes for small children and a hospital to be opened. On the one hand this more humane treatment would make for better relations with the Belgian population; on the other, it would now be easier to gather old people, children and the sick to send them to their gruesome destination when the time was ripe.

In addition to these new measures, there were other reasons for many to have hope. Some prisoners were actually being released. Contacts with the right people, bribes, interventions by Cardinal van Roey and Queen Élisabeth all played a role here and there in loosening the Gestapo's tight grip. If a lucky prisoner was released, it happened in the morning. The most optimistic among the freedom seekers would crawl out of their hutch early, full of expectation. In the washroom their high hopes made more bubbles than the ersatz soap.

"Today is the day, I can feel it, couldn't sleep all night," I heard two B-Numbers whispering behind a towel. "You'll see, they will call my name in a little while. Do you know what I will do first? Go to the Rue Neuve and eat French fries out of a paper bag. Then I will buy fresh walnuts on the corner of the Rue Neuve where they shout: 'Cinq francs les treize.' Of course, I will send you a parcel. Maybe I'll be able to get hold of a piece of sausage." But no name was called. The bubbles burst one after another. At noon during soup, the hope had faded, and when in the late afternoon the whistle blew for the daily walk in the round, a thousand feet listlessly shuffled down the stairs.

⁓

"Cursed bunch of Jews! Can't you get down more slowly? You have it too good here — I'll show you. Up! Back to your dormitories on the double!" Boden infuriated stomped his boot, the guards whistled like crazy. Some of the people were still coming down the steps, when others were already running back up. Ferdekopf, Journée and Moishe

Ear Boxer kicked and hit left and right into the crowd. This up and down relay with blows and curses was repeated four times until the strolling around finally got underway. Walking beside me, Tilly Sachs poked me in the ribs: "What's the matter with that one today?" she winked furtively in Boden's direction. "Maybe his house in Leipzig is kaput, bang, bang?" From the Belgian contingent we heard of new air raids on German cities. Fine. As far as I was concerned, Frank, Boden and the whole Nazi bunch should be bombed into one big hole. But wishing them all the worst, I still felt that little shudder. The duo I knew so well came to my mind, Goebbels' hypocrisies in High German, tatters of Hitler's hoarse threats: "International Jewry. . .if they dare . . . full brunt of the power of the Third Reich . . . will deeply regret . . . vermin . . . exterminate. . .they brought it on themselves." Walking in step with me, Tilly read my thoughts: "Perhaps you can explain why it's our fault? I mean, the British and the French are taking revenge for the Blitz by bombing Berlin and Leipzig? Stay clear of Frank, Irene, since yesterday he's more vicious than his dog." An answer was unnecessary. We both knew why he was livid. After all, everything was the fault of the Jews. Though we imprisoned rejects walking in rows of five around a bare yard were really and truly innocent of the war, of bombs and of defeats, the mere thought of Nazi retaliation gave me shivers. In the final analysis, what did it matter at all as long as Awret and I were together? I really didn't care if the whole world lay in ruins.

Since the last transport we had become inseparable, perhaps because of an event he only told me about years later. One of the schupos accompanying the trains had begun a conversation with him. Awret was working at the storehouse, painting the lettering on the crates that were to be shipped to Germany with the coming transport. The man, a Sudeten German and a member of the S.S., curiously enough seemed to look upon a Jew as a human being. He told Awret about the farm in his homeland, how pleasant life had been there before the war and how much he disliked his present job: What actually was the destination of all those trains, Awret asked.

"Pray to your God you never get there. For most of you the end of that journey is death in the gas chambers, and the only way you can get away from there is as stinking smoke through a big chimney." Like a penitent, the schupo had whispered his confession.

Had Awret's hand trembled? In any event, continuing to paint letters he later filched as many knives as feasible out of a still-open crate to distribute to potential flitzers. He thought the poor fellow was surprisingly decent but was also afflicted by morbid fantasies. To Awret this story seemed as plausible as if the schupo had said that on the Alexanderplatz in the center of Berlin, the Nazis were dancing around an immense cooking cauldron filled with Jews. If there was any truth in that nonsense, would the Kommandant let a pregnant woman (not her husband, however) skip a transport to give birth at the hospital only to have her gassed a thousand kilometers away together with her baby? The Nazis were too practical for such acts of madness. He tried to dismiss the nonsense from his mind. These considerations notwithstanding, since the schupo's story Awret walked about somewhat absent-mindedly. He barely flirted anymore and our relationship took a more serious turn.

All of us inside the camp were one day going to be passengers to the same nameless terminus. Maybe the uncertainty was better for us, especially for women with children or for inmates like Hélène Koen and Evi, whose entire families had been deported. They would learn the truth soon enough. One still could fend off ominous presentiments. To see the letters spelling out AUSCHWITZ naked and glaring, their meaning day and night aflame in our consciousness, would have been of no help.

On an October afternoon Tilly and I walked around the yard for the sixth time, past the toilets, the pigsty and the chicken coop, along the kennel and the punishment cells toward the kitchen, where a delegation of B-Numbers sat in front of the door, peeling potatoes. Out of sheer boredom Tilly searched for Jewish noses.

"Look, Irene, over there by the potatoes. Doesn't that man look like one of the Elders of Zion out of *Der Stürmer*?" What a pity they existed in Streicher's imagination only — Streicher was one of the most infamous of the Nazi Jew haters and publisher of the anti-Semitic

Der Stürmer. We could use an Elder here, a real crafty one to help us escape." She pursued her train of thought in a dreamy tone of voice. I had my thoughts as well. "The Elders of Zion?" I prefered the British and the Americans, they were for real. If only they would land a direct hit on the barracks. But the old brown roof tiles framing our piece of sky had not been damaged by the war — Allied flying formations were still in the realm of wishful dreams. Only a few fleecy lamblike clouds grazed high above in the October blue.

In our ranks down in the yard the scene was less peaceful. Each time the guards did not look in our direction, some prisoners a few rows in front of us belabored a man in their midst with their feet and their fists, a scraggy, unshaven fellow with swollen eyelids from what I could see. To judge from the rage and their hisses, they had recognized him as an informer, one of those miserable creatures who betrayed others to the Gestapo, either to save their own lives or for money, or for both. Could I forget Jacques, the most notorious among them, boxing my ears when I was arrested? The pale, middle-aged man in our row, however, exhibited none of Jacque's aplomb and impudence. As much as he tried to shrink into himself, he was still not invisible, had no way of escape. Under well-aimed blows he staggered right and left, toppling on his neighbors, until a kick hitting his shin sent him as far back as our row.

"Mosser, hanging is too good for you" was followed by a kick in his backside. (Mosser is Yiddish from the Hebrew word meaning informer.) "He has women and children on his conscience. I know him from way back when I lived in the Marolles [the working class district of Brussels] — he never amounted to anything." Using his sleeve, the alleged traitor wiped blood from his nose, when a plain little woman, her hair hidden under a scarf, interrupted the tormenting

"I beg you, brothers, let him go," she pleaded in Yiddish, "if he really is a mosser the Lord will be his judge. Stop it, enough. He is also a Jewish child." As ointment soothed a festering wound, so the words of the old Jewess soothed spirits thirsting for vengeance. "He is also a Jewish child." This last sentence was sinking in — it is hard to describe our state of mind. We continued walking in silence, thinking of what it really meant to be a Jew. At this moment I can almost put my finger on the thousands of years it took to mold us into a group of caring human beings, feeling responsible for each other.

Stars were already twinkling between the clouds when I returned to the painters' workshop and to Awret. The accused and his accusers climbed back to their respective bunks, and as far as I knew the informer was simply ignored until his departure with the next transport. Shortly after this incident the big bell by the gate rang one morning. Peeking through the window, I saw to my astonishment a group of merry young men in uniform instead of a load of prisoners. They were still descending from their truck when Frank and Boden came running to receive these guests with sonorous Heil Hitlering. The leader, his breast covered with brass and visibly excited, lifted his arm for only a brief greeting; he needed his index finger to point at Voss, our Kapo from Cologne. Taller than the officers by a head, he was standing in the background, observing the scene with curiosity.

"Wonderful, the gentleman over there is just what we need," the officer smiled at his men, a class of students of ethnology as I would find out later. He turned to Voss. "I hope you will not object if I take a few minutes of your time, Herr. . . ?

"The name is Voss," said the Jew somewhat embarrassed.

"Nice to meet you, for you are the prototype of a German, Herr Voss, exactly what I need to show my students before confronting them with examples of the Semitic race. Now, gentlemen, turn your attention to Herr Voss, look hard. It would be difficult to find a more striking example for this training course to illustrate our Aryan race. Note the broad shoulders, the erect posture, a sternocleidomastoid almost bursting Herr Voss's collar," he let his finger run from Voss's hairline down to the point of his nose. "And this straight, pure line, please visualize Phidias in your memory. Add the red-blond hair, the blue Nordic eye, the well-marked chin, as I said, a figure out of Nordic mythology, the true primordial German. Would you permit me a few measurements?" He fished a compass-like instrument out of his briefcase. Before Voss could say a word — he was flushed with amused embarrassment — the expert on ethnology managed to lodge each end of his instrument in the apertures of his ear and nose and give some sort of pseudo-scientific explanations on the relationship between the width of the angles of the upper jaw, the root of the nose and the back of the head.

Boden set up his poker face. Frank changed from his right foot to the left and back, apparently seeing no way out of this disgraceful situation but to shut up. The lecture began in earnest only after a number of prisoners were brought into the yard to serve as an object lesson, the purpose for which this class excursion had been planned.

What followed was the identification of Semitic racial characteristics. The pens and pencils kept ready, the copybooks and note pads took me seven years back into the past, to my French class at the Gertraudenschule, to the days Doctor Kadner stood in the door in his brown uniform. On those days he had us shut the French grammar book and instead examine the Semitic racial characteristics listed on the blackboard in place of irregular verbs. Then I wanted to crawl into a mouse hole. Here among Jews, I was at least an integral part of a whole. I compared the situation and knew that I belonged here. Let those students enjoy our characteristics while they can, I thought. On all fronts their brothers were falling, their homeland was burning, but here they were, searching for black, kinky hair, flat feet, crooked legs, flabby behinds, receding foreheads, sly eyes, fleshy noses and protruding lips.

"May they down their meal in good health," Awret, standing near me, said with a wink. After a while the troop left.

———

Despite all the Gestapo's efforts and tricks to flush out Jews, the harvests became poorer and poorer, and the painters' workshop, conceived for the production of numbers and signs, reverted once more into a meeting place for the bohême of the camp. In place of the deported Kopel Simelovitz, our friend Klaus Grünewald now sat on the bench beside us, staring deeply into the cracked glass of a barber's mirror to draw a series of self-portraits. Lon Landau, patiently waiting for the carpenters to finish the wooden theater for the children, familiarized himself in the meantime with the operation of his marionettes. Fixing long, thin threads at the puppets' extremities, and winding them at the other end around his fingers, he tried to drum some talent into his papier-mâché actors, teaching them how to hop, to dance, to embrace and to beat each other up. Despite the deprivations, Nadia Bolotine was a still sumptuous ballerina full of vitality; she helped Lon's work with her stage experience. We had another visitor, the super-svelte actress Dunia Sadow not yet over her thoughts of suicide, posing for me, that is, for Meyer's art collection.

A new and now frequent guest at our workshop was another B-Number, Monsieur Deutsch, a retired art enthusiast, whose clothes made you think the barracks were a backdrop for *La Bohême*. Amiable, polite and unable to grasp the situation, he would be placed in the next cattle train to Auschwitz in his white shirt with an open collar, wearing his huge Basque beret and a flowing black bow, just as he had arrived at the camp. I still use the paint box he left me as a parting gift half a century ago.

I also made new acquaintances in the yard. It was sufficient to be a painter, young and female, to be drawn into conversations with prisoners of superior intellect such as David Kusman, a chemist who recited Russian poetry to me, or with Ilya Prigogine, a young scientist who later received a Nobel prize in chemistry. He discussed aspects of modern art that I had no knowledge of then. We still had to get out of the yard the moment a truck drove through the gate with newly arrested prisoners, though this happened less and less frequently. On the other hand, there were some mornings when one or two inmates were called up and released, like my neighbors the Heibers. The bed beside me was now empty, no more whispering. In place of Maurice Heiber in his white smock cutting an elegant figure in the camp, the dog trainer's red-haired girl friend was now managing the reopened children's kitchen.

At the same time as Maurice Heiber was named director of one of the three new Jewish old-age homes in Brussels, my father was brought there. The Gestapo had finally come to the room with the flower wallpaper and arrested him. But since he had just passed the age limit for deportation set by revised Gestapo regulations (born in 1878, he was now 65), we were spared a reunion in Mechelen. Once again chance had saved us, throwing the lifelines that kept my closest family and me above the waves.

I had wished for a bomb, a well-aimed one to make a breach in the barrack walls. And just as a bomb out of the blue a surprise hit me on an ordinary November morning, a happy event that all the same upset me deeply. All at once, Awret's name was called and he was free. We barely had time to say good-bye.

Seventeen

A LONG WINTER AND MANY MONTHS of yearning were to follow that November morning. Awret's release came about after members of his family petitioned the Queen Mother, who tried to help Nazi prisoners wherever possible. A quite good amateur sculptress, Queen Élisabeth learned from the potter near the palace of Laaken that Awret used to fire his clay sculptures at the same place that she brought hers and in the same kiln. Did she remember his work? In any case it was through her that he obtained his freedom. Helpless in the confines of the yellow walls, I thought of him constantly. Don't feel sorry for yourself, I had to repeat all the time, throwing myself into my work. If until now the Nazis did not get the better of me, I could cope with love too. I now had to paint numbers and signs by myself, since the baron was not much help. Otherwise Herbertchen did what he could to cheer me up. He even got hold of a frame for a drawing of Awret that I made, and carefully set the small portrait on the shelf above the stove. Tilly Sachs also showed unusual tactfulness, refraining from her "I told you so." But help came mainly from a side I least expected. Minnie and I became best friends again, closer than we had been before our rivalry. Every free minute she stole into the workshop, where we talked tirelessly about Awret and every facet of his personality. Since he was now out of reach for both of us, we were rivals no more. With little to do at the Reception, Minnie not only had time to chat but also to write poems. It was rumored that because of the lack of new arrivals the next transport would be composed largely of W-Numbers from the various workshops. Though this was worrisome, we followed our daily routine as before, the transport and B-Numbers keeping each of us occupied in a different fashion. On Sunday afternoons, Albert Clément continued to come up with new improvisations that made us laugh.

If our masters or guards got bored for lack of work, that was not so with their thoughts of sex. Ironically, women were protected by Hitler's Nuremberg laws that decreed any German who "shames his race" through relations with a Jewess was subject to penal servitude with hard work. Thank God we were taboo though the racial laws did not cover voyeurism.

"Health control, women down into the yard!" One early morning in December, Moishe Ear Boxer and Moishe Baby came running into our dormitory with this wake-up call. Not so strangely, only women under thirty had to report to an empty room, there to line up around the walls at regular intervals.

"Take off your clothes. Upper torso bare. Faster. Don't make such a fuss, hands down. This is a consumption checkup." The room was freezing cold and luckily, the inspection was not thorough. Behaving with the self-importance of medical men, a group of uniformed S.S. walked up and down this bosom paradise. But no grabbing — our bare skin was branded with the invisible warning: caution, detention with hard labor! Though I was flushing red and blue, first with shame, then with cold, my eyes, as usual independent, drew comparisons.

Facing me with downcast eyes stood Madame Hamburger, the seamstress for Frank's mistress Lillian. I had always noticed her high-domed forehead, but only now, undressed, she appeared like Lukas Cranach's Eve, with her long, svelte torso, the falling shoulders and narrow set breasts shaped like oranges. The window to my left illuminated a Venus de Milo with arms, Kitty from the kitchen. With her small, perfectly oval face, Greek nose, sturdy neck and the bosom of an ancient goddess, she was the youngest among us. Kitty had class and such "classic" features I thought, automatically crossing my arms over my own bareness.

"Hands down, damn Jew-sows!" shouted someone in a black uniform. Lingering a moment longer in antiquity, I tried to imagine a comparison for Kitty's hair. The Golden Fleece? No, even though curly it was much too short — for good reason. A year earlier, after she had been arrested in an Antwerp hospital, the Gestapo sheared her long curly mane. Why, she didn't know. Perhaps an S.S. had decided such hair would be a fitting trophy to carry back home from the great Jew hunt.

Shortly before her sixteenth birthday, Kitty was forced to leave her family's hideout to have her appendix removed. At the hospital a Gestapo agent had torn up an affidavit confirming that on her sixteenth birthday she would get Belgian citizenship and should not be deported. Even before her wound had time to heal, she was discharged from the hospital and sent to Mechelen. At first she was lucky — she was assigned to glue envelopes at the paper workshop, though soon afterwards prisoners were needed to complete a transport. Her bald head hidden under a scarf, she stood in the yard with those waiting to be handed the dreaded transport number, all of those in line making one last, desperate attempt to convince Boden of their usefulness.

"I am a certified dental technician, Herr Boden."

"In Vienna I used to be the official translator at international congresses."

"Herr Sturmscharführer, I have twenty years of experience in making orthopedic shoes to measure."

"I can peel potatoes!" Kitty had shouted and was told to step out of the line. Since then she worked in the kitchen.

I have mentioned the Negus and his wife, the Viennese couple that slept opposite my bed — he was a good looking fellow in his best years, full of vitality, sunburnt and with flashing black eyes. Was it his job as foreman of the yard workers or as dormitory elder, high positions in the hierarchy of our ant colony that went to his head? In any case he believed himself irresistible. But how he imagined a love affair in the confines of the camp could remain secret was hard to understand.

The ensuing gossip was interrupted by the sudden arrival of several hundred Gypsies, though only for the time being. These completely disoriented men, women and children were apparently needed to compensate for the lack of prisoners and to justify the continued existence of the camp.

One gray winter morning the big bell began ringing as if the camp was on fire. Whistles were blowing from all sides. "Everybody upstairs!" Half a dozen trucks rolled into the yard. People with pitiful belongings and a crowd of children were driven into one of the stairwells without the customary registration at the Reception. Observing the scene from behind one side of our window, Lon Landau squeezed his slight figure between the baron and me. The string tying him to one of his marionettes slid from his fingers: "If they are Jews I will eat my hat. They are Gypsies." Compared to the miserable conditions under which these three hundred fifty people were crammed into two dormitories, our captivity seemed almost humane. Jews were forbidden to have any kind of contact with them, and had to remain inside the building on the occasions they were allowed into the yard.

The more prolonged their stay in the camp, the slower they walked. The children's dark curls became matted, the women's shiny waves grew stringy. Their long, gaily flowered skirts hung limply from hips that became bonier by the day.

Their caretaker was Voss the Kapo, to whose everlasting credit it must be said that he did what he could to help them. He gave them anything edible he could get. He was aided by a Sudeten German who was too decent for an S.S. and remained just a short time in the camp — he brought the Gypsies leftovers from the meals of his comrades. One could not do much for them. The Gypsies probably knew even less than we about what awaited them — all of them down to the last toddler walked about as living corpses. After a few weeks in Mechelen, on January 15, they were put on the same train as the Jews of the twenty-third transport, and on arrival in Auschwitz were immediately gassed I later learned.

A short time after the Gypsies arrived, I sat at our desk painting one sentence on a large cardboard sign: SOILING THE AIR–RAID DEFENSE SAND IS PUNISHABLE BY PARCEL EMBARGO. However hard I tried, my lettering lacked Awret's bravura. The baron watched my efforts.

"Pull your tongue in, Irene," he admonished in a tired voice. Absorbed in wistful thoughts, voices penetrated my reverie, the word "wedding" drove me to the window. Below, Meyer and Voss stood trumpeting out a wedding invitation for all workers. We had to hurry down to the yard.

There we fell in line to form the bridal procession, Boden conducting and one of the yard workers playing Mendelssohn's festive wedding march on his harmonica. The bride, a recent conquest of the Negus, was a lovely girl as vivacious as his wife was quiet — she had a heavy limp, the result of a birth defect. The jailers had of course learned of the affair, and Boden, perhaps for his own perverse entertainment, had decided on a kind of allegorical punishment. Strange as it may seem, when all was said and done we Jews were placed half a step higher than the Gypsies. Even though the same fate awaited us, we were required to go on transport deloused with clean feet and seemingly clean morals.

Flanked by his wife and his girlfriend — by chance both named Trudi — the Negus walked at the head of the column with his tail between his legs. Limping, the younger of the Trudis pushed a baby carriage bearing a doll. The whole to-do was one of Boden's farces — for a moment I believed that the second Trudi would indeed be wed to the Negus' left hand. Then I realized where I was, in Boden's Saxony of the Middle Ages where adulterers were put in the pillory.

To whom did that baby carriage once belong? Who had played with the doll? A mixture of snow and rain began to soften my thoughts and the whole yard into a gray muddle — the faces around me remained stony. Water trickled darkly over the mustard-colored walls, raindrops veiled the black eyes of the Gypsy children pressing their noses against the windowpanes. Staring sightlessly in front of me, the same as the other involuntary guests, I remember only vaguely some kind of tasteless ritual officiated by a pseudo rabbi.

Despite everything, this story eventually had a happy ending. The three principal participants survived the war, the Negus and his wife rejoining their children, and the younger Trudi marrying a man who had been free. Swallowing everything, the legal Trudi remained in their double bed as before, while the Negus, uncharacteristically silent for a few evenings, soon began to circulate dirty jokes again from his vast treasure chest.

A man not to be overlooked in the courtyard was the porter Salomon. It was said of him that he had once been a sergeant in the Prussian army. Perhaps. His bald egg of a head sat ramrod straight over a belly he carried on short legs and flat feet. Such a belly was a rarity in the fourth year of the war and may have been used as padding to grovel before S.S. officers. With his bowing and scraping, his "yes, Sir's" and "very good, Sir's," he apparently wanted to demonstrate the good German he remained despite all the degradation he had suffered. Maybe superior high-toned officers could overlook the little impediment of his Mosaic religion. He was indeed allowed into the casino where he fed on table scraps and was made fun of. It was rumored that he had memorized all the verses of the bawdy song, the "Innkeeper's Wife." Whenever he addressed me in the yard, I gave a friendly nod as I tried to compensate for his lamentable ugliness. It was years before I realized that the true meaning of his pleasantries had been unbelievably obscene.

Toward the end of December, Boden gave Salomon his kind of Christmas present, plying the fat porter with alcohol until he was senselessly drunk. It is a riddle how anybody could have hauled him from the casino to the third floor dormitory, but obviously no effort was too great to bestow a Christmas gift on the girls. Marching in single file, we were ordered to look at the flabby mass overflowing an iron bed in the otherwise empty room — there was the stark-naked Salomon laying on his back, snoring open-mouthed, his whole body smeared with soot.

"Boden's plum-pudding," I whispered, trying to cheer up Dina who was walking in front of me. And in place of a shabby harmonica as with the wedding, a small orchestra made background music for Boden's nativity scene. In the yard below, a handful of Gypsies walked in front of the tattered, hungry column, playing their violins. The music sounded so pitiful and scratchy as though even the fiddles rebelled the Czardas they were forced to play. The loathsome, distorted images, the caterwauling — was I the one going crazy? But if Boden's charade aimed to disgust us, he had overstepped his mark — over time, porter Salomon's apotheosis has simply blurred into a large spot of grease.

———

The New Year brought the charades to an end. From the start of 1944 our masters were otherwise occupied. After four months of a dearth of Jews, the Nazis found in the Gypsies the replacement bodies they needed to fill up a transport. In the middle of January, the train had barely left when the air raids on Mechelen we had so wished for began. I had come down with a serious cold, perhaps caught during the bosom inspection or the wedding in the snow and rain. Of course, the workers tried to avoid the infirmary if at all possible and to appear healthy. Not since my early childhood was I so pampered as during my days of fever. Evi got hold of aspirin, Minnie came with tea and poems, Dina with a lemon wedge. Tilly and Madame Rosenberg warmed me under a mountain of blankets and coats, warming my heart as well while making me sweat profusely. After all that sweating came the luxurious moments of lassitude and weakness when I let myself be taken care of by my nurses. Big-hearted Raymonde the blonde rubbed me down with her precious cologne. Without using the services of the infirmary I was soon back on my feet. The arrival of Awret's first letter around that time also helped lift my spirits.

Was it because of censorship or was it Awret himself who had been slow in writing? Since his release almost two months earlier I had not heard from him. Pitying me and my futile wait for mail, the baron had tried to make me laugh. One day he simply turned Awret's portrait, which he himself had framed, so that it faced the wall.

Reading the letter I was eager to forgive. Awret was a "free Jew" in occupied Brussels. With food rationing, bombardments and continual air raids, he did not have it easy. His letter was warm yet serious, and it reassured me that he missed me and was waiting for me, a certitude I could hold onto come what may.

So we turned Awret's portrait to its frontal view once again. Little had changed except I could now be found in the workshop until late in the evening, often up to the time the guards called "lights out!" Dago Meyer obtained permission for me to work after hours in order to paint for him, naturally. Apparently tired of still lifes with onions and potatoes, and paintings of children with old eyes, he found inspiration in the Gypsies. I should paint a scene from Carmen for him, he said. As much as I hated Meyer, and as little as I felt like painting those poor Gypsies, Carmen it was. To refuse Dago's wishes meant being sent on the transport East under one pretext or another.

Dunia Sadow, the actress who had cut her veins, solved the problem of my blocked powers of imagination. To cut a theatrical pose was child's play for her. It was her profession — besides, she was young, svelte and had dark hair and eyes. Hélène Koen, who had dressed Lon Landau's marionettes, came up with a loose blouse with a lavish décolletage. She even got hold of an artificial rose for Carmen-Dunia to hold between her lips. And as I painted, trying to transform a Russian Jewess into a Spanish femme fatale, I listened for the howling of sirens, hoping for an air raid, for the guards to order us into the cellar. Sitting in the dark, we waited for the humming of the allied planes, the ack, ack of the German air defense, and had to muffle our excitement each time we heard the thud of a hit.

It was during those first air raids on Mechelen that I celebrated my twenty-third birthday, the eleventh anniversary of Hitler's coming to power. Hard to believe that since the day when Hindenburg named Hitler chancellor, eleven years had passed. On that day my last birthday guest had just said goodbye when the news came over the airwaves. I was carrying my mother's mocha cups to the sink when our radio roared with those mighty waves of "Sieg Heil." Good Germans like us had nothing to fear, Papa had soothed me, and anyhow, this whole comedy would be of short duration. Were "we" not the people of poets and thinkers? In a few weeks, at most, all decent Germans would recognize the new chancellor for what he really was, an anti-Semite gone amok, a madman.

I doubt that in Berlin the thirtieth of January continued to be celebrated with jubilation and torchlight parades. Nevertheless, despite bombs and newspapers full of black-framed obituaries, the German people continued to stand loyally behind my father's "madman."

"God with us" was engraved on the belt-buckle of the uniform my father wore marching into the First World War. No more God in this war. "To be German is to be loyal," the new belt proclaimed. At Stalingrad and in the ruins of Dresden, loyalty to the Führer was the motto. Why not add "cruelty does not dishonor, and thinking one's own mind does not bring happiness," I thought with some cynicism, turning the old German adage inside out. ("Armut schändet nicht, und Reichtum macht nicht glücklich.")

This does not mean I spent the whole of my twenty-third birthday chewing on old memories. My second birthday in captivity sticks in my mind because of a sausage, an authentic Hungarian salami, at the time a truly regal present. Schabbes, the house painter, a mute and devoted admirer, had filched the sausage with the help of an improvised fishing rod. Standing high on his ladder he had discovered through a hole in the wall a row of hooks hanging with hams and sausages in the pantry where provisions for the casino were kept under lock. The salami was out of this world — a number of good friends came to congratulate me and, consequently, like all good things, it did not last long.

The last of the salami gone, the baron also went, quite unexpectedly. At the beginning of February his number was called. He arrived at our workshop faster than I had ever seen him run, breezed a kiss on my cheek, took his envelope with the photos of the high society and was gone. The last I saw of him he was carrying a worn-out little snake-skin suitcase.

The "salon des artistes" was now in the past. As the sole remnant of the official painters' workshop, I was transferred to an attic, the kind of place where, from the time I had run after my mother to get a peek at the dolls in the old trunk, I had always felt at home. Attics, for me at least, have a kind of secret attraction. So I was quite satisfied with my new place of work, an abode reminding me of the attic at Uncle Tom's Cabin on Eisvogelweg, and the small world where I had passed a good part of my childhood playing and dreaming. The pine wood coffins the Judenrat provided and the gas masks stowed away between the beams did not bother me. Fitting in the general ambiance, they gave my new refuge a certain cachet.

Tenderly I set my two shells on the windowsill. Seen from high up, the yard lost some of its ugliness. The square sky seemed so near that I could almost touch it. My eyes followed a few rapidly moving winter clouds. Overcome by memories and once more feeling sorry for myself, a passage from Schiller's "Maria Stuart" came into my mind. I tried to piece it together. First haltingly, then more fluently I whispered

> Hurrying clouds, sailors of the airs!
> Could I roam and navigate with you!
> Kindly greet for me the land of my youth!
> I am imprisoned, I am in shackles,
> Ach, I have . . . Ach I have. . . .

There I was stuck. The rest of the unfortunate queen's lament was lost somewhere in my brain. Nonetheless I had to admit that six years of German literature with Miss Vogel equipped me with poetry for any situation.

Eighteen

LIFE IN THE NEW PAINTERS' WORKSHOP was quieter than it was in the old one. Dago Meyer still mustered enough energy to run up and down the stairs urging me to paint, but the guards rarely entered, apparently considering me harmless.

Harmless I was, and also careless. I did something that had I been caught, the Kommandant would have punished me severely. I had been studying Russian, perhaps to spite the Nazis but also because it looked as if the Russians might yet be our salvation. Having experienced the bravery, helpfulness and cooperative spirit of the Communists among us, I had become attracted to things Russian. Awret taught me the Ukrainian songs of his childhood, and I contorted my tongue to imitate the mellow, warm sounds of the Slavic language and so felt closer to him.

When I was in the Zionist youth organization, why had I sung Hebrew songs with such great ardor, not resting until I could also get a songbook in Yiddish? Why had I later plunged head-on into French literature and poetry, if not to prove to myself that I could do very well without my German baggage? German culture had spat me out like a bone sticking in its throat. Now it was my turn. I was going to show those old poets and composers who were obliterated under swastikas just who needed whom! Of course, there were those unavoidable relapses when, as in a fit of self-pity and longing, I identified with Schiller's captive queen rather than with Verlaine in prison. I could not help this.

David Kusman grew up in Lithuania in a Russian environment. He was my willing teacher. He wrote down the Cyrillic alphabet and some grammar on pieces of paper, which I quickly absorbed and then tore the paper into shreds. During the long air raids we passed in the cellar, he repeated little poems, everyday sentences, and the basics of Russian grammar for my benefit as patiently as if he was teaching a parrot. Often the air raid sirens started howling in the middle of the night. In the pitch black, moldy vaults below the barracks, trembling with cold and dead tired, I recited Krylow's fable of the monkey with the glasses, imagining myself as Irina in a literary salon full of plush furniture with tassels.

By day I was engaged in French — Minnie Feldman and I had started writing a novel. In a brew of high school prose, her high-flown poems and my illustrations, we threw ourselves enthusiastically into an epic about the barracks, after every few sentences coming back to ourselves, Awret, and a tangled web of emotions. Surrounded by gas masks, coffins and Lon Landau's merry marionettes, we began to write about two imprisoned women, a poet and painter, who fall for a charming sculptor, despite their tragic circumstances. We kept the manuscript strictly to ourselves and hid it inside the double lid of the paint box that Monsieur Deutsch had given me — the hollow space was for holding canvasses.

Although the absorption in our novel and my cramming of Russian helped get me through the day, I did not get far with either our secret writing or the forbidden language. My Russian lessons would end in May with David Kusman's liberation. Our novel came to a sudden halt with Minnie's release in June, three days after the Allied landing.

Landau's marionettes and I had our refuge under the rafters. In March the carpenters finally set up the theater in a corner of the attic — for Lon, who spent months perfecting the operation of his puppets, this was the time he had waited for. At last he could design the sets — this was his passion. I wish I could once more see the backdrops for the little theater he put together so long ago, especially his "magic forest." Out of remnants from the tailor shop, shreds of fabric and bits of lace, feathers and false pearls, on a watercolor background, he had conjured up a stage that was the most beautiful and imaginative I have ever seen.

My arrival at Mechelen: Minnie Feldman searches my purse at the Reception. A pencil drawing I did in 1944 for the novel that Minnie and I were writing. (Ghetto Fighters' House Museum, Israel)

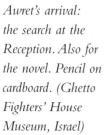

Awret's arrival: the search at the Reception. Also for the novel. Pencil on cardboard. (Ghetto Fighters' House Museum, Israel)

I am sorry to say the puppet show never took place. One morning at the end of May, just as Lon was readying for the premiere, Kommandant Frank sent for him — when he came back he sat for a long time by the two poles that the marionettes hung from. He said nothing. I didn't dare ask what happened.

"Adieu, Irene, I am going on the next transport," he murmured finally, his index finger stroking the crown of the princess. Then he laughed bitterly. "When you are out of luck, you're out of luck. My best friends — and they finished me off with the best of intentions!"

Up to this moment he had not told anyone that from the very day of his arrest his friends and family in Antwerp had been trying to get him out. Having been informed at long last that his family had found a sympathetic ear with the Gestapo, Lon believed he might well have one leg past the gate when the Kommandant sent for him. Seated behind his desk Frank pushed a piece of cardboard at him, one of the new transport numbers I had just painted. Looking through his dossier in view of his eventual release, the Gestapo had come upon information tying him to the Communist party.

"Out!" Frank had said gruffly, and that was it. Had they found in his dossier that he had once raped or killed somebody, then maybe his family could still have saved him. But a Communist — there was nothing anyone could do.

On the fourth of April, the date of the twenty-fourth transport, I had to say goodbye to my good friend, this time forever. With the cattle train on the tracks, Lon came for a last visit — I gave him the woolen socks Awret had left for me, and promised to take care of the marionettes, speaking as if I was sure we would soon see each other again.

Not even at that moment could I overcome my Prussian fear of an outburst of emotions. Why did I act as if I did not know that Lon felt more than friendship for me, that I had not noticed how much the profile of the princess with the little crown resembled mine? Why did I kiss him smilingly with the prescribed three little Belgian pecks, when I was very well aware it was real warmth and a few tears, not woolen socks, he wanted for the journey? Lon had never asked more of me than I was prepared to give. I regret my prudish good-bye to this very day.

Directly after the liberation of Belgium in early fall 1944, when the truth about the camps in the East just started to emerge, I learned that Lon had been found alive in Bergen-Belsen and was shortly expected in Antwerp. A few weeks later he was dead. Lon had volunteered to help with the sick in the camp and in his weakened condition had contracted typhus.

After Lon's deportation, followed by the release of my last remaining colleague and friend Klaus Grünewald, my workshop under the rafters became even lonelier, though unexpected gifts began raining down on my island. The first was two books Ilya Prigogine sent me with colored reproductions of work by Matisse and Chagall. Prigogine was the young scientist who sometimes discussed modern art with me in the yard — he had been freed and not forgotten me. Our censors Mella and Erika did not know what silverware to eat modern paintings with and submitted them to Frank as they did with all questionable packages and mail. In a fit of generosity, the Kommandant let me have them. What evil influence could degenerate art have on someone Jewish anyhow? However, he could not refrain from expressing his opinion on the first page of both books in huge, red, gothic letters, "What trash! Johannes Frank, 29.4.1944."

Prigogine could not have made a better choice to cheer me up. I was hungry for color and Matisse's paintings especially were like the discovery of a portion of juicy roast goose in my tin bowl. That was not all. Awret also began to send me books, *Letters of Vincent van Gogh to His Brother Théo*, and Alain Fournier's *The Grand Meaulnes*. Since these were books Awret had chosen, van Gogh's letters became even more poignant and meaningful to me than they already were, while *The Grand Meaulnes* let me bridge the sordid present into rosy tinted freedom and into the waiting arms of a — at least in the novel — lonely man.

Another of Awret's gifts, Kipling's *Kim*, was a feast day. For a whole week a half-Irish, half-Indian ragamuffin lifted me beyond the most ordinary, the most gray-brown of all barrack rooftops, to explore far away India. Meeting with Hindus, Sikhs and Pakistanis, with holy beggars and wily spies on endless routes and highways, I sniffed the scent of dried dung, of cumin, curcuma and curry, following Kim's flight through the Khyber Pass. I read slower and slower, trying to hold up the unavoidable ending of the story — at last though, I had to leave Kim and company and exchange the green flag with the red bull, the saffron robes of the monks, colorful saris, exotic spices and any imaginable turbans for the barracks.

Apart from Minnie and from Ferdekopf who took an almost human interest in the orphaned marionettes, only Meyer still climbed up the stairs. The relative privacy I enjoyed gave him the idea for a new work of art. Instead of Dunia as Carmen with a rose between her lips, in his last commission he wanted me to paint the actress al fresco, in the nude. If somebody was to come up the stairs, she would have sufficient time to put on a robe, he said without undue concern.

Under normal conditions, it cost me some effort to kill any insect larger than a mosquito. Quail, pigeon, rabbit, any small creature helplessly lying on my plate I could not touch, not even lobster. As a child in Uncle Tom's Cabin, I once went all the way to the park to free a mouse that had been caught in a trap in our cellar. But what happened to the former Irene Paula Dolorosa Sara Spicker alias the dainty baroness, a friend to people and to animals? A W-Number was sitting in her place in the painters' workshop, dreaming with open eyes of blood baths and long, sharp knives. The more time I spent in captivity, the more often my thoughts turned to murder and vengeance. My favorite dream was about joyously thrusting a dagger into Meyer's breast again and again until he swam in blood.

Reality was different. Whether Meyer murmured his demands sweetly and smilingly or barked them in a voice that traveled to the farthest corner of an auditorium, they were to be executed with a semblance of enthusiasm, if one did not want to be sent on transport. Consequently, Dunia had to undress, and I had to paint. And even though the cold in the attic affected her flesh tones, Meyer got his nude — with somewhat bluish colors.

In addition to daydreams about murdering Meyer, I also began to rack my brains about possibilities for a breakout. In the middle of May, sirens were driving us more frequently into the cellar. The British or the Americans were probably aiming their bombs at the neighboring railway network and bridges. Even though the hits were coming closer, the barracks remained untouched. Once, around midnight, we all jumped up, so powerful was the bomb that had struck near us. The cellar walls were swaying as in an earthquake, but the longed for cave-in did not follow. That gave me an idea. Bombs would not do the job, but might there not be a more silent way to break out? Kusman who was still in the camp not only knew Russian, he also was a chemist familiar with solvents. I speculated that all we needed for our flight was a hole in the wall, night and fog.

"Kusman, do you know of chemicals that can dissolve bricks?" I asked, keeping my voice low. The darkness was alive with animated talk. To regain their balance after the shock of the near hit and the disappointment that followed premature shouts of joy, people told stories or anecdotes. While Kusman weighed my question, Nadia Bolotine, the sumptuous ballerina, described her past in a Brussels corps de ballet:

"My second husband was Russian and a marvelous dancer," she began to giggle. "Once during a pas de deux he had to lift me up and swing me around. It should have been easy, like lifting a feather — after all, he is the prince and I am sleeping beauty. But it was hard work after my good dinner. 'Nadia, mooo, you're dancing like a cow!' he hissed in the middle of a passionate embrace. 'Nadia, mooo. Du tanzt wie eine Kuh!'" She was still shrieking with laughter when Kusman whispered an answer to my question.

"You want something that can dissolve bricks? Sure, caustic soda. That eats everything, including your hands. It dissolves in water, it's cheap and easy to find, but for what in God's name do you need it?" I explained my idea. "You cannot mean that seriously, Irene," he said, feeling the clammy wall we leaned on as if to gauge its thickness. "Do you know how much of the stuff would be needed to chew out a hole the size of a man's shoulders?" He squatted down on the flagstones listening to the Negus telling one of his dirty jokes. But just when

Count Rudi and Viscount Bobbi met in the Vienna tramway, the sirens sounded the end of the air raid and we returned to our dormitories.

Not only this night, but for a whole week until Kusman's sudden liberation, I dreamt of a caustic soda miracle. A magic formula was working for me, a gooey mass, relentlessly wearing away the wall in the darkest corner of the cellar. Would it eat a hole big enough to crawl into freedom? But how, under what pretext, could I obtain a large quantity of caustic soda? How could I explain that I needed it to paint?

Still racking my brain during the afternoon walk, I did not notice that Evi looked more absentminded than usual, her round, brown eyes full of worry.

"What is the matter Evi, what happened?" I asked.

"I would not be astonished if Boden ships me off with the next transport," she said. "Some days ago, right after he mailed a parcel with the pick of our packages to his family in Leipzig, he was in a good mood. Thinking this was my chance to ask him for a favor, I went up to him and requested a coupon for a head of lettuce for the witches' den. I did not remember anymore what fresh vegetables taste like."

"All right, Fräulein Efa," he looked me up and down, "You are a little pale around the gills, but at the same time you are rising like a yeast-cake." Furtively glancing at Evi, I had to admit that Boden was right. Bloated by twenty months of rutabaga soup and potatoes she was no longer a squirrel. She still ran more than walked, but her little feet were not so nimble anymore.

Boden, in any event, had given his authorization for a head of lettuce. Evi naturally used her one-time entry into the vegetable cellar to take two lettuce heads, filling her basket with carrots, cucumbers and onions too. Bad luck had it that on the way back to the witches' den she met Boden. He obviously noticed the kerchief covering her basket, but did not say a word. "That was only the prelude, Irene, the worst is still to come. Boden is finished with me. Finished, out! Now he dictates his reports to Anna Landes, and I am no Fräulein Efa anymore. I am thin air." How did she so suddenly fall out of favor?

A few days later when Boden sent Evi to get a bar of soap for the Reception, she dared to plead for a coupon for two bars, one for her personal use. Receiving only Judenrat packages, and those rarely, she found it difficult to depend on her fellow prisoners' good graces for her personal hygiene. If lettuce then why not soap too, she thought, and indeed, Boden acquiesced.

"Let's see yours," Boden pointed to Evi's apron pocket when, on her return, she deposed a bar of soap by a basin in the reception.

"My bar was bigger and why not?" As if to justify herself with me, Evi gripped my arm. "In the storeroom they have piles of soap that were taken from Jews — all for Germany. This errand was a unique opportunity. Don't ask what a scene Boden made! Still waters run deep and dirty. Good that he's at last got to know me, the most selfish, the most ungrateful person he's met in all his long career. You will see, Irene, he will put me on a transport!"

But things would turn out differently. Boden's preoccupation with soap would soon fade in the face of the Allied landing.

In the middle of May, David Kusman's release brought more than just my Russian language study to a halt. Deprived of his expertise, my chemical hocus-pocus — caustic soda eating holes through prison walls — went up in air but to be supplanted by more concrete hopes. Toward the end of May talk in the dormitories, in the workshops, and in the yard centered on rumors about papers on Frank's desk — according to a list sent from Berlin, a number of prisoners from our camp would be exchanged for wounded German prisoners of war in British hands.

Excitedly we speculated on how many and whose names might be on that list. Altogether our motto was, "waiting." Waiting for the next transport, waiting for the next piece of bread, waiting for the next bowl of soup, waiting for the next package. We had been waiting so long for the Allied landing that we had no breath left, not even a second wind. While one cattle train after another took Jews East without hindrance, the string we so desperately clung to slid out of our fingers; the ballon going with it faded into an almost invisible dot in our square of blue. If only the Allied bombers would destroy the railway tracks.

A list of names to be released, on the other hand, was tangible, maybe not a great hope, but one that could become reality. How many names were there, six, seven, eight, and perhaps even a dozen? The camp buzzed with rumors as a handful of prisoners were let go, among them Madame Ehrentreu with her three sons. That was said to be only the beginning, soon to be followed by a second batch.

In the meantime we were in the last days of May, unaware that a gigantic armada with the British, American and Canadian armies, as well as French soldiers, was putting to sea for the Continent. Many thousands would give their lives to liberate Holland, Belgium and France from the Nazi yoke. One more week of the seemingly endless waiting and these thick stonewalls would almost burst with our joy.

We first learned about the Allied landings from Arnold Dobruszkes the electrician. Usually repairing at least one radio for the S.S., he was the first to know the latest news. Our captors were in the worst of moods. After the fiasco of the German army in France, more than a hundred newly-caught Jews were brought into camp, an action that we took for some kind of helpless, vengeful counter-offensive. These people were from Liège. The remnants of the Jewish community in Brussels and Antwerp were too well hidden to let themselves be taken by surprise raids. Against whom else could the Nazis vent their rage if not the Jews? Who else could so easily be made accountable when things went wrong?

Yet strangely enough and despite everything else, at the very time the Jews from Liège were arriving — exactly three days after the Allied landings — the rest of the prisoners on the exchange list were freed. A list was a list, and order was order. Once more I had to say goodbye. Left, right, left, three quick Belgian pecks on both cheeks, and Evi, Minnie and her sister Miriam were gone. All three worked at the Reception from the day the camp had come into existence.

Much as I missed my friends Minnie and Evi, in the bustle of the barracks and among the many new prisoners, I could not feel lonely for long. Also, the rapid unfolding of events did not let anyone sit and mope.

"What do you think, Tilly, what will they do with us when they are cornered?" Handing my neighbor a bucket full of water with so much

energy that it slopped over, I glanced in the direction of Moishe Baby
and Moishe Ear Boxer's black uniforms.

"Better pay attention to what you are doing, Irene. My stockings
were soaked, and Moishe Baby was looking at us." We stood in a long
line reaching through the open gate to a pump and freedom, passing
buckets from hand to hand. A bomb damaged the water supply to the
barracks and we were sitting high and dry and beginning to smell.
"What will they do with us?" Tilly wiped a few gray strands from her
forehead. "Why should I worry over unlaid eggs? Have you ever seen
things happening the way you thought they would? After all, an end
with terror is better than terror without end, don't you agree?" I
agreed.

Not only from Arnold had we heard how successful the Allied landing had been, but the growing nervousness of our jailers spoke for
itself. The best sign of their mounting fear was the ditch they were digging in the yard. I never understood what they needed it for. Some
prisoners said that while we were down in the cellar during an air raid,
Frank, Boden and the other S.S. would jump into that ditch at the
approaching sound of the bombers.

Did they consider jumping into ditches more manly than running
into a cellar? Or was it their intention to defend the building from that
last stand in case of an infantry attack? To be driven into the cellar with
the first howl of the sirens was clearly not only for our protection —
we had no illusions about that: it was probably a precaution against our
flight in case of a hit. That under certain conditions we could be
driven into the ditch instead of into the cellar, there to be shot and
buried, never entered my mind. For me the ditch was a symbol of
defense — hurrah! At last the Nazis were forced into the defensive.
Nevertheless, and to our general astonishment, our jailers did not treat
us more roughly than before. On the contrary. While they were
drowning their worries in French cognac, we were left more to ourselves. But with all that, the well-oiled deportation mechanism still
continued its work just as efficiently as before, undisturbed by drunken
S.S. or the slowly approaching Allied armies. For the dozens of prisoners on the exchange list that had been freed, hundreds of new ones
were delivered in those summer weeks that followed.

One morning a tall man with a white mane of hair and sharp eyes stood in the door of my attic. He presented himself as "Jacques Ochs, from Liège." My visitor was the caricaturist of the *Pourquoi Pas*, a masterful draftsman, whose signature I had seen often on the title page of the best-known Belgian satirical monthly. For the first time since Lon Landau's deportation and the release of the painter Klaus Grünewald, I had a colleague who was an experienced artist I could learn from. A virtuoso, he caught his model with a few simple lines, cutting through contours and superficial resemblance to the quick of a person's true nature. I looked on as he immortalized Ferdekopf, Meyer and Judith the Spider on paper at the painters' workshop, feeling flattered that a draftsman of his stature treated me as an equal. Naturally I enthusiastically accepted his proposal to bring the slightly retarded but picturesque "Napoléon" to my garret, so we could paint his portrait together. Wine colored cheeks, a cerise nose and a scarlet scarf made a violent contrast with the cobalt blue shirt and the jellyfish eyes of the one-legged former slaughterhouse assistant. A touch of yellow was added by a mouth full of giant teeth. Needless to say, this feast of color paired with my eagerness to equal Ochs transported me to fields of garish brightness I had never reached before. Not yet very critical, I sat in the saddle of a merry rainbow, for a while forgetting where I was.

Shortly after meeting Jacques, I was circling the yard for the umpteenth time with Madame Rosenberg who called my attention to a thin newcomer in our ranks. Silently plodding along, this taciturn new prisoner was the most famous artist I was to meet in the camp.

"Give him some paper and lend him your watercolor box for a few days, Irene," pleaded Madame Rosenberg, always eager to help. "The man is the painter Felix Nussbaum and he is from Germany like you. His wife hopes that paints and a brush might bring him out of his despondency." Said and done. Nussbaum came to my workshop to get the box, but painted only in his dormitory. To judge from the still lifes he showed me afterwards, even painting did not seem to cheer him up. Neatly rendered on the tiniest bits of paper lay a lone, dimly lit pear, a gray apple. Even a lemon boded gloom. Unfortunately the artist's hopelessness and dark premonitions were well founded.

While high under the rooftop I was delighting in a red scarf, a blue shirt and yellow teeth, great battles were being fought on all fronts. As the German army retreated, I sat in my garret spooning up beet soup, receiving here and there a package with real food and much that was supposed to be real food. Irresistibly driven from Northern France in a southeasterly direction toward where we were, the Wehrmacht was forced to give up one town after another that it had occupied four years earlier. At the same time the Gestapo was still making frantic efforts to ship as many Jews as possible to Poland — no obstacle was too great for this end. Even though railway tracks were jammed with troop transports, air raids were constant and surveillance personnel were lacking, one more empty cattle train arrived in front of the barracks at the end of July. It was here to transport the several hundred prisoners the Gestapo had scratched together with great difficulty since the last transport in May.

Jacques Ochs was a Belgian subject and a renowned artist — with many contacts, he was spared deportation. This was not so for Felix Nussbaum. An unknown refugee whose name art lovers and critics outside Germany had never heard of, he and his wife were herded into a wagon to disappear forever. The tiny watercolor of a gloomy lemon was very likely his last painting. At the time I did not pay much attention to Nussbaum's small still lifes. Only many years later, leafing through a book of German art, I understood just whom it was I had met.

We W-Numbers, about 500 of us, would have been enough to complete what could have been a twenty-seventh transport from Belgium eastward — often during the month of August, my stomach was upset at the thought. Still I went on in my workshop as if all was well with the Third Reich, which was the impression the Gestapo wanted to maintain in the camp and among the general population. Fortunately. Although they might have wanted to simply close up shop and run, how could the Gestapo do so when the Wehrmacht was fighting nearby for every town and village? Of course we were not told of plans for our eventual evacuation, or of other lethal alternatives in case of a general retreat.

We veteran slaves continued groping in the dark for our future, any future. One moment, full of hope, I propped up my ears, imagining cannon thundering in the distance. The next, recalling the photos of the dead flitzers and the furniture van carrying suffocated corpses, I tried to prepare for the worst.

There was not even enough work for one painter. New numbers were no longer needed. Too impatient to paint, my models too jittery to pose, waiting became my main occupation. But what was I waiting for? Better an end with terror than terror without end, Tilly had said. For now all was calm, not even a swallow sailed through the sky. And so I began reading the last book Awret sent me, *The Wonderful Adventures of Nils Holgersson.* Children's classics are a proven antidote for feeling blue. Soon I was accompanying the wild geese North on their flight over Sweden. But when we were over Lapland I heard steps approaching on the stairs. Too soft for Ferdekopf coming to visit the marionettes, too slow for Meyer, I closed my book anyhow, taking up a pencil. My visitor was not the guard in his black uniform that I expected. Wearing field gray, Lieutenant Noppenei the supervisor of the storehouse opened the door. With a polite nod, he looked at some of my work quite patronizingly, then began to lecture me about his family. According to his description they were an old, widespread clan of patrician extraction settled on the Rhine. What did he want of me with his fine, pure Aryan ancestors? Still I listened like a serious, equally proper young lady, nodding from time to time until he finally explained the reason for his visit. He wanted me to draw the family tree of The Noppeneis in a hand-bound booklet, in color and in Gothic calligraphy.

An old Yiddish saying came to mind, "Your worries are the kind I would like to have." Here we were in the third week of August 1944, the German defense of Paris had been breached, and Lieutenant Noppenei stood here, this wooden martinet with rosy little cheeks and Delft blue eyes, cool as a cucumber, describing his precious family tree down to its smallest twigs.

"Next week I shall bring you the parchment paper already bound. Until then, get your sketch ready. You know, some beautiful oak tree, my family rising up from strong old roots, my ancestors, and most

Flemish S.S. guard Lodewijk van Col, whom prisoners called "Ferdekopf." Pencil drawing by Jacques Ochs. (Ghetto fighters' House Museum, Israel; photograph of van Col, Jewish Museum of Deportation and Resistance, Mechelen, Belgium)

Dago Meyer. Pencil drawing by Jacques Ochs. (Ghetto Fighters' House Museum, Israel)

Judith, "The Spider." Pencil drawing by Jacques Ochs. (Ghetto Fighters' House Museum, Israel)

Drawing of an inmate. Crayon drawing by Jacques Ochs. (Ghetto Fighters' House Museum, Israel)

important I want clean work!" The man was to be envied. He wore invisible blinders, I thought to myself. A fool's cap too, doddering over that stuffy, pink face. Don't look up or you'll burst out laughing.

"Yes Herr Noppenei, nice and clean," I promised. The following week, however, the Kommandant received a visit of such importance that even Lieutenant Noppenei, still loyally believing in the Führer's secret wonder weapon, forgot to water his family tree. For two whole days Frank sat from early morning until late at night, closeted with a Gestapo envoy from Berlin. It was rumored that they were fine-combing each one of the E-Numbers, meaning prisoners who were not yet deported, because it was unclear whether or not, according to the Nuremberg laws, they were Jews.

Today I know the name of that mysterious courier — he was Anton Burger. Having overseen the mass deportation of the Jews of Greece, he had hurried to Brussels to organize a quick eleventh hour "final solution" for the remaining Belgian Jews. Burger and Frank scrutinizing all E-Numbers through a magnifying glass implied a transport. These were the last, oppressively hot days of August — so near to freedom, we were yet on the threshold of despair. For who except a few dozen E-Numbers was still available for Herr Burger's transport? Only we W-Numbers. But Herr Burger had others besides us in mind. It later came out that all of the more than 500 inmates of the camp, together with the occupants of the Jewish old age, children and infant homes, were to be shipped from the Brussels South railway station to Bergen-Belsen on August 31st.

Had a telephone call not suddenly ordered Herr Burger to Berlin, then this story would in all probability have never been told. Since trains cannot be conjured up and since there was no gasoline for trucks to replace them, Herr Burger would not have hesitated to march us on foot to Bergen-Belsen. And it was well known what that would have meant. Instead, with all 500 Jews in the barracks, I was once more incredibly fortunate. The very moment the gate closed behind Himmler's courier, Frank stood in the yard raising both his hands. "Ugh! Thank God he is gone," he exclaimed in earshot of the girls of the Reception and of many workers.

The news about Frank's gesture got around the barracks, and a collective load was taken off our minds. Would Frank have executed any given order at the time, I sometimes ask myself, including one to kill us all? I believe that the answer is yes, even if reluctantly. What may have prompted that hardened S.S. officer's public sigh of relief? Fear for his own skin in view of the advancing Allies? Too much trouble to organize a death march? A belated touch of humaneness?

The telephone ringing in Frank's office had not only called Herr Burger back to Berlin, it had rung the bell of freedom and a new lease on life for the old people and the babies in the Brussels homes and for the inmates of our barracks. Quietly, without shouts of "faster, faster," the prisoners were assembled in the courtyard the next morning. Standing with crossed arms on the edge of his trench, Frank made a speech that was short and to the point. If we would calmly go about our work we had nothing to fear, we were not going to be deported. In a few days the garrison would leave, in which case we must stay in our dormitories and wait. Whom we should wait for was obviously too embarrassing for him to detail. Listening from a place where I saw his backside, I was fascinated by the flat cognac bottle sticking out of his trouser pocket.

Was Frank preoccupied with our safety while he himself had to take to his heels? It was too good to be true. As in a dream floating up into my workshop, I was called back down into the yard a short while later to listen to Boden's long-winded exhortations. To our amazement, we found that we were no longer Jew-sows, that today was not "Shabbes" for him, that it did not "rain" anymore whenever a Jew asked for something. Where in his broad chest had he hidden so much paternal benevolence? Visibly trying to convince himself of our good treatment at his hands, he told us how he had always done his utmost to be just. "Don't ever forget who has been the Mamme of this camp!" he ended unctuously. We were, of course, not in a position to reply, not to mention the fact that we were speechless.

Evidently Boden believed what he was saying. From his point of view he may have been right. Had sadists like Major Schmitt and his helper Krull remained at the helm of the camp, things would undoubtedly have ended worse. Even if the whole world went up in flames,

and even if not all Jews were reduced to ash, Boden might have speculated, the rest of them still remained Jews — and to whom did we
then owe our lives?

The Nazis fleeing and we staying? We could barely believe it,
though Frank's assurances and Boden's fatherly outpouring were not a
dream. The guards passed as usual. Each of us stuck to our job.
Nobody wanted to attract attention at the last moment. Hélène Koen,
her husband and a whole band of tailors lodged in a dormitory with
an alcove. Through its small window one could see the outside world
— that is, the upper floor of a house in the Joodenstraat. (It is ironic
that one wing of the barracks stood in an alley which for hundreds of
years has been called Jews' Street!) Risking arrest themselves, the
Flemish inhabitants of that house tried to encourage us with good
news, coming faster and thicker with one bulletin after another. As
soon as they saw one of us in the window, they exhibited a blackboard
freshly chalked up with the daily reports from Radio London. Patton
in Chartres! Next day in Dreux, then Orléans, Fontainebleau, Troyes.
Then at last "American Tanks in Paris!"

When the British and Americans also breached the front in the
North — the German armies had to defend not only against the Allies
but also against a hostile civilian population bearing down from all
sides — we got visitors. As the big bell by the gate rang almost unin-
terruptedly, we had to drop everything and were ordered to go up to
our dormitories.

"Everybody upstairs! Whoever looks through the window will be
shot!" How could one miss the view we caught peeking sideways
through the panes? Military vehicles, motorcycles, trucks were driving
in and out, the courtyard transforming itself into a forest of antennas.
The entire general staff of the Gestapo from the North of France under
General Constantin Canaris sought refuge in the barracks before continuing into Holland, the only way left open for their attempt to reach
Germany.

Tilly pulled me back from the window at the head of our beds.

"Want to die a heroic death in action at the last minute?" But the
guards only shouted. Even they had other things to worry about.

"Arras and Tournai in British hands" had presumably been chalked on the blackboard. "Tomorrow it's the turn of Brussels." Who could sleep? All night the dormitory was whirring with plans for the future. With morning light, activities in the yard became even more hectic than the day before. Soldiers getting in and out of trucks repacking and reloading, others calmly sitting with their headsets and their radios amidst the noise and the comings and goings. One scene, which took place in the afternoon at the time when the jubilant population of Brussels greeted the first allied troops, remains more distinctly imprinted on my memory than others. A young woman, probably known in Mechelen as the lover of one or several German officers and fearing retribution at the hands of enraged patriots, tried unsuccessfully to be accommodated in one of the crammed trucks. (Maybe the men inside simply wanted to get rid of her.) Fully aware that at the very least, the next day her head would be shorn, despair gave her the courage to climb on the roof of the already rolling vehicle. As the truck disappeared through the gateway, she lay on her stomach on the tarpaulin, trying frantically to get a grip on the canvas.

On the other hand, Herr Noppenei, momentarily deflected from his genealogy, remained a rock of faith in the chaos of flight. The same as the fortunate ones among us, trusting in God's help in any situation, he, the master of the storehouse, continued to cling to his belief in the Führer's secret weapon. The following took place between him and my friend Arnold, Noppenei's right hand man, on that same afternoon. In contact with the underground, Arnold was charged with providing potential flitzers with tools he had to steal from the storehouse.

The owner of the hardware store where Arnold used to shop was in collusion with him, so that he always received more tools than shown on the receipt. On the other hand, each time Noppenei checked the storehouse inventory, which he did frequently, Arnold was the one responsible for the numbers. Since Arnold could not always remember how many files, saws, knives and crowbars he had distributed to the transport numbers, he preferred to produce too many rather than too few tools for Noppenei's inspection. Arnold's lists did not arouse suspicion, quite the opposite. Noppenei was happy when the numbers were on the plus side.

On this day preceding our liberation, when everything was upside down, Noppenei and Arnold had the following exchange:

"Now listen, Arnold, I will be away on a trip for a short time. In two weeks at the most I shall be back. I count on you to stay here. Watch the store well. I don't want anything missing, do you hear!"

"Herr Noppenei, I cannot promise you that I will stay, but nothing will be missing."

⸻

At nightfall the courtyard below was still swarming with vehicles and uniforms. Our guards however were invisible, no one patroled the dormitories where we shared what was left of our packages. Again too excited to sleep, toward midnight I dropped fully dressed on my bed, dozing until sporadic crackling made me sit up. It was dawn. I could hear shooting from outside the barracks; otherwise everything was quiet. Looking through the windows we saw no reaction. The yard was empty. Only a few hardy souls dared to go down at first, soon to be followed by all of us. Cautiously reconnoitering the staircase leading to my workshop, I noticed that the door to Doctor Parnes' place, a room the camp physician shared with his wife, stood open. The room was empty, the whitewashed walls punctured by bullet holes. Trying to get nearer the window to see what was going on outside, something flitted by. Ping, ping — a few more pockmarks in the wall, and Tilly and I ran down into the cellar.

In relative safety there, we could piece events together. From all appearances a small engagement was taking place in the street above between the German rearguard and the first British soldiers. Since all we saw through the cellar windows were boots running along the barracks wall, all of them black, we could not distinguish who was who. Later it appeared that the German rearguard was to have blown up the bridge over the canal nearby, but had been too late. The shooting finally stopping, everybody met in the yard to discuss whether we should try to break out. One thing was certain, with Frank, Boden and the gray, green and black uniforms gone, we were alone in the barracks.

Arnold who had been listening to a radio in the storehouse all morning, came running.

"Brussels is free. The Germans have fled!"

"We've waited enough. GA BUITEN (Flemish for GO OUT!) shouted Meier Koen, Hélène's husband, pointing upward in the direction of their dormitory. "That's all that the people from the other side of the street have written on their blackboard, only two words, GA BUITEN!"

Should we simply disregard Frank's warning not to open the gate? Even before a decision was made, Napoléon stamped to the gate on one good and one wooden leg, drawing the crowd behind him.

"After me!" he shouted, swinging his cane high into the air and then with all his might against the heavy gate. Was it unlatched? As in a biblical miracle, the wings flew open. Roaring "Vive Napoléon!" five hundred twenty-seven Jews streamed into the streets of Mechelen.

⟶

What more can I say of that moment? My life has had many beautiful days, but September 4th, 1944, has remained the most beautiful of all. Simply to walk along a street straight into the horizon was such a heady adventure. It took my breath away. On all sides inhabitants of the neighborhood invited us into their homes. For the first time, I saw the neighbors among whom I had lived for a year-and-a-half. Their small houses were spick and span, even their dishes, down to the coffee cups, taste of green soap. Jews from the barracks were sitting in entrances, pubs and stores, drinking coffee, the last of the reserves each good Belgian had saved for the day of liberation.

The excitement heightened by the coffee and paired with lack of sleep took effect. My heart, whose existence I had been aware of only metaphorically, was suddenly fidgety, a rather harmless, nervous syndrome, in German popularly called "Zappel Herz." Since such a condition was unknown to me, I resigned myself to an early end. Fate in its typical irony, I thought. The beginning of the end had to come on the very day of liberation. All right, I shall die young — what does it matter? I was free, everything else was unimportant.

Beautiful as it was outside, I returned around noon to the barracks to pack. For the first time in three days I set foot in the painters' workshop. The attic looked undisturbed. The coffins and the gas masks, which fortunately were not needed, the paint box, my paintings and my books, everything was in its place. The theater was also still there — but the backdrop and the marionettes were gone. The only one left, hanging from his pole as if to mock me, was Till Eulenspiegel.

I suspected that Ferdekopf, who had shown the puppets more interest than the living beings — interest verging on affection — was responsible for the yawning gap. But when the police went to his house to look for them, Ferdekopf already sat in prison and his wife claimed she had never seen any marionettes.

Public transport had not yet been reinstated on that fourth of September, but where help was needed, nothing was impossible for Maurice and Esther Heiber. In the afternoon, my former neighbors from the W-dormitory arrived at the barracks to tell us that on the following morning the Judenrat was sending trucks to bring us back to Brussels.

I could have easily slept one last time on my old straw mattress. However, Flemish hospitality would not have it. Never before and never again have I slept in a bed as I did that night. Was there a custom where the lady of the house kept bedding as a memento of her wedding night? That in any event was what my bed looked like, snow-white, heaped pillows, a feather bed, lace, ruffles and pink bows, not to forget a nightgown printed with rosebuds. Uncharacteristically, I do not recall what I ate that evening or on the following morning either — only that I took a bath. And I remember sinking, sinking into that feather bed, gently gliding into sleep as into a bottomless cloud.

Some clatter came from the kitchen — they must have been doing dishes. A plate was smashed, a coffee cup? The flannel nightgown was soft, and I smelled good, clean, like a baby.

"Shema Yisrael. Dear God, make me meek, so I shall enter Heaven," I used to pray a hundred years ago. I was there now, and the liebe Gott from the lock house in the Tiergarten opened the floodgate. Waters rushed out, flushing all those sad and ugly images. Frank's gold teeth,

Boden's whip and Ferdekopf's mean grin were crumbling. Only Meyer did not yet dissolve — may my paintings stick in his throat, especially when he is singing. Sinking deeper and deeper into the feather bed, I saw Awret, ever so tiny, winking from a white cloud. Then came dreamless sleep.

Epilogue

Only recently I learned that the Dossin army barracks in Mechelen were built by Queen Marie-Therese in the 18th century when Belgium and the Netherlands were not yet independent states, but provinces of the Austrian Empire. I suppose that when I was imprisoned there neither my fellow inmates nor I were interested in the history of a place we abhorred. On that September morning of 1944 when the ancient barracks gate swung open, I saw the most beautiful, the most fascinating world of unlimited possibilities. For a while at least. For those streaming out into the streets of Mechelen the sweetness of freedom would soon be laced with a heavy dose of bitterness. The survivors kept waiting for their families and friends who would never return.

Those couples who had found each other in captivity married and stayed together for life. Dina and Sam, Evi and Arnold, Awret and I, and many more. Evi's parents and three brothers did not return, neither did Dina's, nor more than 25,000 others. All the "childless" couples among the slave labor force were reunited with their offspring, most of whom had been hiding with Belgian families in the countryside. In many cases the children had been raised as Catholics and had to be coaxed back to Judaism. Maurice and Esta Heiber, true to form, adopted a teen-age girl whom they had befriended in the camp and they put her through college.

Not everyone was lucky. When a former inmate met Tilly Sachs and remarked on her protruding belly, she said mockingly that she was going to have a baby. A few weeks later she succumbed to cancer. In his absence, Napoléon's job at the slaughterhouse was apparently taken by someone else. One day Awret met him begging in the street.

What became of Major Schmitt, nicknamed the "Butcher of Breendonck?" The Allies sent him back to Belgium where he was tried and executed. The advancing Allies also captured Kommandant Frank and Max Boden in Holland on their flight to Germany. They were imprisoned in Brussels. About two years later Evi testified at their trial in Antwerp. She told me that when she entered the courtroom the pair bowed almost to the floor. She ignored them. She was not vindictive in her testimony, but simply told the truth as she did at Schmitt's trial earlier.

I gave a deposition only against Dago Meyer, in a judge's chamber, not in open court. Though a dossier thick as an encyclopaedia was lying on the judge's desk, " Meyer was never tried due to a "lack of evidence."

In 1943, the Judenrat opened orphanages and old age homes for people over age 65. My father, born in 1878, just qualified and went to live there, where I found him after my liberation in September 1944. I rented new quarters and he came to live with me. He died in March 1945, just before the end of the war. It was the winter of the desperate attempt by Germany to stage a comeback at the Battle of the Bulge, and V1 and V2 rockets rattled over Brussels, sometimes exploding in my neighborhood. Food was still scarce, and I would have been happy to receive a package with anything edible, rice, sardines or corned beef. Instead I received a letter from Aunt Hanna in California who promised to send me a silver salamander brooch if only I would write back.

After the German defeat, the Jewish community's first task was to open orphanages for the many children left without families. Awret and I decorated a number of walls there — on condition that we use happy themes and bright colors — and this assignment helped us through difficult times.

Directly after my liberation I went to re-register at the town hall of my district in Brussels, expecting the registrar to welcome my resurrection. I was told that since the former German occupants had declared the Dossin barracks in Mechelen to be an "ex-territorial zone" I was no longer a resident in good standing. Because I had left Belgium, I was a new, stateless immigrant who was at liberty to travel but would not be readmitted to the country! I did leave. In 1949 Awret and I with our three-year-old daughter shouldered two knapsacks and left for the newly founded State of Israel where I would not have to admonish my children that because they were Jewish they had to behave better than anyone else.

An Afterword on Mechelen

Germany invaded Belgium on May 10, 1940; less than six months later, all Jews were ordered to register with the German authorities. A little more than two years after the invasion, the country's Jews were ordered to wear the yellow star. In Malines (called Mechelen by the Germans), located midway between Antwerp and Brussels where most Belgian Jews lived, the Nazi S.S. converted the Casern Dossin barracks into a transit camp for deportations to extermination camps in the East. The barracks consisted of a single three-story building, which surrounded a courtyard. For the Nazis, the Mechelen camp was a strategic location because of its proximity to a rail line — on August 4, 1942, the first transport of 998 Jews was shipped to Auschwitz. Mechelen was one of a number of transit stations the Germans established in Europe for moving Jews to the East. The most well-known were in Drancy and Gurs in France and Theriesendstadt in Czechoslovakia.

Memoirs of Mechelen by survivors have been limited, largely because most Jews were imprisoned there for a brief period before being deported. Survivors had little experience at Mechelen to write about. Irene Awret was among the exceptions — she was made part of the Malerstube, the painters' workshop, after her arrest in March 1943 until the camp's liberation on September 4, 1944. As she writes, Jews were assigned to work details, for example, in the "Reception," in the various workshops, the sick bay and the showers. Only a handful have written memoirs that even refer to life in Mechelen; *They'll Have to Catch Me First* is the one book that gives a detailed first-person account of conditions there.

Scholarly works on the Holocaust in Belgium have also been limited. Historian Dan Michman argues that serious scholarship on the war itself was held back for several reasons, among them restrictions on the use of government documents that may have shed light on alleged cooperation with the Nazis by the Belgian King. A historian of Belgium must also know a number of languages to fully use archival materials, Michman writes, which complicates research. In addition, the character of Belgian Jewry was not encouraging for academic studies: many Jews had migrated there from Eastern Europe before the war, and their ties to the country were not as strong as the ties of German, French, and Dutch Jews to their countries. Unlike neighboring Holland, for example, where 85 percent of the country's Jews were citizens, only ten percent of the Jews in Belgium were citizens. Lastly, Michman speculates that the relatively small number of Jews in Belgium (estimates are between 60,000 and 90,000), making up less than one percent of the country's population before the war, may have implied "historical insignificance" to scholars. Clearly, this was not true for Maxime Steinberg, who has published rigorous studies on the Holocaust in Belgium.

Steinberg examines many aspects of Jewish life during the occupation, among them, the Jewish resistance. In the early period, 1940 to 1941, he writes, resistance was manifested in attempts to maintain "the official Jewish community and Jewish life." These efforts were led mainly by Zionists. With the onset of deportations from Mechelen, Jewish communists and other extreme leftists established the Comité de Défense des Juifs (Jewish Defense Committee); the Jewish Resistance, unlike in Eastern Europe, was able to join forces effectively with non-Jewish underground organizations to plan actions that led to the hiding of about 4000 children (approximately 2500 by Catholic institutions) and some adults, while at the same time engaging in armed resistance.

In the *only* successful attack on a train to Auschwitz, the 20th convoy from Mechelen, which Mrs. Awret writes about, 15 deportees were freed and 261 escaped. Though many escapees were captured and killed, the attack was a source of great pride to resistance organizations in the country. Claire Prowizur-Szyper writes about these events in her memoir, *Looking Backward: A Jewish Fighting Woman in Belgium* (in Hebrew). She and her husband were among the underground activists captured by the Germans and sent to Mechelen; they were also among those who escaped from the 20th convoy and then continued in the resistance until the war's end.

The table summarizing Jewish deportees from Mechelen shows that in 26 transports over a period of two years, 24,906 Jews — men, women, and children — and 351 Gypsies, were sent to Auschwitz. The terrible trip usually took two days. Some deportees were sent to forced labor, but in the end only 1,335 survived.

~

In November 1941, Adolf Eichmann's Reich Security Main Office in Berlin gave orders to establish the Association des Juifs en Belgique (Mrs. Awret refers to the AJB as the Judenrat). The S.S. intended that the AJB like Judenrats established in the East would assist the Germans in solving the so-called "Jewish Problem." Though the Nazis had ordered anti-Jewish decrees a year earlier, they were not immediately enforced because of some opposition from Belgian government agencies and because the Germans wanted to maintain the stability of the Belgian economy.

The AJB'S role was far less crucial in the deportations than that of other European Judenrats. Though it distributed notices in July 1942 summoning Jews to Mechelen for labor services, children and the elderly were not included. Later on the AJB received funds from the American Jewish Joint Distribution Committee and as a result was able to send packages of food to Mechelen and even supplies for the artists who were imprisoned there. As Mrs. Awret writes, the AJB also maintained Jewish orphanages and old age homes. When the Germans did not get full cooperation from the AJB in gathering Jews for deportations, the S.S. convinced some that their lives would be spared if they cooperated in identifying Jews in the streets. The informer Jacques who accompanied the S.S. when they arrested Irene Spicker [Awret] was one of the notorious collaborators.

Much remains to be documented about Belgium and the Holocaust. Though research has lagged that of other countries, Dan Michman writes, Maxime Steinberg's work, new studies such as a

JEWISH DEPORTEES FROM MECHELEN

Transport	Date	Males	Females	(Children)	Total No.
			1942		
I	8/4	570	428	140	998
II	8/11	486	513	147	999
III	8/15	428	572	172	1,000
IV	8/18	498	500	287	998
V	8/25	486	509	232	995
VI	8/29	422	578	179	1,000
VII	9/1	444	556	344	1,000
VIII	9/8	500	500	238	1,000
IX	9/12	507	493	228	1,000
X	9/15	534	514	264	1,048
XI	9/26	796	946	523	1,742
XII	10/10	446	553	281	999
XIII	10/10	325	350	206	675
XIV	10/24	440	555	250	995
XV	10/24	342	134	71	476
XVI	10/31	704	118	50	822
XVII	10/31	673	201	87	874
			1943		
XVIII	1/15	460	485	182	945
XIX	1/15	290	320	105	610
XX	4/19	628	772	262	1,400
XXI	7/31	781	772	208	1,553
XXIIa	9/20	331	300	86	631
XXIIb	9/10	379	415	152	794
			1944		
XXIII	1/15	346	311	62	657
Z (Gypsies)	1/15	176	175	175	351
XXIV	4/4	333	292	54	625
XXV	5/19	257	250	58	507
XXVI	7/31	300	263	47	563
TOTAL					25,257

Adapted from Maxime Steinberg, *Dossier BruxellesAuschwitz*, 1980.

recent collection that he edited and memoirs like Mrs. Awret's have begun appearing in recent years. Among those, very few are in English.

⟨⟩

Mrs. Awret writes about the fate of some of the Nazi officers in her epilogue, in particular, Kommandant Schmitt, the "Butcher of Breendonck," Kommandant Johannes Frank and Max Boden. Little is known about the fate of the others, though it is likely that they lived as free people after the war.

What of Fritz Erdmann, who saved Mrs. Awret's life after interrogating her at the Gestapo headquarters and jail on the Avenue Louise in Brussels? According to Rudi van Doorslaer, a Senior Researcher at the Centre for Historical Research and Documentation on War and Contemporary Society in Belgium, Captain Erdmann headed up different sections of the Sicherhertpolizei, a section of "Jewish Affairs," in Brussels, beginning on December 29, 1942. He died in Germany on May 5, 1955.

In a recent memoir Noah Kliger writes about an astonishing encounter with Erdmann. Kliger's father was arrested by the S.S. in Brussels and Kliger wrote letters to the Gestapo headquarters, naively requesting that they release his father because he and his mother needed him. He was summoned to the Avenue Louise; arriving there, he was escorted to meet Erdmann who asked how he had the audacity to write and ask for favors — "my father is not a criminal," Kliger replied.

Erdman did not respond but started speaking to him in a language that Kliger did not understand. "You don't understand your own people's language?" Erdmann asked in surprise. "I was in shock," Kliger writes. "Isn't it strange that you, a Jew, don't know the Hebrew language but that I, a German, do?" He then went on to say that he learned Hebrew in Palestine where he grew up. Two weeks after that strange encounter, the author came home to find his father at the kitchen table. "I didn't recognize him," he writes.

Erdmann was evidently from a Templer family and though he was born in Germany, on March 23, 1900, he spent some years of his childhood in Palestine. Founded in 1868 in Haifa, the German Templers wanted to bring "God's people together so that each person would become a living spiritual building block in the temple of God" in Palestine, the holy land (from *Templer Society, Australia*). By 1910, German Templer settlements and communities were flourishing in Jerusalem, Bethlehem, Sharona (now in the middle of Tel Aviv) and Waldheim near Nazareth. Templers founded the first agricultural enterprises in Palestine and, in addition, are said to have made major contributions in the building of roads, crafts, trades and businesses. During the 1930s Palestine-Germans of military service age were ordered to return to Germany for compulsory military training.

Erdmann became a member of the Nazi party in 1931 and in 1938 he signed a certificate testifying that he believed in God but did not belong to any organized religion. In April 1940, according to van Doorslaer, Erdmann was dismissed from his functions in the S.S. in Spring 1944, and "shortly afterwards was condemned by the S.S. for neglecting his duty (and remarkably 'for corruption by Jews') and sentenced to 4-1/2 years in prison." Whether he was part of the smuggling ring that Mrs. Awret writes about is unknown. Van Doorslaer also writes that Salomon Van den Berg, president of the Brussels section of the Association des Juifs en Belgique, noted in his private journal, "Ce Ertman [sic!] est plus poli que les autres et semble être un peu plus humain." (This Erdmann is more polite than the others and seems to be a little more human.) Van Doorslaer observes that "this attitude served also to fill Erdmann's private pockets." Maxime Steinberg has commented that "Erdmann seemed 'plus humain' to the Jewish leaders in the AJB because he could be bought."

What Erdmann did after the war is unknown and just why he chose to save the lives of Noah Kliger's father and Irene Awret still remains a mystery.

Bibliography

Belgium and the Holocaust: Jews, Belgians, Germans, edited by Dan Michman (Jerusalem, Yad Vashem, 1998).

Brachfeld, Sylvain, *Ha-hayim Be-matanah: Hatsalat 56% Mi-Yahadut Bel-
giyah Bi-zeman Ha-kibush Ha-Natsi. (Life as a Gift: The Saving of 56%
of Belgian Jewry During the Nazi Occupation)*. (Israel, Yedi'ot Aharonot, 2000, in Hebrew).

Encyclopedia of the Holocaust, Israel Gutman, editor in chief. (New York,
Macmillan, 1990).

Kliger, Noah, *Shetem Esreh Lahmaniyot La-aruhat Boker/ 12 Rolls for
Breakfast* (Tel Aviv, Yedi'ot Aharonot, 1995, in Hebrew).

The Malines Museum of Deportation and Resistance. www.cieb.be

Prowizur-Szyper, Claire. *Be-mabat Le-ahor: Lohemet Yehudiyah Be-Belgi-
yah Ha-kevushah (Looking Backward: A Jewish Fighting Woman in
Belgium)*. (Sifriyat Po'alim, 1981, in Hebrew).

Steinberg, Maxime, *Dossier Bruxelles-Auschwitz: La Police SS et Le
Extermination de Juifs de Belgique Suivant de Document Judiciares de Les
Affairs Ehlers.* (Bruxelles, LeComite, 1980).

Steinberg, Maxime, *L'Etoile et le Fusil — La Traque des Juifs 1942-1944*
(Bruxelles, Vie Ouvriere, 1986).

Credits

The publishers thank Michlean Amir and Amy Derin for their assistance in preparing *They'll Have to Catch Me First* for publication. They also extend their appreciation to the following who have given permission to publish photographs and artwork. Permission to reprint any of these works must be obtained from the copyright holders.

Evi Fastag-Dobruszkes, France, for the portrait of Arnold Dobruszkes (Plate 9).

Ghetto Fighters' House, Israel, for the drawings by Irene Awret, Lon Landau and Jacques Ochs on the following pages: i, 169 and front jacket flap, 227 (bottom), 228, 237, 238, 239, 247, 248, 289, 301, 302 and the paintings: Redhaired Girl in a Green Coat (Plate 4), Playing Cards (Plate 5), The Train Is Coming (Plate 6), Distribution of Packages (Plate 7) and Napoleon (Plate 10). These works are ©Art Collection Ghetto Fighters' Museum (Beit Lohamei Haghetaot), Israel, donated by Irene and Azriel Awret.

Jewish Museum of Deportation and Resistance, Mechelen, Belgium, for the photographs of a Jewish shop (P001283), p. 15, Courtyard of the Mechelen camp (ref. P000749), p. 173, prisoners' numbers, p. 229, Flemish S.S. guard Lodewijk van Col ("Ferdekopf"), p. 301 and Till Eulenspiegel (Plate 3); and the paintings: Sara Yampolsky (Plate 1), The Two Seashells (Plate 2 and back cover), The Youngest Brother Ehrentreu (Plate 11) and Pieteke Anger (Plate 12).

Musée Juif de Belgique, Brussels for p. 227 (top).

Stiftung Archiv der Akademie der Künste, Germany, for Onkel Tom's Hütte, p. 1.

Yad Vashem, Israel, for the portrait of Painter Kopel Simelovitz (Plate 8).